Contents

AWAKENING TO LITERACY

*The University of Victoria Symposium on
ildren's Response to a Literate Environment:
Literacy Before Schooling*

Edited by

Hillel Goelman, Antoinette A. Oberg, and Frank Smith

*University of Victoria,
Victoria, British Columbia, Canada*

Heinemann Educational Books

4 Front Street, Exeter, New Hampshire 03833
22 Bedford Square, London WCIB 3HH

EDINBURGH MELBOURNE AUCKLAND
HONG KONG SINGAPORE KUALA LUMPUR NEW DELHI
IBADAN NAIROBI JOHANNESBURG
KINGSTON PORT OF SPAIN

First published 1984

Cover design by Ryan Cooper

Library of Congress Cataloging in Publication Data

University of Victoria Symposium on Children's Response
  to a Literate Environment: Literacy before Schooling
  (1982)
  Awakening to literacy.

  Bibliography: p.
  Includes index.
  1. Children—Books and reading—Congresses.
2. Reading (Preschool)—Congresses. 3. Literacy—
Congresses. I. Goelman, Hillel, 1951–   . II. Oberg,
Antoinette A.   III. Smith, Frank, 1928–   .
IV. University of Victoria (B.C.)   V. Title.
Z1037.U74   1984   028.5'30543   84-727
ISBN 0-435-08207-8

Printed in the United States of America

Introduction

Frank Smith

Awakening to Literacy is the written language product of a symposium at the University of Victoria, where fourteen researchers with extensive and overlapping backgrounds in anthropology, linguistics, psychology, sociology, and education met in October 1982 to discuss preschool children and literacy. The participants came from Canada, the United States, Mexico, and Britain, and their professional experience ranged from Alaska to Latin America, from West Africa to New Guinea. The theme of the symposium was "Children's response to a literate environment: Literacy before schooling."

Why a Symposium?

Why should the familiar topics of children and literacy warrant the time, effort, and expense involved in putting together yet another international symposium and yet another multidisciplinary book? What new ideas could possibly be presented? A first and most obvious justification might be that, despite several decades and many millions of dollars expended in concentrated worldwide research, the teaching of literacy continues to be a widespread concern. There is still a great deal about literacy that remains to be understood. Before the University of Victoria Symposium, I probably would have written that literacy was a universal concern. I probably would also have said that literacy was a universal good and that it was to the advantage of every child to be taught to read and to write. Whatever I might still feel about the value of literacy personally, I can no longer regard the benefit of its acquisition as axiomatic. Rather, the proposition that literacy is desirable and worth the effort of learning has to be argued and defended—especially, perhaps, with the children we so egocentrically expect to follow our example (or our precept) in the development of literate skills and interests. If the jolting of prior conceptions and the illumination of alternative points of view was one of the purposes of the University of Victoria Symposium, then it succeeded for me. I believe that many readers will have a similar reaction to chapters in this book, especially those written from a perspective different from the reader's own.

Bringing together authoritative researchers from different disciplines was a second and perhaps equally self-evident purpose of the symposium. Opportunities for such multifaceted exchanges are infrequent and scattered. A third, particular reason for organizing such a symposium was its focus on children who achieve literacy before they receive formal instruction in it, a phenomenon still insufficiently studied or appreciated. I shall give more consideration to the last two reasons (in reverse order) before elaborating on the organization of the symposium and of this book.

Literacy and the Preschool Child

The past 10 years have seen a growing interest among educational and psycho-linguistic researchers in the substantial number of children who attain a significant understanding of reading, and sometimes of writing also, before entering school. The psychological and linguistic interest focuses on the nature of such children's interaction with the signs, labels, and other ambient print in their environment, on supportive adult activities such as story-telling, and on children's own insights into the structures and functions of written language. Case studies tend to show that children who become literate before schooling are not otherwise precocious; they need not be favored intellectually or economically. In other words, it is to particular conditions of these children's experience that one must look for explanations of their facile progression into literacy.

Such conditions clearly demand educational consideration beyond the simple but impressive demonstration that children do not always need formal instruction to become literate. (The opposite side of the coin—that children who receive formal instruction in reading and writing do not necessarily succeed in becoming literate—unfortunately is also quite frequently demonstrated.) The study of untutored literates may provide a better understanding of the insights and experience that children require to make sense of written language and thus, presumably, of formal instruction. What these children have succeeded in discovering for themselves is what education must build on and, if necessary, provide. From such studies we may learn what children who achieve literacy possess, with or without formal instruction, and what those who fail may lack.

There are more technical reasons for literacy researchers to focus on the preschool child. Unless ambitious parents have deliberately anticipated the teacher's role and introduced classroom paraphernalia and activities into their homes, preschool children, uncontaminated by schooling, are a rare source of research material for students of child development. The effects of formal education are profound, especially in matters related to literacy. Children quickly come to perceive reading and writing in terms of the material and tasks they encounter in school (just as later they may become reluctant to engage in reading and writing unless recompensed in the educational currency of marks or grades). Even parents and teachers can become convinced that literacy is what is done in the name of reading and writing in classrooms rather than in less conspicuous transactions with print in the world at large. Only unschooled children can offer an undistorted perspective of the direct impact of written language in use.

The Disciplinary Gulf

There can be little dispute that professionals in various academic disciplines do not communicate well with one another or indeed attend very much if anything is offered from outside their boundaries. Even when there appears to be considerable overlap in interests—between cognitive psychology and linguistics, for example, or between anthropology and economics—interactions tend spontaneously to generate specialized and relatively independent subgroups, such as psycholinguistics, which further isolate areas of common ground. It could be argued that contributors to the University of Victoria Symposium were at the leading edge of their disciplines but few were in the mainstream. The psychologists, for example, tended to adhere to the relatively new "cognitive science" orientation, which concerns itself with structures of knowledge rather than patterns of behavior, with intentions rather than responses. Nonetheless, the predominant educational thrust at the symposium was toward enlarged opportunities for experience rather than programs of instruction.

It also is undeniable that different disciplines can exhibit very different points of view which, even if not contradictory, rarely may coincide. When the topic is literacy, completely opposite perspectives can be adopted, with anthropologists looking in one direction at entire cultures and psychologists looking the other way toward individuals. Anthropologists tend to be concerned with what literacy does, and psychologists with what individuals need to know. One might think that such complementary approaches would draw together professionals in the two disciplines whose particular interest is literacy, but in practice there is often a peculiar disregard, as if nothing studied outside a discipline can be relevant to it. It is not easy for many psychologists to accept that the particular interactions children have with other people or their artifacts may have more to do with whether the children become literate than their own intellectual strategies and abilities. (Paradoxically, psychologists at the University of Victoria Symposium demonstrated their interest in the individual with a strong preference for universal statements, and the anthropologists asserted the need to respect differences and unpredictability.)

Given the preceding truisms, it is clear that a particular motivation is required for another attempt "to bridge the gulf" between disciplines, to impel specialists not only to talk to one another but to listen. The motivation on this particular occasion was education. Perhaps the only concern shared by all the symposium participants was the education of children, and particularly the belief that formal schooling (in the Western middle-class tradition from which most participants came) should be based on a broader, cross-disciplinary view of how children learn and of how they might fail. It is not coincidental that the symposium, despite its focus on the preschool child, was organized under the auspices of a faculty of education.

Although it is widely accepted that education and its institutions are primarily sociocultural in origin and purpose, educational research during the past 2 or 3 decades has turned almost exclusively to psychology for theoretical support of its practices and solutions to its problems. Not that other disciplines have been reluctant to make statements about education. Cultural anthropology has a long history of observation of educational practices in many cultures and of direct attempts to influence policies in prevailing systems. Sociologists have taken an increasingly vocal role, not just in claiming their relevance to educational theory and policy-making but in striving to achieve change in particular directions.

Nevertheless, educational theory and practice have traditionally been dominated by psychology. The reason for this seems clear enough to me. The logistic triumphs of space exploration and of information management systems generally, added to an earlier respect for the standardized achievements of mass production, consolidated the belief among educators in authority that success would result from delivering to children the right amounts of the right instruction at the right time, with constant monitoring and quality control. The belief still has not been totally discredited that learning is a simple matter of individual ability and effort applied to appropriately organized and presented subject matter. Thus for literacy, educators occasionally turned to linguists to ascertain what should be taught but primarily to psychologists for how the instruction should be delivered. Success has not been conspicuous, but the failures of managed instruction continue to be attributed to the child or teacher rather than to the philosophy. Improvement still is sought through better and more extensive programs. The persistent underlying conviction is that if reading and writing are analyzed into component elements of basic skills and knowledge which are presented and rehearsed under appropriate conditions of incentive and reinforcement, then every relevant factor has been attended to. From this perspective, learning is essentially a series of inevitable psychological processes.

Of course, forays into other disciplines have taken place, especially as the huge expenditures on psychological research and development in education have failed to produce universal literacy, or even to ameliorate traditional problems in major Western countries. Sociologists, particularly their own specialized group of sociolinguists, were drawn into literacy education in the 1960s and 1970s because of the realization that children who did not speak the language of the dominant social group or school failed to benefit from the advantages of its education. However, there still is a widespread belief that such children suffer from various kinds of psychological deficit rather than from a mismatch of social understandings and expectations. Psychologists rather than sociologists have been called on to interpret the new data, which they assimilate into conventional procedures instead of using the data to re-evaluate the procedures themselves.

Educational research also has turned more to anthropology in recent years, but what has been adopted is a method rather than a new perspective. The method is *ethnography*, the employment of independent or participant observers to provide "naturalistic" descriptions of situations and relationships. Classrooms and the interactions between teachers and children have become fashionable objects of study, even among teachers. But the descriptions are used primarily to shore up or reorganize existing procedures. The predominant use of ethnographic methodology in educational research is by psychologists rather then by anthropologists. Psychology still claims and receives monopolistic rights in instructional development.

Organization of the Symposium

At this point the discussion must become personal. The presence in Victoria of fourteen qualified individuals at the right time and place to discuss literacy before schooling was not a happy accident. I invited them. I mention my role not to claim credit (since the symposium would not have taken place without the effort of many people who will be recognized in due course), but because objectivity requires acknowledgment of the bias in the arrangements that were made. What transpired reflected my own beliefs about how literacy and children should be most productively discussed, beliefs that the other participants were not slow to contest. With well-intentioned counsel from my colleagues—some of which actually was accepted—I suggested topics because I thought they were interesting and important. Participants were invited for the same reasons. Participants I did not know personally were recommended by people I did know. Not everyone I would have liked to invite could be invited, and not everyone I invited was able to come.[1]

I could not and did not try to bring together representatives of all the prevailing views on literacy in all the disciplines. Instead, my aim was to bring together, within bounds of practicality and budgetary constraint, individuals who would say something about literacy that was current, relevant, possibly controversial, and unlikely to be familiar in other disciplines. My intentions were to make a contribution to the various disciplines through the interaction of the participants themselves, to contribute to the University of Victoria through the participants' presence on our campus, and to serve a broader audience, particularly in education, through this book. All of these considerations played a part in how the symposium was organized. The participants were asked to prepare and circulate drafts of their papers in advance and, surprisingly, everyone did. They also were asked to read one another's papers before sessions and, even more remarkably, they did that, too. Symposium participants could not have responded more industriously and conscientiously.

For the 4 days in October 1982 that most of the participants were in Victoria, the main obligation placed on them, and the main entertainment offered to them, was to talk to one another. They were lodged in the same hotel off campus and ate most of their meals together. They were protected from other engagements and demands on their time (much to the envy of some colleagues in other departments who thought we were far too possessive of our distinguished visitors). The audience was kept small and unobtrusive, so that participants might not be tempted to make long and formal speeches. Even the weather collaborated: It was too wet and cold during most of the formal sessions to entice thoughts of diversion elsewhere, but the sun came through with appropriate warmth on the last afternoon so that we all could go sailing together.

At the working sessions, each participant was allowed to speak briefly about an aspect of his or her paper that wanted highlighting or elaborating, and a general discussion followed. Inevitably, the discussions digressed from the theme established by the speaker and the framework imposed by the organizer. The order of presentations resisted any obvious or arbitrary organization because of the divergent and overlapping nature of the topics and interests of the participants. It surely says something of the nature of literacy that it resists tidy compartmentalization. The eventual program sequence was only slightly more meaningful than the alphabetical order which was seriously considered, and the confining program labels were properly disregarded by the participants. Since the order of presentations at the symposium was different from the order in this book, it might be of interest to outline the symposium program here:

General Topics	*Participants*
The cultural setting	Anderson, Jacob, R. Scollon and S. Scollon
Family and friends	Heath, Bissex, Bruner, Schieffelin
The child's perspective	Ferreiro, Olson, Smith, Donaldson
Methodological issues	Leichter
Educational implications	Clark, Goodman, Teale

The final two sessions proved to be particularly inappropriately labeled. Almost all the participants talked about methodology and education, and the participants assigned to those topics spoke of many other matters as well.

At the end of each session, there was an opportunity for interaction between the participants and the audience, a changing population consisting primarily of thirty or forty graduate students and professors from the language arts section of the university's Faculty of Education. In the concluding period of the final session, members of the audience were given the floor, at which time they offered to the participants their views of where the symposium had been and where it might more profitably have gone.

Preview of This Book

After the symposium, participants revised their papers into the form in which they appear (after editing) in this book. The papers have been reorganized and grouped according to central themes which are as logical as the editors can make them, given the broad concerns and overlapping interests of all the authors.

The first five chapters are grouped under the general heading of Literacy and Culture. These are the papers concerned primarily with literacy in its social and cultural settings, especially in family environments, and with the impact of literacy on children. They are concerned with the pressures of literacy as well as with its possibilities. There is also a significant and important emphasis on research techniques in these chapters.

The next five chapters are broadly concerned with learning to be literate. Again, these papers reflect an interest in the interaction between children and their environments, but there is more of an emphasis on the use that children make of literate adults and literacy artifacts to learn to become readers and writers themselves. A consistent theme is the initiative and inventiveness that children frequently display in coming to terms with literacy early in their lives. These chapters also include valuable reviews of recent research and of research methods.

The final five chapters focus more precisely on literacy and cognition. These pages are concerned primarily with the difference that literacy might make to the thought of a child, the power of written language competence, and the demands that literacy might make on thought. Chapters 13 through 15 in particular argue the controversial concept that literacy requires using language in a specialized way— namely, to talk about itself.

Finally, as David Olson asserts, one characteristic of literacy may be the ability to distinguish what was meant from what was said. In the concluding part of this book, Goelman and Oberg have provided commentaries on the symposium discussions and on the meaning of the event as a whole.

All of the references for the fifteen chapters have been collated into one list which appears at the end of the book. This list should prove a useful bibliography of current theory and research on children and literacy. There are also author and subject indexes.

It is impossible to summarize a book such as this or even to provide a comprehensive overview of its contents. Therefore, in the following paragraphs I shall give a brief description of the major content of each chapter and an even briefer description of the backgrounds of the authors.

I. Literacy and Culture

1. *Learning to Read Culturally: Literacy Before Schooling*, by Bambi B. Schieffelin and Marilyn Cochran-Smith.
Literacy is never a simple matter of knowing how to read and write. What literacy is and how it is learned and used depend on many cultural factors. Schieffelin, who teaches in the Graduate School of Education, University of Pennsylvania, and her co-author discuss recent work on literacy as a social and cultural phenomenon. They examine three disparate examples, involving a tribe in Papua New Guinea that is just moving into a literate world, a group of middle-class suburban North American children, and some Chinese immigrant children who are newly arrived in the United States from Vietnam and who are responsible for bringing a new culture as well as a different literacy to older members of their families.

2. *Social and Institutional Influences on the Development and Practice of Literacy*, by Alonzo B. Anderson and Shelley J. Stokes.
The authors, members of a research team of social scientists at the Laboratory of Comparative Human Cognition, University of California at San Diego, ask questions that are basic: What are the life experiences that lead to literacy, and why, in an extensively literate country such as the United States, do the poor, and especially ethnic, minorities tend to fall short of others in literacy and school achievement? A careful and innovative research technique shows that, contrary to stereotypes, low-income minority preschool children spend more than 80 minutes every day of their lives in literacy activities, as much time as do more "privileged" children. Anderson and his co-author argue that the impediments to literacy are social and institutional rather than cultural, economic, or ethnic.

3. *Families as Environments for Literacy*, by Hope Jensen Leichter.
The manner in which families educate children into literacy and the methodology by which such environments can be studied are the concerns of Chapter 3. The author is Elbenwood Professor of Education and chairperson of the Department of Family and Community Education at Teachers College, Columbia University, New York. She argues that education is a naturally occurring process within families that should not be evaluated in terms of narrow school practices or outcomes. She describes the findings and methods employed in a number of intensive studies of families in their natural environment and comments on some of the difficulties and consequences of the presence of outside observers.

4. *The Achievement of Preschool Literacy for Mother and Child*, by Shirley Brice Heath with Charlene Thomas.
An anthropologist in the School of Education at Stanford University, Heath tells a remarkable story of how an untutored 16-year-old high school dropout achieved literacy herself while struggling to find ways to teach her son to read. Before his second birthday, the son was demonstrating reading to his 4-month-old brother. Many of the insightful and careful observations of how the child is learning to talk and to make sense of books come from the mother herself, who illustrates the role of "parent-researcher" which Heath argues must be part of new approaches to literacy research. The mother is Heath's collaborator in this chapter.

5. *Learning Literacy through Play: Puerto Rican Kindergarten Children*, by Evelyn Jacob.
An anthropologist in the education department of George Mason University, Vir-

ginia, Jacob also has an appointment at the Center for Applied Linguistics in Washington, D.C. She describes spontaneous "literacy activity" observed in the play of 5- and 6-year-old Puerto Rican kindergarten children. In this play, and in the absence of any adult guidance or direction, children engage in actual and pretend reading and writing activities, refining skills and developing appropriate social behavior. Jacob's chapter is interesting for its clear picture of untutored children exploring roles for literacy in their personal lives. It also offers a detailed description of a careful data-collecting technique appropriate to many research settings.

II. Learning to Be Literate

6. *The Child as Teacher*, by Glenda L. Bissex

Many children not only seem capable of teaching themselves to read and write but frequently demonstrate a remarkable talent for teaching adults around them how to assist them in their learning. In this chapter, which focuses on two young boys, one "advanced" and one not, Bissex, a former schoolteacher now on the English faculty of the University of Vermont, argues that children can invent possibilities for every aspect of language, from the graphic symbols to the syntax. They use as resources the people and print in the world around them and organize their own learning "like a textbook." Bissex's conclusion is that "children are small but their minds are not."

7. *The Development of Initial Literacy*, by Yetta Goodman

Even children who fail to learn to read in school have an extensive knowledge about written language, argues Goodman, a teacher and teacher educator at the University of Arizona at Tucson. She identifies three roots from which children are able to invent literacy for themselves as they participate actively in a literate society—the functions that written language serves, speech that children hear that refers to written language, and children's conscious awareness of the functions, forms, and contexts of writing. The author observes that some children as young as 3 years are confident they will learn to read easily, but others at the same age already believe that it will be difficult for them.

8. *Reading to Young Children: Its Significance for Literacy Development*, by William H. Teale

Reading to children is almost universally recommended as a desirable practice in leading children to literacy, but whether and why it has this consequence has not been studied intensively. Teale, who teaches in the Division of Education at the University of Texas at San Antonio and who was a member of the research team to which Anderson belongs (see Chap. 2), has found significant variation in the ages of subjects and the materials and manner used by parents reading to children. In this chapter, Teale relates these differences to what children learn and to their subsequent success with schooling generally. His conclusion is that although reading stories to children generally is beneficial, it is by no means a necessary preliminary to literacy.

9. *Literacy at Home and at School: Insights from a Study of Young Fluent Readers*, by Margaret M. Clark

A former teacher in a primary school, Clark is professor and head of the Department of Educational Psychology at the University of Birmingham, England. Her chapter begins with a reexamination of data gathered in a classic study of early readers 7 years previously, emphasizing the wide variation in the children's backgrounds and the important sharing and supportive role played by parents. Follow-up studies showed that, despite their precocity in literacy, a number of the children experienced some difficulty in school. Clark also discusses aspects of the children's writing, noting contrasts with some of Bissex's observations (see Chap. 6) but drawing on recent research to agree with Bissex that the basis of literacy learning must be the hypothesis-testing nature of children.

   10. **⊦RUN TRILOGY:** *Can Tommy Read?*, by Ron Scollon and Suzanne B.K. Scollon

The juxtaposition of computer programming language and a traditional literacy question in the title of this chapter typifies the broad and provocative approach of the Scollons, who work at the Center for Cross-Cultural Studies, University of Alaska, Fairbanks. They doubt whether literacy always has benign effects and contrast their own "modern consciousness" with the "bush consciousness" of Alaskan tradition-bearers. They also are concerned with the socialization of children and the role that computers might play in education. In particular, they see the possibility of a new form of discourse developing around computers, a discourse which, paradoxically, might integrate well with discourse values that existed before print and which might provide a basis for mediation across the gulf they see between contemporary individuals and bureaucratic institutions.

III. Literacy and Cognition

   11. *The Creative Achievement of Literacy*, by Frank Smith

Rather than viewing society as an irresistible force that molds children into its own forms, this chapter looks at how children use adults and their peers as resources for achieving their own creative ends through literacy. The chapter also relates literacy development to the manner in which children learn and make use of their understanding of spoken language. Children learn what is demonstrated to them but only when what is demonstrated is something they will want to achieve. Collaborative and vicarious aspects of literacy learning are discussed from the points of view of children, parents, and teachers.

   12. *The Underlying Logic of Literacy Development*, by Emilia Ferreiro

A Piagetian scholar and researcher in the Department of Educational Research, Center for Research and Advanced Studies at the National Polytechnic Institute in Mexico City, Ferreiro gives examples from carefully devised experimental research into the development of children's understanding of literacy. Her concern is with the "psychogenesis" of literacy before children acquire the insight that letters are related to sounds, illustrating the ingenious hypotheses that children generate when first learning to distinguish writing from drawing. Working with contrasting groups of middle-class and slum children in Mexico City, Ferreiro finds that all are capable of asking profound yet untutored questions regarding the nature of writing systems.

   13. *Speech and Writing and Modes of Learning*, by Margaret Donaldson

In a chapter which introduces some challenges to assertions of Goodman and Smith, Donaldson argues that written language presents a number of unique difficulties to children. She examines specific problems that children might have in understanding communicative functions of writing and the relation of written language to reality. Donaldson, who is professor of psychology at the University of Edinburgh, concludes with a description of some parallel difficulties children experience in making sense of fundamental arithmetic processes.

14. *"See! Jumping!" Some Oral Language Antecedents of Literacy*, by David R. Olson

Another former grade school teacher, now professor of applied psychology at the Ontario Institute for Studies in Education in Toronto, Olson argues that the roots of literacy and of school success lie in how children learn to talk. To a literate person, language exists as an object, an artifact, which can be analyzed, discussed, and intentionally taught. In literate and "school-advantaged" homes, Olson claims, parents talk differently to children about spoken and written language. Olson's abstract metalinguistic and metacognitive emphasis[2] is controversial among psychologists, but it has many links to the anthropologic and sociologic observations of earlier chapters.

15. *Language, Mind, and Reading*, by Jerome Bruner

An eminent student of children's thought and learning, Bruner also believes that the movement from spoken to written language depends on a specialized use of language, namely language that talks about itself. In this paper he analyzes his belief by reexamining the manner in which spoken language is learned, arguing for a connection between the creative story-experiencing aspects of both speech and written language. His conclusions lead him to one of the few strong implications for instruction voiced at the symposium—that language instruction should be dramatic, even melodramatic, and personal, the antithesis of the simplistic and decontextualized "mechanics" approaches. Bruner is George Herbert Mead University Professor at the New School for Social Research, New York.

Commentaries

i. *The Discussion: What Was Said*, by Hillel Goelman

The fifteen papers constituted only part of the University of Victoria Symposium, a part which, like an iceberg, was largely below the surface but massively present. Although never formally read or presented in their entirety, the papers were the basis of most of the discussions and the source of most of the issues that were raised at the symposium. Goelman, an assistant professor in early childhood education at the University of Victoria, describes how early questions concerning definitions of literacy and culture remained unresolved as the interplay of ideas and positions moved from abstract issues to questions of conflict, tension, and power, then to profound political and social issues, to negative aspects of literacy, and, at one point, to a frustrated silence.

ii. *The Symposium: What It Meant*, by Antoinette A. Oberg

Despite all the discussions and thousands of written words, no single definition of literacy, description of how preschool children become literate, or set of guidelines for how reading and writing should be taught emerged from the University of Victoria Symposium. Oberg, an assistant professor at the University of Victoria who specializes in curriculum theory, examines some of the impediments to mutual understanding among authorities from different academic disciplines even when the topic of discussion is a common concern. But she concludes that the complexity of literacy itself defies simple analysis. The main implication for education must be that, although many disciplines have insights to contribute, none can be expected to provide final answers. Literacy can never be separated from the individual child or from the child's own culture.

Acknowledgments

Two weeks before the symposium was due to begin, when most of the financial and personal commitments had been irrevocably made, a sudden budgetary squall threatened to founder the symposium before it was afloat. The rescue was organized by the Dean of the University of Victoria Faculty of Education, Dr. John J. Jackson. Valerie Abbott, hard-working departmental secretary, coped with the paperwork and the negotiation of travel and accommodation arrangements, and I thank her.

My colleagues in the Faculty of Education, especially Terry Johnson, Walter MacGinitie, Norma Mickelson, Lloyd Ollila, and Arthur Olson, were enthusiastic from the start and took care of much of the daily running of the symposium.

For the participants, an especially memorable contribution was made by graduate students who accepted responsibility for many different aspects of "hospitality"—meeting participants at the airport, driving and escorting them around town and university, and generally making them feel at home in Victoria. The students also did much to keep the sessions lively and intellectually honest. I am particularly grateful to Gordon Alexander, Donald Boyes, Stanley Byrne, Valerie Collins, Charles Crocket, Anne Davies, James Field, David Haslett, Margery Littley, Joy Maxham, Paul Montgomery, Carol Onushko, Eileen Pangman, and Carole Poy.

Finally, I thank the participants themselves. It was a pleasure and an education to meet them.

Victoria, B.C.
October 1983

Notes

1. In particular, Margaret Donaldson was prevented by illness and Shirley Brice Heath by commitments in Europe, but both contributed drafts of papers for consideration at the symposium. Their papers are included in revised form in this book.
2. *Metalanguage* is language about language (like much of this book) and *metacognition* is thought about thought.

PART I. LITERACY AND CULTURE

1. Learning to Read Culturally: Literacy Before Schooling

Bambi B. Schieffelin and Marilyn Cochran-Smith

In the past few years, investigators from a variety of disciplines and with different goals in mind have undertaken research on literacy. While there is still a strong interest in the cognitive and psycholinguistic aspects of reading and writing, more recently the social, political, and educational consequences of literacy have been taken up as topics of investigation. Researchers at a number of different universities have adopted an ethnographic perspective to investigate what literacy means to those who are acquiring and using it. Amidst the debates about oral and literate cultures (and about the nature of orality and literacy in general), an important literature has developed concerning the relationships between schooling and becoming competent in literacy skills both within and outside the United States. When the investigation of the organization of literacy activities and talk in the classroom did not supply sufficient answers or raise the "right" questions, researchers sought other contexts and modes of investigation. They went into homes, observed children playing at recess, talked to children about their ideas concerning literacy, interviewed parents, and examined children's writing samples.

From a different perspective, developmental psychologists such as Ninio and Bruner (1978), Miller et al. (in press), and Snow and Goldfield (1981) have been looking at interactions involving books and literacy-related activities in connection with the language acquisition of very young children. Although the number of children focused on is small, the descriptions offered by these researchers are provocative, suggesting the importance of these activities that involve using books for both social and linguistic development. However, there is a gap between the research that focuses on the 2-year-old and that which analyzes interactions in reading groups and changes in writing assignments in the elementary school years.

At this time it is well worth investigating the home contexts where the beginnings of home-based and nursery school-based literacy may be located before the child receives more formal instruction often found in kindergarten and first grade. Once we do begin to examine these early literacy activities, we must examine the

The report on the Kaluli of Papua New Guinea was based on ethnographic fieldwork carried out by Bambi B. Schieffelin. Support for this research from The National Science Foundation and The Wenner-Gren Society for Anthropological Research is gratefully acknowledged.

The report on the Sino-Vietnamese refugees was based on ethnographic research carried out by Bambi B. Schieffelin. Support for this research from the National Institute of Education is gratefully acknowledged. In addition, appreciation and thanks are extended to J. Buchanan, for allowing participation and observation in a wonderfully open classroom and for sharing so many insights.

3

ways in which children, as well as the adults around them, organize and use the literacy skills they have to perform their own social functions, and how this changes across social and cultural context as well as developmentally.

The focus in these studies is on literacy as a social and cultural phenomenon, something that exists between people and something that connects individuals to a range of experiences and to different points in time. Literacy skills are acquired in a variety of ways and contexts and have an equally wide range of meanings. It is becoming clear through research reports that many children are socialized to go to school and participate in school activities. Some are socialized to become literate. For some, becoming literate and enjoying books is something that is assumed. For others, it may not be. Some children receive assistance in becoming literate from their parents or siblings, some receive help from individuals outside the family, and others may receive very little or no assistance at all.

An Ethnographic Perspective on Early Literacy

The best way to investigate literacy as a cultural phenomenon that interacts with certain social processes is by adopting an ethnographic perspective. By *ethnographic*, we mean descriptions that take into account the perspective of members of a social group, including the beliefs and values that underlie and organize their activities and utterances. An ethnographic perspective allows the researcher to find out the meanings of events for those who are involved in them. Since we are concerned with the variety of ways in which children do and do not acquire literacy skills, we must investigate what literacy means to both children and the adults with whom they interact.

Many topics can be investigated from an ethnographic perspective to account for and understand the meaning of literacy before schooling. In this chapter we focus on several that seem relevant in formulating some of the dimensions of our understanding of what literacy means and what it achieves for different individuals. Our use of data from three different cultural groups is meant to raise questions concerning our assumptions about literacy and what literacy means to the individuals involved. We suggest that a careful examination of cross-cultural material may allow us to reevaluate the way we have formulated prerequisites for the achievement of literacy which have been based on the experiences of a relatively small number of social groups. We intend to demonstrate how an ethnographic perspective allows us to find evidence of recurrent patterns in particular social groups and then to investigate what these patterns mean for the individuals and groups involved.

We focus on three groups: a group of educated, school-oriented parents and their preschool-aged children from a Philadelphia suburb, a family in a traditionally nonliterate society in Papua New Guinea, and a number of Chinese families who left Vietnam and recently settled in Philadelphia. For these three groups, we sketch the values and beliefs concerning literacy, the different roles played in literacy activities, some of the functions of literacy, and finally, some of the relevant contexts that organize, shape, and promote certain types of literacy experiences.

The first description concerns preschool literacy in an educated, school-oriented community in Philadelphia. A careful look at this group is especially important, because researchers, readers, and subjects of studies of children's early experiences with print have tended to be from the same social group and thus share many unstated assumptions about the value and course of development of preschool literacy. Whether consciously or not, we researchers tend to use school-oriented, middle-class literacy values and patterns as the baseline against which we compare other patterns of literacy use. Therefore, one of the goals of our first account, which is based on ethnographic research, is to make explicit that which is implicit in and organizes the early literacy experiences of these young school-oriented children.

If You Don't Read, How Do You Know?
Learning to Read in a School-Oriented Philadelphia Community

During the 18-month period in which it was studied, Maple Nursery School served a group of fifteen to seventeen Philadelphia families. Their cultural and ethnic backgrounds included white Eastern and Western European, Jewish, Indian, Filipino, Egyptian, English, and Black American. Two of the children in the group were bilingual (Bengali and English and Filipino and English), and one was monolingual in Arabic; the others were monolingual in English. Although there were many differences among these families, there was also a great deal that they had in common. Most of the Maple Nursery School children were from two-parent families and had one or two siblings. Similarities were especially striking in the educational backgrounds of the families (fathers had undergraduate or advanced college degrees and held professional positions, and mothers were college-educated and held current or former professional positions, especially in teaching) and in the parents' values concerning schooling and literacy. Adults in this community took literacy for granted in their own lives. Consequently, they also took for granted the eventual literacy of their children and assumed that their children's early print interests emerged "naturally" as part of their normal, routine development.

Many of the literacy values and beliefs of this particular community are those often shared and assumed by scholars and researchers in early literacy. For this reason, it is somewhat difficult to acknowledge and examine the learning that underlies literacy behaviors that our own communities tend to take for granted and hence regard as "natural." It is a premise of this chapter, however, that particular ways of using and interpreting print are not "natural" but develop as part of early social learning within particular cultures. In the community studied, an important part of that early learning included a print-reliant approach to knowledge acquisition, entertainment, mental stimulation, and everyday social interactions and transactions.

The description that follows details some of the dimensions of the early print experiences of one community. This description peels away some of the layers of meaning of early literacy for this particular Philadelphia group and provides a sense of literacy as something that was used and organized by members of the community for their own social purposes. The description draws from a larger study concerned with the ways adults help children acquire and develop the literary and social knowledge needed to appropriately interpret and use texts and other printed materials (Cochran-Smith, 1983).[1] The larger study particularly provides insights into how the adults in this setting acted on their assumptions about how children learn to make sense of print, especially written texts.

Without exception, the families in this community read stories to their children frequently and regularly. Children also were encouraged to look at books independently. Bedtime reading was favored and considered particularly appropriate, because it allowed close physical contact and encouraged a calm and peaceful kind of interaction between parents and children. Cross-culturally and cross-nationally, the bedtime story cannot be considered a "given" (for example, see Heath, 1982; Scollon and Scollon, 1981). However, to understand the Maple Nursery School community it is necessary to recognize bedtime reading as much as a taken-for-granted part of raising children as is attending to physical needs. Within this community, book-reading provided a prominent framework within which one-to-one adult-child social interaction occurred. Book-reading was also a favored and encouraged solitary activity for children and adults. Underlying both kinds of book-reading—social and solitary—is the assumption that reading is a valued and approved way to spend time and that it brings to the reader many kinds of rewards. Likewise, books were treated as valuable possessions in the community.

The children of this community were constantly surrounded by books and book-related items, including games, records, items of clothing, and room decorations. Children also were provided with a wide variety of writing utensils and materials. These were available to the children just as toys were available. Children were encouraged to play and experiment with these materials and frequently saw adults using them. Parents emphasized, however, that they did not push their children to learn the alphabet or to practice printing techniques. Rather, parents simply assumed that their children would become literate and that their interests in literacy were part of normal child development.

The point we wish to stress is that the print interests of the children in this community (or in any community) do not emerge "naturally" at all. Rather, in this community, they emerge out of a particular cultural orientation in which literacy was assumed and which organized children's early print experiences in particular ways. The children of this community were being socialized to be literate and to come to print to meet a variety of goals. Storybooks were used in an especially wide range of contexts and for a large number of purposes in the community. Adults read storybooks to their children as an entertaining leisure-time activity, a way to initiate problem-solving discussions, a way to verify and introduce new information, and a way to relax and calm their children. Parents believed that books in general offered a source of valid information about, as one parent claimed, "just about everything": That is, in this community, book information served to legitimate experience and to verify other sources of information. Parents believed that printed sources of knowledge were significant to their children's learning in many areas of development—social, cognitive, psychological, and philosophic.

In addition to using print to meet a wide variety of goals, families used printing and found print to be appropriate in a large number of contexts. In this community, unlike some other social groups, there was no single context in which literacy could occur and no single purpose to which it could be put. Rather, literacy-related activities occurred in the two major contexts of preschool children's lives—the home and the nursery school—as well as in the church, in the general community, and in almost any social setting.

Perhaps the most striking characteristic of the literacy orientation of this community was the authority accorded printed materials and books to verify and extend primary experiences and to legitimate oral information. With the authority vested in them, books and other printed materials functioned to provide the community with a primary way of knowing, which was supported and extended by dozens of nursery school experiences. As one parent questioned at the conclusion of her interview, "If you don't read, how do you know?"

The adults in this Philadelphia community did not believe in emphasis on academics for nursery school children, and indeed all of the 3- to 5-year-old children who attended the school were nonreaders in the conventional sense. Nevertheless, each day at the nursery school contained dozens of literacy events, and the nursery school environment was laden with printed materials. Children were invited regularly to identify their belongings using printed name labels, to use books and other printed materials to introduce or verify new information and experiences, to express their own ideas by dictating printed stories, to relax and be entertained by the fictional narratives of storybooks, and to use the environmental print of posters, signs, and labels to learn about their everyday world.

For the members of this community, however, there was no incongruity between a nursery school philosophy that deemphasized early reading and writing and a pervasion of printed materials and print-related activities in the nursery school setting itself. There was no incongruity, because the context of nursery school literacy events almost never was instruction or situations wherein adults attempted to teach children to read and write. Rather, literacy events consistently were embedded within the routine social interactions of adults and children. For participants, the literacy events themselves were not noteworthy.

It was the social context itself that was the key to peeling away the layers of meaning of these nursery school literacy events. For example, one kind of social context in which print functioned involved situations where children expressed strong emotions of one kind or another. In these situations, adults frequently wrote down the children's words or encouraged the children to join them in a cooperative writing session wherein adults transcribed as children dictated. Adults used print in this way to acknowledge and reflect children's feelings and to give them credibility; the adults later read the children's words back to them and invited discussion.

Underlying this use of print is a model for the functions of literacy that includes using reading and writing as a way to sort out and work through strong feelings and emotions. However, for nursery school participants, what was noteworthy about these literacy events was not their print orientation but their function in helping the children deal with their emotions. In other words, what was foregrounded in these events was the children's emotional well-being and not the adults' seizing of convenient opportunities to teach ways that literacy functioned. Reading and writing were used to help children express their emotions, because the adults of this community saw written expression as an effective way for people to deal with their feelings and not because the adults were deliberately instructing the children in the development of literacy skills.

The children were being oriented to a kind of literacy that functioned in many ways: It could be used for oral substitutions, as an instrument that provided information about the everyday world, as a social interaction, as a memory support, as a way to present information efficiently, as a way to acquire knowledge, as a way to clarify status, and for self-expression (see Cochran-Smith, 1983). The children were exposed to all these functions of literacy within the everyday interactions of nursery school life rather than within contexts constructed for instructional purposes. Hence, these preschoolers were not so much surrounded by print as they were surrounded by adults who routinely chose to use print because it was effective in many contexts and for many purposes in their everyday lives.

Both children and adults participated actively in literacy events in the nursery school community. Adults took on the roles of teacher-helpers or what I have called intermediaries between children and print: That is, they completed whatever parts of literacy events that children asked them to complete or that they assumed the children were unable to complete. The shape of the adult intermediary role in these events varied according to the degree of adult initiation, guidance, control, verification, and termination of uses of print and the decoding or encoding of print. Adults took larger or smaller intermediary roles depending on the needs and skills of individual children. With very young children who adults assumed had little control over the uses of print, the adults used print by initiating literacy events, encoding or decoding the necessary printed words, and following through for or with children with the appropriate responses or interpretations of the print. Through adult intermediaries, for example, children's possessions were retrieved, art works were identified, written messages were substituted for oral ones, or feelings were expressed.

In some literacy events, even though children were directly involved, adults were dominant; they initiated and controlled both the mechanical processes of encoding and decoding the print and the way in which the print was used. However, even in situations where adults completely controlled the uses of print, children were not merely observers but were, in a sense, consumers of print. That is, these events occurred to meet the needs of the children, and adults behaved as if it had been the children's intentions to use print for particular purposes. Fulfillment of the perceived or anticipated needs and wishes of children themselves was, in most cases, the purpose of literacy events initiated by adults for children.

Studies of children's language acquisition and development indicate that, in cultures where adult-child dialogue is characteristic of language learning, children's caregivers initially accept almost any response as the child's part in a conversation. Thus, adults respond to gurgles or coos as if they were children's conversational turns, they take children's perspectives in conversations, and they act as if the behavior of infants carried meaning and intention.[2] These actions provide some insight into the way the nursery school children were acquiring literacy. Adults initially played all the parts in literacy events, completely producing and comprehending print for the children and behaving as if the children themselves intended for print to be used in particular ways and as if the children themselves were using the print. Little by little, however, the nursery school children took over the various roles in literacy events and needed less and less help from adult intermediaries. In these literacy events, children's control of the uses of print preceded their control of the mechanical skills of decoding and encoding.

Although there were some literacy events that were completely controlled by adults, the majority of nursery school literacy events were accomplished through the joint and active participation of adults and children. In addition to an image of the adult as intermediary, what emerged from the data was an image of the child as constant learner, sorting out the rules for interpreting and using print effectively by organizing and using it for his or her own social purposes. Although many of the nursery school children could recognize their own names and some environmental print, they could not read and write in the conventional sense. All of the children, however, were regular participants in social situations in which adults used reading and writing for and with them for a variety of purposes. The most significant characteristic of these uses of print was that the children were exposed to them on a daily basis and gradually were acquiring great facility with them. Although they could not encode or decode, nursery school children *did* know much about contexts in which print could be used, purposes which print could fulfill, and the ways that print was to be interpreted in relation to its context.

In some instances, adults were intermediaries only as instruments for the children. That is, the adults encoded messages specified by children, but there was little doubt that the children themselves controlled the uses of reading and writing. Children initiated, directed, and concluded entire literacy events. Their actions indicated that, to a certain extent, they had internalized many of the uses of reading and writing that were common in the nursery school or in their homes.

It is evident that the role of the nursery school child in literacy events was not a passive one. Rather, the child was very actively involved in employing print for his or her own social purposes and, in the process of doing so, was sorting out the rules for using and interpreting print in various situations. In dozens of nursery school literacy events, children were experimenting actively with kinds of print as they employed or attempted to employ it to effectively fulfill their own needs.

Underlying adult-child interactions around print was a clear model for ways of using and interpreting various kinds of print. The children were beginning to internalize the ways of using reading and writing that were accomplished or modeled for them or explained to them by adults in the community. The children gradually were acquiring ways to use print as well as some of the initial skills of encoding, decoding, and printing. Their exposure to and involvement with the uses of print, however, generally occurred apart from involvement with the more or less mechanical skills of literacy. Consequently, a child who could successfully decode only his or her own name could, nonetheless, request that an adult intermediary transcribe an oral message that was to be used for the child's own purpose and in a particular context stipulated by the child. It is not surprising that the children in this community expressed an interest in print. Print enabled them to do things. Print was very meaningful and functional in their nursery school lives and in their home lives and, hence, played an essential role in their early social learning.

Nursery school story-readings were literacy events that were very different from those that were embedded in routine social interactions. Story-readings were the only literacy events in which children were required to participate and, as such, were pivotal to their literary socialization and to their larger literacy socialization. Story-readings were adult-dominated and adult-controlled. However, the texts of storybooks never were simply read to children, and children were not expected to be only listeners. Rather, story-readings were characterized by cooperative negoti-ation of the story by the reader and listeners. The story-reader was aware of the response of her particular group of listeners, and individuals' responses influenced the story-reader's guidance of interactions around the text. The meaning that the listeners seemed to be making of texts directly shaped the story-reader's role. Through verbal interaction between child listeners and adult reader, the decon-textualized language of storybook texts was given a context. The story-reader essentially instructed the listeners in how to use various kinds of world knowledge as frameworks within which particular parts of texts could be read. In this way, she transformed the reading of decontextualized texts from a one-sided to a joint sense-making process.

This transformation was accomplished through a network of verbal give and take in which the story-reader mediated between child listeners and text. To do so, the story-reader continuously monitored the "match" between the readers implied in texts and the real readers-listeners who sat before her listening to texts. To help them make sense of texts, the story-reader guided the listeners to take on the characteristics of the readers implied in individual works. To shape these real readers-listeners into implied readers, or whenever a mismatch between the two seemed to occur, the story-reader overrode the textual narrator and became the narrator herself, annotating the text and trying to establish some sort of agreement between real and implied readers. The story-reader was constantly mediating by alternating between two roles—spokesperson for the text and secondary narrator or commentator on the text.

The strategy used by the story-reader in this community effectively turned story-reading into a negotiated, interactive event. Very young readers-listeners were not faced with the task of making sense of an author's one-sided text. Instead, they received a great deal of instruction through confirmation of their correct attempts and negation of their incorrect attempts at sense-making. If they misun-derstood or became confused, they were allowed to try again; specific textual passages or pictorial spreads that caused confusion were recycled and the proper ways to make sense were explained.[3]

Underlying story-reading interactions was a model for how to make sense of and use texts in the world. The verbal interactions around story-reading essentially transformed the usually internalized and automatic reading process of the literate adult readers of this community into an outwardly explicit and very gradual sense-building process for a group of young literary apprentices. Hence, in this com-munity story-reading was a special literacy event that provided a transition between the language strategies used to make sense of oral face-to-face communication and the language strategies used to make sense of the decontextualized print of story-book texts.

The preceding description makes explicit some of the values, assumptions, and practices of a particular group that has been considered effective and successful in preparing their children for school literacy. In this school-oriented Philadelphia community, it is assumed that children will become literate, and so literacy activi-ties often are taken for granted or are backgrounded in relation to the social functions and interactions in which they occur.

For many of us (as researchers, educators, and parents), the experiences of these children are predictable, familiar, and even desirable. However, in many parts of the world and even in the United States, these values, assumptions, and practices are not predictable, familiar, or desirable. Therefore, we would argue that it is premature at present to attempt to understand literacy before schooling in a general way. Rather, we need to become more fully informed about its particulars. For those of us interested in literacy before schooling, the task is to investigate directly the similarities and differences in the meanings, functions, roles, and contexts of literacy in given social groups.

The following brief sketches of work in progress concern literacy before schooling in two different social groups. These sketches, particularly in comparison to the familiar patterns of literacy drawn above, raise questions about cultural variation in literacy and how this variation affects both the ways that literacy is organized and the ways that literacy organizes and shapes social experiences.

Learning To "Read" In a Nonliterate Society: The Kaluli of Papua New Guinea

The Kaluli people (population 1200) live in the tropical rain forest on the Great Papuan Plateau (E.L. Schieffelin, 1976; Feld, 1982; B.B. Schieffelin, in press). These monolingual speakers of the Kaluli language (non-Austronesian) are traditionally nonliterate. Their society may be characterized as an egalitarian one in which face-to-face interactions predominate. Kaluli have extensive gardens and hunt and fish to provide food for themselves. Until 1971, they were relatively isolated from outsiders and Western influences, such as the national government and Christian missions. Research on the Kaluli before this time documents their traditional activities, belief systems, patterns of language use, and other socio-cultural aspects of their lives. Although the Kaluli observed three anthropologists reading and writing, they never expressed interest in learning about these activities for use in their own lives.

In 1971, the Kaluli began to experience social and cultural changes which included the introduction of adult literacy classes by evangelical Christian missionaries who settled in the area. The main reason for the introduction of literacy was to enable the Kaluli to translate and eventually read the Bible so that they could be converted to Christianity. The introduction of literacy classes for adults was only one of a number of previously unavailable services offered by the missionaries. Others included a medical clinic, a store, and religious services and instruction. In addition, mission presence provided the Kaluli with the opportunity to earn small amounts of money by cutting grass on the airstrip and performing other domestic tasks. The missionaries taught mainly young adults who were interested in becoming part of the Christian movement. Writing was not emphasized as much in their teaching program as was reading, nor was literacy connected with other kinds of educational topics such as social studies or science. Reading in Kaluli was taught by syllabication, and a few Kaluli learned to read aloud, very slowly, and with clear enunciation. The missionaries developed simple booklets with line drawings illustrating traditional and new cultural items, such as tins of food, clothes, and nontraditional dwellings. They developed English-based words for the new items and printed the labels under the drawings.

Another arena in which literacy events took place was the small government boarding school for older children (ages 10 to 16 years). This school was part of the government system in that teachers were paid by the government and their careers advanced through the government system. However, in this part of Papua New Guinea, teachers were trained in mission-run schools. Furthermore, the school and teachers were not located in any village but on the mission station. Given this arrangement and the other social services offered by the mission, the lines between government and mission were not always clear. In two classrooms, Papuan nationals taught basic reading, writing, and mathematics in English and Tok Pisin to monolingual Kaluli children. Most Kaluli children who attended school did so for only a few years and predictably learned very little. There was no evidence that these children and adolescents brought literacy back to their villages to which they returned for the weekends. Thus, the only print found in the area was in the worksheets and copybooks from the mission school, the adult literacy booklets, chapters of the translated Bible, and the labels from the few introduced canned foods from the mission store. In addition, there were no logotypes, photographs, or other pictorial representations in the society that could have been seen as part of an ambient print environment.

After 5 years of literacy classes, there was little evidence of an impact of literacy on the organization of everyday village life. For example, in the village in which one of the authors (B.B.S.) did ethnographic field research (the largest Kaluli village, populated by approximately 100 individuals), only one couple and a few of the younger men were able to read the literacy booklets and Bible passages that had been translated. Most village people did not think of literacy as something relevant to their lives, and only those with strong interests in mission activities actually devoted any time or attention to literacy. A major consideration was that the adult literacy classes took individuals away from the village since it was a 2-hour walk to the mission. Those villagers who were interested and participated separated themselves from those who continued to lead more traditional lives. An interest in literacy meant that one had to rethink some of the basic issues of domestic organization. For example, anyone attending the mission would have difficulty gardening and performing other food-collecting activities, and so other family members who did not participate in literacy activities would have to provide food for those who did become involved in literacy and mission activities. This could present a problem in a society where people are organized to supply food for members of their households.

A second consideration was that literacy for the Kaluli was tied directly to mission matters and subject material. Literacy skills meant access to mission life and involvement outside village politics and social life. Interest in literacy tended to separate individuals from one another in fairly significant ways and changed the usual patterns of organizing social activities. The Kaluli also did not assume that their children would benefit from the ability to read or write. Literacy was not seen as something of value for children just as it was not considered relevant for the majority of adults. In addition, literacy was believed to be difficult to achieve. Given the limited nature of the literacy materials, the difficulty and cost of obtaining them, and the general irrelevance of the literacy activities to traditional social life, it is not surprising that most Kaluli were not particularly interested in or curious about literacy. Therefore, those few individuals who were acquiring some literacy skills did not extend them beyond the purposes for which they were presented by the mission program.

Within this framework of an essentially nonliterate society in which schooling plays no role in village life, we can examine the "book-reading" activities that were observed to occur regularly in the one family in which both parents were acquiring literacy.[4] This family consisted of mother, father, a daughter named Meli (who was 24 months old at the beginning of the study), and an infant son. They lived in a small dwelling with another family and a grandmother. The first question to consider is whether the situations in this family in which activities involving books occurred should be regarded as a recognized, recurring cultural context of interaction. For the mother in this family, Osolowa, book-reading took place when she was not occupied with child care or food preparation. Osolowa would remove her literacy booklet from its special bag and practice reading aloud. There was no regular time of day that this activity took place, but because there were only limited means of artificial lighting (lanterns), most reading was done in the daytime.

In general, adults did not want children handling the literacy booklets or even looking at them because the booklets were valued and could be damaged easily. Osolowa was the only adult in the village who looked at books with her child. The few men who were learning to read and who practiced their reading at home did not share the booklets with their children. Given that men in this society do not spend time with small children, to focus on them in this way or to share the reading activity with them would have been socially inappropriate. Likewise, Osolowa's behaviors were consistent with the Kaluli women's role of caregiving and paying attention to small children.

Meli always initiated what became a joint book-related activity with her mother. When she heard Osolowa reading, Meli would ask to look at the pages with her. At those times when Osolowa cooperated, she would have Meli sit beside her while she controlled the page-turning. Each black and white page consisted of several line drawings of objects and animals with their names printed in Kaluli. Since this Kaluli mother was not particularly interested in encouraging her child to look at the book, she did not use any of the attentionals (such as "look!") as described by Ninio and Bruner (1978) and Miller et al. (in press). However, to a limited extent, Osolowa did use the remaining key utterance types—queries, labels, and feedback—when looking at the pictures and naming them. Pointing occurred in some sequences, and occasionally the mother used the names of the pictures (animals, people, or objects) to "touch off" conversational topics related to real-life experiences. For example, when Meli pointed to a picture of a banana and said, *"Magu!"* (banana), her mother would ask, "Do you eat bananas?" What is important here is that discussion of these topics as well as naming the pictures was in a conversational speech register: That is, the mother and child would say the name of the picture, but the fact of the printed word that was next to the picture was essentially ignored. The printed word never was referred to or pointed out, and it was never said in this conversational context in its clearly syllabified form that would indicate reading.

From a cultural perspective, what is particularly interesting about these interactions is that they are inconsistent with traditional Kaluli patterns of oral language use. The Kaluli do not encourage naming or labeling when children first begin to speak or at any other point in their development. In fact, a child who simply names objects is considered not to have begun to use language. Kaluli adults do not elicit the names of objects to make conversation or to instruct their children in the names of things. When Kaluli children use two words appropriately, *no* (mother) and *bo* (breast), the Kaluli say that language has begun. At this point extensive verbal instruction is begun within ongoing dialogue and interaction (see B.B. Schieffelin, 1979, for details). When Meli and Osolowa are looking jointly at pictures in books, Meli names the pictures and her mother further elicits the names of other objects and animals. Thus, for the Kaluli, there is discontinuity between the patterns of language used in this specific book-looking context and the language used in all other contexts. The Kaluli language patterns are unlike those documented by researchers who focused on Anglo-American society, in which naming and labeling are valued in early language and are used to form the basis of extended discourse between adults and young children. These same patterns of language use are drawn on when a child looks at a picture book. However, when Meli did not name an object correctly, her mother corrected her and requested clarification until Meli either produced the correct name or it became obvious that she did not know it. When the child did not know the name, the mother would provide it and tell her to say it.

In contrast to looking at books as a social activity, there were a few occasions when Meli was able to look at the literacy booklet by herself. This occurred when her mother was involved in other activities but was nearby to monitor Meli's handling of the book. Just as her mother did when she read alone, Meli slowly pronounced the names of the pictures, breaking each word into the appropriate syllables, pausing between each, and articulating clearly. In doing so, she was using a reading register that was different from the conversational register she used when involved in the social activity of book-looking with her mother. Thus, at a very early age (27 to 30 months), Meli was sensitive to and producing different styles of language appropriate to each activity. She seems to have distinguished between the talk used when naming pictures, which is conversational, and reading, which is marked by slow enunciation of each syllable. This is a relevant distinction in terms of language use in this society.

When asked about these activities in which books were involved, Meli's mother would laugh and say that what Meli was doing was *ba madali* (to no purpose). This phrase was used to describe other vocal activities, such as babbling (which was said to have no relationship to language development) and sound play (which was thought to be harmful to the young child's language development) (B.B. Schieffelin, 1982). (The phrase *ba madali* was applied to other verbal interactions that did not have social or cultural meaning.) We can analyze these book-looking and reading sequences from a Western research perspective and consider what they suggest about the child's metalinguistic development and sensitivity to the sociolinguistic and appropriateness rules of language use. However, if instead we take a Kaluli view of these situations, we must conclude that the book-looking and reading sequences are not contexts with the meaning and function of book-oriented activities in the ways that story-reading is for the Philadelphia children described earlier. These literacy activities for the Kaluli are very suggestive, but they have little connection to other aspects of Kaluli social life. Looking at books is seen as neither instructional nor entertaining. The length and frequency of these interactions between Meli and Osolowa were determined by the child's persistence and interest, never the mother's. It was not a regular context of interaction. Most importantly, although it resembled the *form* of similar activities described for school-oriented, educated mothers and their similarly aged children in the United States, it did not share the *functions* nor have the *meaning* that those interactions had for the school-oriented American participants.

Nonetheless, book-looking activities did have an important effect on the language use of Meli and her mother. Unlike the children in the traditional Kaluli families in whose lives books played no part, Meli elicited the names of household objects and occasionally managed to draw her mother into interactions based on object naming. However, from an examination of the data, it is very clear that Osolowa never initiated these activities or particularly encouraged them. She tried to distract Meli when Meli tried to start these types of interactions. In effect, she found this activity to be "to no purpose."

Who Is Doing the Reading?
Literacy in Sino-Vietnamese Families in West Philadelphia

This study of literacy in the lives of a Chinese family from Vietnam is based on ethnographic fieldwork in a West Philadelphia community and school. In this study, literacy has been examined as a social process, as something that is organized by the cultural conventions individuals bring to the task and as something that organizes individuals in dealing with a new set of tasks. The focus is on a 9-year-old boy, V., and his family and friends. One of the important findings of this study is that V., like other Chinese children who have arrived in the United States in the last several years, has developed a number of successful strategies for getting help with school-related and literacy-related activities. Because he cannot receive assistance in school-related activities from his non-English-speaking parents, his requests for assistance are directed primarily to English-speaking adults who are outside his family network. The networks of assistance certainly are available to V. and other Asians who have recently arrived in the United States. However, in eliciting assistance, the non-English-speaking child must develop a range of social relationships that are very different from those of the English-speaking child, who may expect to receive assistance from family members.

Another important finding of this study is the extent to which V. and his older siblings transmit important cultural material to their non-English-speaking parents because of their school-based literacy skills. The children must act as translators and mediators in dealing with a range of forms (such as school-related, job-related, medical, and tax forms) that present a vocabulary and structural organization different from the types of written materials with which young English speakers of a comparable age usually deal. The assistance in coping with written and spoken English that the children give to their parents can be seen as a literacy role reversal. The young Sino-Vietnamese children are facilitating their parents' entrance into a new society and are acting as socializing agents, a role usually restricted to parents in English-speaking families.[5]

An issue raised in this study concerns the notion "literate environment" and its role as a prerequisite in school-based literacy skills. There was no evidence of early parent-child book-reading and later casual reading by school-aged children, and yet the children in this study used books as resources and became literate in the course of being acculturated. Letters are another literacy resource in these study families, as both an important genre and a source of information.

Finally, an important consideration throughout this ethnographic research concerns the role of the researcher as an instrument of the research and as a literacy resource for those being studied. Only by letting the members of these families inform the researcher (B.B.S.) of what they needed to know was it possible for the researcher to learn what they needed and wanted.

V. and his family come from Saigon and now live in West Philadelphia. Members of their extended family living in Philadelphia often visit, and recent arrivals stay with the family for varying lengths of time. Cantonese is the language of the home, but V.'s parents also speak Mandarin and Vietnamese. V.'s father speaks some English, and his mother speaks less. Most of the reading material in the home— books, magazines, and newspapers—is in Chinese though occasionally the family buys an English newspaper. The children younger than 12 years cannot read Chinese, but V.'s parents and the members of the household older than 12 do read Chinese. V.'s mother has taught him approximately half a dozen Chinese characters, but V. says that it is hard to learn them while he is working on his English. The family owns a television, and on the weekends they often go to Chinatown to see Chinese movies.

When V. arrived from Saigon, he started school in the second grade at one of the largest Philadelphia elementary schools, located in West Philadelphia. Approximately 40 percent of the students are nonnative English-speaking children. Most of these are Asian refugees from Vietnam, Laos, and Kampuchea (Cambodia) and speak a number of different languages including Vietnamese, Laotian, Hmong, Cambodian, and various dialects of Chinese. These refugees began to settle in the area in late 1978 and continue to arrive at this time. Most of the other students are Black, with a minority of Indian, Haitian, Ethiopian, and white pupils.

V. and his older siblings are asked to give a great deal of assistance to adult members of their family who are learning to speak and write in English. Whereas, the usual situation with a school-aged child is for the child to seek and receive help from an adult, in these families the child is asked to assist the adults. In establishing helping relationships with adults, the child learns a different set of interactional and literacy-related skills than do children who are primarily in situations of receiving assistance.

V. also offers help to adults outside the family and this assistance involves a wide range of contexts. There is continuity of behaviors observed at home and at school both with English and non-English speakers. For example, on one of the first days that I (B.B.S.) was observing in class, V. asked what I was writing in my notebook. I told him that I was interested in the games that the children were playing during a free choice time. He volunteered to spell the names of the games to me and began, "*c-h-e-s-s, o-u-t-w-i-t,*" but then said that he would make a list of the games. During free choice time, V. wrote a list of the names of the games on the shelves. When asked if I could keep the list, he said he would copy it neatly and then give it to me. V.'s confidence in writing, his presentation of a list to me, and his ability to consider what I needed were impressive.

V. often was interested in what I was writing in my notebook in the classroom. Sometimes he would correct me if he thought I had misspelled a name. For example, when I had not wanted to write out the teacher's full name but chose to refer to her as Miss K., V. corrected me, pointing out that I had forgotten the other letters. My abbreviations were very confusing to him and required several detailed explanations.

V.'s offers of assistance were not limited to me but were part of many interactions he had with his classroom teachers and the reading aid who came to the classroom. V.'s offers to help were taken well. His manner of providing correction was more an indication of interest than an inappropriate comment. This behavior was part of a much larger pattern of helping adults with literacy-related tasks, which I would see repeated with V.'s parents at home on a regular basis.

From classroom observations, it became clear that V.'s offers of assistance were not limited to adults but extended to other members of his class. He would point out spelling errors made by both Black and Asian children and these would be well received. V. was proud of his spelling ability and would ask the teacher if he could take the spelling tests of lower-level groups because he wanted to see how he would do with material that he was supposed to know already. V. did this for himself and perhaps also to receive praise from the teacher, but he did not show these tests off to his peers or even discuss the tests with them.

The most extensive assistance V. gave was to his parents, cousins, and other nonnative English-speaking relatives. This was evidenced first in the classroom when V. gave to his teacher a note that was written by his father. He accompanied it with a long apology for the way the note was written and for the misspelling of the word *lunch*. V. explained that his older sister had helped his father, but his father had not written it correctly. V. later told me that he often would help his parents with reading, filling out forms that came from school, and writing notes in English. His sister and older brother helped also, with tasks that included dealing with materials related to V.'s father's employment. V. would be asked to act as a translator in conversation with his mother's employers, the people whose homes she was cleaning. He would accompany his mother on different errands to help with map-reading, instructions, and reading and translating a wide range of forms, such as those used at the bank. During the time that I have been visiting V.'s house, he and his older siblings have helped their parents and older cousins to interpret and complete a variety of forms (school-related, job-related, medical, and dental forms, permission slips, and tax or other financial forms). They have had to read and translate announcements that covered a wide range of topics and that were issued by a number of different institutions. All of these interactions involve a reversal of the expected roles of assistance and a certain level of sophistication in literacy skills.

V. and other children in a similar situation cannot rely on their parents as resources for direct assistance with school-related tasks, such as homework and test preparation, or for participation in school trips, special programs, and special projects. Instead, they seek help from adults outside their familial networks, adults who they meet at school or through church associations, community volunteers, or the occasional anthropologist. They must ask for assistance with literacy tasks for themselves directly as well as to enable them to help others.

One question raised by this research concerns what it entails (and means), in terms of the quality of emotional involvement and type of assistance given, to get help from someone who is not a family member. Furthermore, what does it mean, in terms of how information is organized and presented, for a nonnative English speaker to receive assistance from someone who does not share membership in the same social group? What strategies does the child develop to obtain the necessary information to complete an assignment or to elicit an explanation that is comprehensible given what the child already knows? How does the child develop and manage social relationships that are built on requesting help so as not to overburden those relationships? How does the child structure interactions to get information for himself or herself as well as on behalf of others who use the child as an intermediary or translator? Finally, what aspects of language must the child understand in these exchanges that are different from the typical interactions that English-speaking children have with printed material? For the non-English-speaking child, the social requirements for success in school and the achievement of literacy skills are of a different nature from the social requirements for the English speaker. The development of these social skills must be viewed as part of the acquisition of literacy.

V.'s home environment presents challenging data to the current debates concerning the importance of a literate environment for the achievement of school-based literacy skills. A literate environment usually is characterized as one in which there are books and other forms of print in abundance, as well as writing materials. It would be difficult to categorize V.'s home as a literate environment in these terms.

On the first floor of V.'s family's house (comprising the living room, dining room, and kitchen), there is a notable absence of books in bookcases, coffee-table books, and other reading materials. Sometimes, there is a folded-up Chinese newspaper and a Chinese popular magazine but little else for reading. There is a tape deck with a box of cassette tapes, and the walls are decorated with posters of Asian movie stars, but there are no bookshelves. On the second floor are the bedrooms, and here, too, there are no books on the night tables or magazines on a rack. The television is on the second floor, but there is no television guide.

V. shares a room with his older brother and has made a bookcase of an old toy refrigerator. A few books, magazines, and old games are on its shelves. A stack of old *National Geographic* magazines was given to V. by a neighbor who found them on the street. V. says they are too hard to read, but sometimes he looks for a picture to cut out when he has an assigned school report. There are half a dozen comic books that a teacher gave him and a couple of Golden Book editions of *Peter Pan* and *Pinocchio*. There is a small desk by the window where V. does his homework and on which his quarter-sized school violin and music books are stacked. V. says he likes to play the violin and enjoys the school lessons but never practices at home.

V. reports that he likes to read and does read fiction during the daily sustained silent reading time at school. However, he does not read casually at home. This is not to imply that he never uses books as a resource. I have observed V. and one of his friends (who is also Chinese from Vietnam) follow the directions in paper-folding books to make airplanes, dragons, boxes, and a variety of other elaborate objects. When playing chess, another of V.'s favorite activities at school with his male classmates and at home with his older siblings, V. will consult a chess book when there are differences in interpretation of rules. V. also will use the dictionary when doing his homework. However, I have not seen V. or his siblings casually reading non-school-related fiction or nonfiction at home.

V.'s family did not look at books together and it was not customary to read to the children. In fact, when asked directly if his parents ever read to him in Chinese from any books, V. asked in surprise, "Why would they do that?" No one reads in English or Chinese to V.'s younger siblings, and there are no books especially for them. V.'s parents have never bought him a children's book. All his books and magazines were given to him by neighbors or teachers. Occasionally, V.'s parents do read Chinese novels when the children are watching television or playing.

Although V., his siblings, and some of the other Asian children are not involved in frequent or extensive book-reading sessions, they live in a very literate environment. They are part of a culture with one of the oldest traditions of literacy in the world. Reading and writing letters are important in their lives and in the lives of other Asian refugee children as well. V.'s father reads to the family letters from family members in Vietnam and other places, and letters are exchanged frequently, but V. and his younger siblings do not write them.

However, a tutor who had helped V. with his homework last year and who had since moved to California writes to the children, and they occasionally write back to her in English.

S., a Chinese boy from Vietnam, wrote in his school writing book about receiving a letter from his mother and sister, who are still in Vietnam. He wrote about the contents of the letter, thus translating from Chinese to English a letter that was read to him because he does not read Chinese.

Children in V.'s class have pen pals in another school with whom they regularly exchange letters. Literacy skills often are mentioned in self-description when these letters to pen pals are written. They also are mentioned in other writing assignments when children describe their relationships with one another. For example, in a story V. wrote, he described his best friend as follows: "He can do math and spelling and handwriting and write very well too." The story continues in a narrative mode about the boys' joint success in apprehending a robber. Similarly, S. wrote a story about a magic book found by two boys:

the magic book January, 5, 1981.
once up on a time, there was a boy. Tre
boy was named Peter, Peter went out
to play. with his friend. his friend
named Joe, then Joe and Peter walk
then Peter and Joe find a magic book

then Peten and Joe look in side of
the book, then they don't know how to
read, the magic words, then they go
to aske the man, the man said this
book is a magic book, then they
wish they can read, then the
book said your wish is my
command, then they can read....

The stories of these nonnative English-speaking children often mention the desirability of having certain literacy skills. In contrast, the theme of literacy competence does not appear in the stories written by the native English speakers in this classroom.

Literacy skills are used frequently by these Asian children to build and maintain their social relationships with others, particularly adults. Letters were written and cards with messages often were created and sent to principal, assistant principal, and office staff, to teachers, and to the ethnographer. Cards sent for Christmas, New Year's Day, and Valentine's Day often were elaborate and made with school materials at home.

The skills that these children develop are contextualized in their social relationships and social life. They are developed within the sociocultural context of their families and must deal with the sociocultural context of their new society. One wonders how far-reaching literacy role reversal is in terms of other important areas of social life. The child with nonnative English language and literacy skills transmits important knowledge about the new culture to his or her parents and thus can be seen as a socializing agent. For this particular population, the Chinese from Vietnam, this reciprocal relationship is encouraged. In terms of assistance, children may be on the giving as well as on the receiving end. It seems that these particular cultural values are adaptive in that information is translated and exchanged and family members can benefit from a wide range of institutional services including education.

To understand the observed behaviors of any social group we have to know what literacy means to that group. We have to understand which genres are seen as appropriate to master at different points in time. For immigrant and refugee populations, we must explore the ways in which schooling and different aspects of literacy are related. As seen from the results of this initial report on literacy among Sino-Vietnamese refugees in West Philadelphia, developing and maintaining relationships of assistance with literacy-related tasks and devising strategies of resource use may be key factors in succeeding in a number of critical social arenas.

Discussion

We have examined three very different types of literacy experiences. In the first community, literacy is long-standing and is an integral part of many activities. Adults introduce and lead their children into literacy through a wide range of experiences and media. In the second community, literacy is being introduced into a society, and the role played by the introducers (the missionaries) is different from the middle-class, school-oriented parents in scope, function, and meaning. The future of literacy in terms of integration into Kaluli society is as yet undetermined. In looking at interactions involving a mother, a young child, and books, we saw that it was the child who initiated all of the activities, since for the Kaluli, literacy was not seen as relevant to or having any impact on the lives of children. In the third sketch, we examined a refugee family in which adults and children are becoming literate in English. This is a situation that is becoming increasingly common in the United States. The notion of a "literate environment" does not apply to the home environment of these Sino-Vietnamese families. Yet, once children enter elementary school, they make remarkable progress in acquiring school literacy. They are part of a literate culture. Even if their environment does not have a variety of books and reading material for them to explore and is not literate in some sense, their ideology is.

The variation among the three social groups we have examined demonstrates that the concept of literacy has many different meanings and has many implications. Children and adults learn a number of different kinds of literacy in different ways and for different purposes. The children in the Philadelphia nursery school were learning a broad kind of literacy, one that included familiarity with their own literate heritage as well as what is commonly referred to as *functional literacy*. These children were learning to use print in their everyday social transactions with peers and adults, to acquire or share information about their world and for more personal and private purposes of self-expression, problem-solving, enjoyment, and knowledge acquisition. For this social group, the children's acquisition of this broad kind of literacy is desirable and assumed.

In contrast, the Kaluli do not see their children's acquisition of literacy as particularly desirable. In fact, they discourage the children's interest in books. Furthermore, the kind of literacy that a small group of Kaluli adults were learning was quite unlike the broad literacy of the Philadelphia community. Their experience of literacy was not indigenous but was brought in by members of a radically different culture who had their own agenda for its use. For the Kaluli, the purposes of literacy are restricted to limited contexts and users.

Finally, for the Sino-Vietnamese families in Philadelphia, an English literate tradition is being added to an even older Chinese one. For recently arrived refugees, the acquisition of functional literacy in English is a priority. Their involvement in English literature for personal expression and enjoyment was not evident, and its eventual development is not certain.

Given these three variations in the forms and functions of literacy (and we know of others), there are two additional questions we would like to raise. First, what can we mean by the phrase *literacy before schooling*? Our first example of school-oriented families comes closest to our initial expectation of the meaning of the term, because there we are looking at the early print experiences of young children who eventually will attend school and become involved in formal efforts to teach them reading and writing. For this group, many uses of literacy are acquired before formal schooling takes place. For the Kaluli, literacy is considered something for adults who are interested in developing connections to the Christian mission. It is literacy before schooling in the sense that it is not part of a wider educational context, but neither is it part of everyday social transactions. In this society, there is no ambient print. Literacy is very restricted both in terms of the contexts in which it occurs and of the number of individuals involved. For the Sino-Vietnamese families in West Phila-delphia, the home was not like a literate environment, even though these people were members of a literate culture. Books and a general interest in print did not organize activities of preschool-aged children. For these recent arrivals to the United States, a main concern is literacy in English. Although the children develop their literacy skills in a school context, their parents are being introduced to literacy before schooling through their children. Clearly, it is crucial that we not equate the form, function, and meaning of literacy events across cultures, communities, or social groups. For example, the form of book-reading in the Philadelphia nursery school resembles the form of the book-looking activity of the Kaluli mother and her child. However, as we have argued above, the functions and meanings of these two literacy events are very different.

Having observed variation in the ways individuals do and do not achieve literacy and in what constitutes a literate environment, we pose our second question: How can we talk about *prerequisites for literacy* in a meaningful way? One theme that emerges from all three of our study examples is that, for an individual to become literate, literacy must be *functional*, *relevant*, and *meaningful* for individuals and the society in which they live. It must be able to meet the needs of individuals for their own social purposes and goals. For both the Philadelphia preschool children and Sino-Vietnamese adults and children, literacy is meaningful, and individuals show a strong interest in it. For the Kaluli, on the other hand, literacy is not yet relevant and is still restricted to a very narrow context. Future research will need to address this issue. If Kaluli become more generally literate, what form will this take, and what functions will it serve in their everyday lives?

There are many questions and issues raised by the three configurations of literacy before schooling that we have outlined. What we wish to impress on the reader is the importance of an ethnographic approach to studying the complex relationships involved in the acquisition and evolution of literacy. Without serious consideration of what literacy means and does not mean for those people who are introduced to it, it will be impossible to make sense of the ways literacy organizes and is organized by different social groups.

Notes

1. The larger study carried out by Marilyn Cochran-Smith focuses on adults and children observed over a period of 18 months at a private, cooperative nursery school in a residential section of Philadelphia. The study highlights both what these children seemed to know about print and some of the ways they seemed to be coming to know it. The research strategy for this study, constructed and adapted during a 4-month phase of

exploration, combined audiorecordings of more than 100 story-reading events, informal and formal interviews with nursery school parents and teachers, and longitudinal partici-pant observation of a broad range of nursery school activities. The study focused on group story-reading, which emerged as a key aspect of early socialization for literacy in the community, and, equally importantly, on the network of literacy events that surrounded and supported story-reading.

2. For an insightful discussion of communicative development in Anglo-American, middle-class households, see Ochs and Schieffelin (in press).

3. For a more detailed discussion of mediated story-reading, see Cochran-Smith (1982), which includes extended transcripts of actual story-reading interactions.

4. As part of a larger study on the development of communicative competence, three children were selected for longitudinal study from families that represented different points along a continuum of social change. One child was from a family in which both parents had recently been baptized and were learning to read. In the second family, there was an interest in Christianity but not in literacy. The third family was traditional and did not participate in either Christian activities or literacy classes. As part of this study, the spontaneous conversations of three children (ages 24 to 36 months) were tape-recorded for 1 year. Detailed contextual notes were taken while recording. These conversations took place between the child and those people with whom the child usually interacted. In this way, data on language acquisition as well as data on the contexts of language acquisition were collected. After recording, the conversations were transcribed by B.B.S. with the assistance of the mother (the primary caregiver), who provided additional information. In addition to 83 hours of transcribed and annotated conversations, extensive interviews and observations were part of the ethnographic research design. For this chapter, the tran-scripts were examined for those contexts in which looking at books and all other print was a focus of activity. These behaviors were found only in the Christian family, even though another family owned a literacy book and had the same access to the labels on canned food.

5. It is beyond the scope of this chapter to address the question of why some social groups are comfortable with this literacy role reversal and others are not, but it is an important question to raise and eventually investigate.

2. Social and Institutional Influences on the Development and Practice of Literacy

Alonzo B. Anderson and Shelley J. Stokes

This chapter inquires into the sources of life experiences that lead to the development of literacy. We address this question because we share a concern with many fellow citizens and scholars that the scholastic achievement in the United States of the economically poor, particularly those people usually referred to as *ethnic minorities*, falls short of that of the country's mainstream students. We also share a belief in the relevance of literacy to schooling; only in exceptional circumstances are the two separable (see Scribner and Cole, 1981). However, we do not share two key assumptions that seem to characterize much of the literature about the sources of high levels of literacy and scholastic achievement in children. These assumptions are that books provide the only valuable source of literacy experience for preschoolers and that ethnic or cultural factors mitigate against literacy development and practice.

The Equation of Literacy with Books

Few people would argue with the assertion that the United States is a literate society. Writing and its associated technologies are central to scientific discourse and the organization of industry, government, and education. "Get it in writing" is not merely an adage; it is the accepted legal practice. Literacy also is used extensively by businesses in their dealings with the public. Advertising, product labels, billing systems, directions, and receiving and distributing the family income all make use of written language. In the United States, literacy is an integral part of food gathering, the acquisition and maintenance of shelter and clothing, transportation, entertainment, and other recreational activities. Literacy seems to be involved in many of the essential domains of human activity as they are organized in this society.

Despite the obvious importance of literacy to everyday functioning in many different contexts, it has appeared plausible for social scientists to concentrate their attention on only a few of these contexts, especially cases in which parents engage their children in reading in a deliberate and planned manner. Book-reading, storybook time, and other experiences related to books (Wells, 1981; Scollon and Scollon, 1979; Varenne et al., 1981) are not the only sources of literate experience, although these are the ones typically focused on when the child's preparation for school is being considered. In summarizing this body of research, Heath (1980b,15) informs us that children with book-reading experience at home arrive at school

This research was supported by grants from the Spencer Foundation and the National Institute of Education.

already socialized into the school-preferred approach to teaching literacy. With such socialization, the school can best capitalize on what the child has already learned about print and its functions and meaning through early exposure to books. Thus, one predominant source of poor school performance of lower-class children is considered to be a lack of experience with books.

However, as we will demonstrate later, book-reading, storybook time, and other experiences related to books are *not* the only sources of literate experience even among the urban poor of the United States. In fact, these book-related experiences represent a minority of heterogeneous activities involving print. Lower-class children have considerable experience with print in addition to books.

Everything we know as social scientists suggests a very simple truth—that the literate practice observed within a group can best be accounted for by examining the external restrictions on the uses of literacy within a community. In West Africa, Scribner and Cole (1981) show this to be true of the Vai. The extent and structure of literate skills practiced by the Vai matched the range of contexts and functions encountered in their daily lives. Vai literacy is restricted because many of the contexts in which literacy would be functional are controlled by government agencies, schools, and modern economic institutions. Insofar as United States communities also are defined by such constraints, the contexts in which literacy is practiced and the links between local contexts must be known if much is to be said about literacy development. In fact, we see the whole notion of levels of literacy development as contingent, in this case, on the overwhelming power of schools for determining entry into a wide variety of important contexts. Consequently, we sought not only a principled, reproducible, description of different learning contexts but some notion of the frequency of various types of events as a basis for characterizing the patterns of different fundamental kinds of literate activity in homes where young children are being raised.

We already know from the work of Heath (1980a, 1980b) that even among working-class people there are many ways, in addition to reading books, that adults arrange for their children to come into contact with print. Her reports are detailed and suggestive with respect to the deliberately constructed contexts in which parents teach their children about print. She notes different orientations toward the kind of reading that one will need to do in school, which split along both class and ethnic lines, and arrives at three different configurations of home literate activity with three resulting patterns of school-home correspondence.

Based on such evidence, we may conclude that literacy is not absent in these working-class families' homes. Literacy encompasses a wide range of everyday practices, and these practices are important aspects of the knowledge people acquire about literacy.

Ethnic and Cultural Aspects of Literacy Development

As an ethnically and socially diverse group of social scientists, our research team[1] is very concerned with seeking to clarify the basis on which such phrases as *ethnic group differences in literacy* or *literate practices associated with poor people* are used. In our opinion, far too much emphasis has been placed on the cultural impediments to literacy, making it difficult to see the ways in which social and institutional forces operating on groups of people structure these groups' exposure to and uses of print.

Hence, in our analysis we have taken special care to link practices in the home to the social sources from which they spring. In effect we ask, "When we see a literate practice in the home, where did it come from?" When we see cultural forces at work, we see resources for coping with print as part of the mix.

The Study

Our work, undertaken at approximately the time that Heath's work was beginning to appear in print, shares with hers a concern with ethnographic description. Although we were interested in the situations stressed by Heath, which we might term *instructional* in the broad sense, we also had a greater interest in a variety of events in which print enters all but unnoticed by the participants. That is, we wanted a description of those literate events that were so much a part of people's lives with one another that they pass largely unnoticed. It was our belief, based on the work of Goody (1977) and Scribner and Cole (1981), that many mundane uses of print, if described carefully, can yield evidence of important elements of literacy practice that, although differently structured than the pure essayist style of literacy which is so much a part of formal teaching situations, represent a very important part of what it is that adults pass on to their children.

We conducted approximately 2000 hours of observation of our sample over a period of 18 months. The average number of home visits per child was thirty-four and the average number of hours of observation per child was 91. All of the families lived in the metropolitan area of San Diego and equally represented three ethnic groups (Black American, Mexican-American, and Anglo-American). Observations were focused on the preschool children but also included the daily activities of their families when the child was present to observe or participate in them.

Data-Gathering

Ethnographic participation in everyday affairs as a member of the community is an ideal way to experience the community members' point of view. Ethnography often has yielded descriptions about the details of mundane events, but it often is vague as well. "Spot observations" are a contrasting tradition, in which behavior samples are taken from time to time by someone who is normally a member of the community in question. Spot observations offer the advantage of repeated systematic observation, which allows ethnographers to make statements about the relative frequency of different kinds of events of importance to them. In our research, we attempted to link the best of the ethnographic and spot observation techniques; in other words, we employed *emic observations*[2] which are grounded systematically.

Our basic approach was to make observations in the homes and community which were preserved by detailed field notes. By this approach, we attempted to describe as fully as possible all literacy events that occurred during observation periods. We defined a literacy event as "any action sequence involving one or more persons in which the production or comprehension of print plays a significant role." Any time a target child or anyone in the child's immediate environment directly used any type of literacy technology (such as a book, a pencil or a newspaper) or was in any other way engaged with written language, the observer described the event in detail. The focus was on providing a description of the actions that took place, the contexts in which the event arose and was played out, the participants in the event, any activities that occurred simultaneously or alternated with the literacy event, and the activity that took place after the event ended.

Observations were made at various hours of the day during which the child was awake over the 7 days of the week. We attempted to interfere as little as possible in the normal activities of the families and thus assumed the role of passive observers. The presence of an observer in the homes seemed in no way to stifle the reading and writing of the members of the household. On the contrary, in a few families extra literacy events almost certainly were staged for our benefit until the novelty of having an observer around had worn off. Also, some events were clearly inspired by the observer's presence. These two types of events were not included in our analyses. One such event is presented here:

> The target child (T.C.) notices the observer (O.) taking notes. He asks O. what she is doing. O. answers, "Writing." T.C. responds: "I want to write." O. gives T.C. a sheet of paper. Mother (M.) hands him a pen. T.C. asks O. to draw him a happy face. M. tells him to draw one himself. M.: "You know how." T.C. draws. (He wanted to make a happy face, but the shape came out rectangular so he called it a pillow.) T.C. turns the paper over and makes what he calls a happy face. T.C. notices the print on his pen and studies it.

The Research Population

Our attention was focused on preschool children to attempt to uncover what constitutes their experiences with literacy. In particular, we wanted to know whether there were kinds of literacy experiences other than story-reading that provide these preschoolers with systematic and useful sources of learning about print. Since the family unit represents the smallest and most familiar social organization that transmits early knowledge of literacy, we selected the family as the focal setting for our observations. We were especially sensitive to the way patterns of literacy related to the total configuration of people's lives. We hoped to build a broader notion of literacy practice in the home, not only for the sake of ethnographic description but also for use in future research as a source of either independent variables (to predict school success) or dependent variables (to measure the effect of some intervention).

The Analytic Framework

The wide range of literacy events we ultimately observed represented a major coding problem for us. Before we could begin analyzing, we had to figure out what there was to analyze. Our field notes were not check sheets. We had no prespecified categories to guide us. Storybook time might be considered an exception, but it serves only to illustrate the problem we faced. Suppose that we agree that we know what is meant by *storybook time* and that it is a reliably scorable unit of activity to be observed in any home. What other categories are there? *Homework* might suggest itself, but we were working with preschoolers. The fact is, there was no accepted taxonomy of home literacy events that might involve 2- to 4-year-olds. We had to build a descriptive scheme and then, using this scheme as a starting point, we could code each event for purposes of data aggregation.

The results reported in this chapter represent our solution to the complex problem of building a descriptive scheme that was both faithful to the everyday experiences of our study sample and comprehensive. The analytic framework we present evolved from a detailed analysis of the more than 1400 literacy events observed. We have attempted to maintain the descriptive focus of our ethnographic methods and, at the same time, to present a summary of the major configuration of literate practice within the present sample which could be generalized to similar populations of low-income people in the United States.

Domains of Literacy Activity

Our data clearly indicate that literacy events function not as isolated bits of human activity but as a connected units embedded in a functional system of activity generally involving prior, simultaneously occurring, and subsequent units of action. In other words, the literacy events we observed were socially assembled transactions. Through a careful analysis of the literacy contexts we obtained from our field notes, we were able to identify several elements of these complex literacy situations: the materials, the people, their goals, the participant structure,[3] behavioral rules and expectations, the physical setting, and prior and subsequent units of action. Based on this qualitative analysis of the context surrounding the literacy event, we were able to construct an analytic system of *domains of literate activity*.

Once we began the detailed qualitative analysis of our field descriptions, we noticed that the types of literacy technology being used and the actions constructed around them were linked in nontrivial ways. First, the content of the material could be linked to organizations and institutions outside the home. That is, the originating point of the material involved in most literacy events could be traced directly back to particular segments of the society, such as the trade economy, the school, the church, or the welfare system. Second, various materials involving different kinds of text structure entered differentially into various kinds of contexts. For example, television or movie lists were used in an instrumental way to select entertainment; biblical narrative was used to learn or teach the Word of God; a list of food items was used for shopping; and isolated alphabets, the names of family members, and isolated words were used to teach phonics, letter identification, and word recognition lessons to young children. Very often these kinds of activity carried a familiar label (such as "shopping," or "paying the bills"). Within each of the domains of literacy activity, we attempted to characterize how print mediated the activity.

Consideration of these aspects of the literacy context enabled us to organize our literacy events into the following nine domains of literacy activity: daily living, entertainment, school-related activity, religion, general information, work, literacy techniques and skills, interpersonal communication, and storybook time.

Daily Living

Literacy events coded into the domain of daily living were embedded in activities that constitute the recurrent practices of ordinary life for the families in our samples, including obtaining food, maintaining shelter, participating in the requirements of social institutions, and maintaining the social organization of the family. Literacy events appeared in daily living activities such as shopping, washing clothes, paying bills, getting welfare assistance, preparing food, and dressing the children.

Entertainment

Literacy events coded into the domain of entertainment were embedded in activities that passed the time of the participant or participants in an enjoyable, constructive, or interesting manner. Literacy was observed to occur in a wide variety of activities in this domain. However, depending on the activity, literacy itself was (1) the source of the entertainment (for example, reading a novel, or doing a crossword puzzle), (2) instrumental to engaging in the entertainment itself (for instance, reading the television guide to find out what programs will be on, or reading the rules for parlor games), or (3) a facet of media entertainment (such as reading that occurs in the course of a television program or film).

School-Related Activity

In most cases, the material that served as the focal point of the events coded into the domain of school-related activity came directly from the school. In other cases, the direct link to the school was provided by the event participants' labeling of their ongoing activity as school-related. For examples, literacy events were coded in this domain when siblings were "playing school," or when parents were getting their children "ready for school," or when parents were helping their children "do better in school." Parents or siblings organized these types of events around workbooks purchased at the supermarket or other literacy technology such as tablets and cutout pages of magazines.

Religion

A distinguishing feature of literacy events coded into the religion domain is that they typically involve more sophisticated literacy skills than do events in most of the other domains. For example, it was not uncommon for these events to require individual or group text analysis skills as a part of Bible study sessions.

General Information

The information being accumulated in general information literacy events covered a wide range of topics and may or may not have some future use.

Work

In most cases, the literacy events related to employment were associated with producing a product, performing labor, or providing a service that was exchanged for monetary resources. However, in some cases the literacy event was associated with either gaining or maintaining the opportunity to earn money in this way.

Literacy Techniques and Skills

Literacy events coded into the domain of literacy techniques and skills were those in which reading or writing was the specific focus of the ongoing activity: That is, print is the thing that initiated and organized the activities. Specifically, these activities were organized to teach or learn literacy techniques, skills, or information. The events sometimes were initiated by a literate person, but more frequently they were initiated by the child. In either case, at least one participant in an event (and sometimes both) is required to shift abruptly out of some unrelated ongoing activity to participate in the new literacy event.

Interpersonal Communication

Literacy events classified as interpersonal communication involved printed communication with friends or relatives, usually in letter form.

Storybook Time

The domain of storybook time comprised those literacy events in which a caregiver read to a child or children in the family as a part of the caregiver's *routine* activity. Of course, not all events in which a caregiver read to a child involved narratives (stories). Typically the books involved in these events were alphabet books or books that have objects pictured with their corresponding labels; such materials contain no story line in the conventional sense. However, the category storybook time included such readings and emphasized the planned regularity of the event.

Evaluating Literacy Within the Domains

The nine domains of literacy activity organize the literacy events we observed according to salient features of the contexts within which they occurred. Within each domain, we first wished to know the frequency of events and their duration. The *frequency* of events is expressed as a proportion to standardize it across all families in the sample. This proportion was obtained by dividing the total number of literacy events by the total hours of observation. The *duration* of events is measured in minutes and also is expressed as a proportion for purposes of standardization. This proportion was obtained by dividing the total minutes of literacy events by the total hours of observation. Using the parameters of frequency and duration, we could compare the patterns of literacy activity in the different ethnic groups being observed.

Results

Frequency and Duration

Table 2-1 summarizes the frequency and average duration of literacy activity that occurred in each of the nine domains. In the interest of representing the data more accurately, we have differentiated two of our domains in this table. The entertain-

Table 2-1.   Average Duration and Frequency of Literacy Events per Hour of Observation, by Domain

Domain of Literate Activity	Duration		Frequency	
	Average Minutes	Percent of All Literacy Activity	Average Frequency	Percent of All Literacy Activity
Daily living	1.28	17.1	0.17	23.9
Entertainment				
Source	1.66	22.1	0.11	15.5
Instrumental	0.26	3.5	0.09	12.7
Media	0.03	0.4	0.01	1.4
School-related activity	1.16	15.5	0.08	11.3
Religion	1.27	16.9	0.02	2.8
General information	0.68	9.1	0.06	8.5
Work	0.09	1.2	0.01	1.4
Literacy techniques and skills				
Adult-initiated	0.19	2.5	0.03	4.2
Child-initiated	0.58	7.7	0.10	14.1
Interpersonal communication	0.17	2.3	0.02	2.8
Storybook time	0.13	1.7	0.01	1.4
Total	7.50	100.0	0.71	100.0

ment domain has been subdivided according to the three ways print enters into this activity: one in which print was itself the source of entertainment, one in which print was instrumental to entertainment, and a special category in which print was provided through the television media. We have differentiated the literacy techniques and skills domain according to who initiated the event (the adult or the child being studied).

Interpretation of Table 2-1 is facilitated when the reader keeps in mind that the averages represented in the table are proportions based on the number of literacy events or the time (in minutes) spent in literacy activity *per hour of observation*. Table 2-1 reveals that, on the average, the preschool children who participated in our study either observed or participated directly in 7.5 minutes of literacy during every hour of observation. Also, nearly once every hour a literacy event occurred and our preschool children either observed or participated in it. If we take into account that the average low-income child who participated in our study is awake 10 hours per day, we then can estimate, if our sample is representative, that this child is going to observe or participate in nearly eight literacy events or approximately 75 minutes of activity involving print virtually every day of his or her life. However, these events are not organized one after another, and all the reading or writing time is not condensed into one period. Rather, the frequency and time of events is distributed across the nine domains.

Inspection of Table 2-1 also reveals that the domains of activity in which print most frequently becomes involved are daily living, entertainment (where print is both the source of and instrumental to the entertainment activity), literacy techniques and skills, and school-related activities, respectively. Regarding the amount of time spent in literacy events, the highest percentage is committed to entertainment (especially where print is the source of the activity), followed by daily living, religion, and school-related activities.

Ethnic Group and Cultural Contrasts

When we compared the experiences that families in our population had with literacy across the domains composing our analytic framework, we found considerable variability distributed across all families in all ethnic groups. However, all families did come into contact with print. In turn, the frequency and duration of particular experiences that a preschool child has with print apparently are determined in large part by the interactions that his or her parents and other literate people in the home have with various organizations and institutions that exist outside the home. These experiences do not seem to be determined by the cultural arrangements particular to each ethnic group.

Table 2-2 and 2-3 indicate that the patterns of activity by ethnic groups differ across the nine domains. However, the differences are statistically significant in only four of the domains of activity: In the domains of daily living and entertainment (where print is instrumental), there are significant differences between the ethnic groups in the duration of activity, and in the domains of religion and literacy techniques and skills, the frequency of activity is significantly different.

Table 2-2. Average Frequency of Literacy Events per Hour of Observation, by Domain and Ethnicity

	Anglo-American		Black American		Mexican-American	
Domain of Literate Activity	Average Frequency	Percent of All Literacy Activity	Average Frequency	Percent of All Literacy Activity	Average Frequency	Percent of All Literacy Activity
Daily living	0.22	21.1	0.16	30.2	0.12	20.3
Entertainment						
Source	0.13	12.5	0.12	22.6	0.09	15.25
Instrumental	0.21	20.1	0.02	3.8	0.03	5.1
Media	0.01	1.0	0.002	0.4	0.01	1.7
School-related						
activity	0.10	9.6	0.05	9.3	0.09	15.25
Religion	0	0	0.05	9.3	0.02	3.4
General						
information	0.10	9.6	0.05	9.3	0.03	5.1
Work	0.01	1.0	0.01	1.9	0.02	3.4
Literacy techniques and skills						
Adult-initiated	0.06	5.8	0.01	1.9	0.03	5.1
Child-initiated	0.13	12.5	0.06	11.3	0.13	22.0
Interpersonal communication	0.06	5.8	0	0	0.01	1.7
Storybook time	0.01	1.0	0	0	0.01	1.7
Total	1.04	100.0	0.532	100.0	0.59	100.0

Table 2-3. Average Minutes of Literacy Events per Hour of Observation, by Domain and Ethnicity

Domain of Literate Activity	Anglo-American		Black American		Mexican-American	
	Average Minutes	Percent of All Literacy Activity	Average Minutes	Percent of All Literacy Activity	Average Minutes	Percent of All Literacy Activity
Daily living	1.31	18.4	2.03	20.1	0.52	9.9
Entertainment						
Source	1.42	19.9	2.88	28.5	0.68	12.9
Instrumental	0.55	7.7	0.15	1.5	0.08	1.5
Media	0.05	0.7	0.02	0.2	0.02	0.4
School-related						
activity	0.97	13.6	0.94	9.3	1.57	29.9
Religion	0	0	2.68	26.5	1.09	20.7
General						
information	1.47	20.6	0.41	4.0	0.15	2.9
Work	0.02	0.3	0.21	2.1	0.05	1.0
Literacy techniques and skills						
Adult-initiated	0.27	3.8	0.07	0.7	0.24	4.6
Child-initiated	0.40	5.6	0.72	7.1	0.63	12.00
Interpersonal com-						
munication	0.36	5.1	0	0	0.14	2.7
Storybook time	0.31	4.3	0	0	0.08	1.5
Total	7.13	100.0	10.11	100.0	5.25	100.0

Of these four differences, the most interesting occurs in the domain of literacy techniques and skills. The events we observed in that domain focused on the production or comprehension of print symbols. Many of these events also provided the preschool child with value statements regarding literacy, such as "it is better to write than to color." Although all the events in this domain could be characterized as literacy lessons, only a portion of them followed the familiar initiation-reply-evaluation sequence (Mehan, 1979). Our findings regarding the frequency of these kinds of events generally replicate those reported by Heath (1980b). It is the case that Anglo-American parents more frequently ($p = 0.07$) initiate activities that specifically communicate about the value of literacy or its techniques and skills. It also is interesting to note that, as Heath (1980a) found in Tracton, literate adults in Black families usually wait for the preschool child to initiate this kind of interaction rather than initiating it themselves (see Table 2-2). However, our data suggest that when preschoolers did initiate events in this domain, the events tended to last longer in Black families than in Anglo-American families (see Table 2-3).

A final point should be made regarding the overall differences in patterns of literacy activity between the three ethnic groups that participated in this study. Inspection of the totals presented in Tables 2-2 and 2-3 reveals that, overall, members of Anglo-American families involve print in their activities more frequently than do members of Black or Mexican-American families. However,

Anglo-American families do not spend more time involved with print. Thus, preschool children in Anglo-American families can be expected to observe or participate in a comparatively larger number of literacy events than do their Black or Mexican-American peers. However, these events can be expected to be of comparatively shorter duration than those that occur in Black or Mexican-American families. By contrast, preschool children in Black and Mexican-American homes can be expected to observe or participate in comparatively fewer literacy events than their Anglo-American peers, but for Black children, these events can be expected to last for comparatively longer periods of time than they do in Anglo-American families.

Rethinking the Notion of Culture and Literacy

We began our study by asking what were the sources of life experiences that lead to the development of literacy, particularly among ethnic minorities and the poor. We were aware of the large body of social science research that suggests that the culture of the poor and ethnic minorities in the United States accounts for these people's failure to develop sufficient skills in reading and writing to do well in school (for reviews, see Downing and Thackray, 1975; Cullinan, 1974; Simons, 1974). Thus, from the beginning we thought we would find that culture exerts a significant influence on a child's development of literacy and that this was likely to be true even within our lower-class sample.

We were careful to select our research sample in a way that would allow us to investigate this hypothesis. At the outset we reasoned, as many social scientists before us, that any variability in literacy activity resulting from ethnic group membership may reflect cultural differences in literate practice. However, when comparing the patterns of literacy practice presented by the three ethnic groups in our sample, we found it difficult to conclude that ethnicity was a uniformly significant source of differences.

Social Institutional Influences on Literacy

The elements of the context used in building our descriptive scheme of domains of literacy activity were the source and type of material involved in the literacy event and the sequences of action that were clustered around the particular function of the material. Using these criteria to define the relevant features of the contexts in which literacy occurs suggests that *literacy is influenced largely by social institutions and not cultural membership.* In fact, the closest we came to a source of cultural influence on literate practice concerned religion. Even there, the organization of religious practice was not consistent with traditional accounts. In our study, the Black and Mexican-American families who practiced religion were not engaged in "oral tradition." On the contrary, the churches our families attended encouraged and even required an active, assertive approach to print. A statement from a Black mother accurately captures the role of literacy in the way most of our study families practiced religion:

> Reading the Bible builds up your faith. The more knowledge you take in the more faith you have. It helps you build a better relationship with God. . . . Besides, scripture says that from babes you should inculate them with the Word.

In this woman's church, the congregation is responsible, under the leadership of the minister, for reading, analyzing, and applying the Word of God. The Word also instructs the woman to read the Bible to her children from the time they are infants until they can read for themselves. This religious imperative led many of our parents who practice religion to include the children in their semi-weekly Bible study sessions conducted in their home or at the home of a friend. Sometimes Bible study groups were specially organized for the children. Also, one of our mothers conducted regular bedtime Bible-reading events for her children. In these events, the child we studied either pretended to read along with a literate person or said the Lord's Prayer while pretending to read it from the Bible.

Another factor that would seem to be a possible source of cultural influence is language or dialect. Some of our families spoke Spanish, and even more of our families frequently spoke vernacular Black English. However, these factors seemed to exert relatively little influence on the patterns of literacy use that we observed during the study.

It became increasingly clear over the course of the study that many of the businesses and institutions of society exert a strong influence on literacy practices of low-income people. Aside from using print to carry out official and routine activities, social institutions also were involved in the recreational activities of the people who participated in the study. Many of the businesses in United States society design and distribute printed material for use during leisure-time activities. The proliferation of print for entertainment includes such items as children's and adults' games. Instructions and rules for playing games, comic books, paperbacks, all varieties of television listings, some television game shows, and the theater guide. In the United States, the production of print for entertainment purposes can be a very profitable enterprise. With such a wide availability of print for entertainment, people at all income levels in the United States are provided the opportunity to interact with print on a regular basis. In fact, in low-income homes we visited during the past 2 years, entertainment represented the most frequent use of literacy. We have observed both children and adults using printed materials to entertain themselves alone and jointly.

Anticipatory Preparation for Schooling

More prevalent influences on literacy seemed to be the parents' anticipation of their preschoolers' attendance at school, the routine requirements of daily life, or passing time in recreation. Perhaps the most dramatic example of social influences was demonstrated by our one nonliterate mother who exhibited a strong orientation toward literacy. Despite what would seem to be extreme impediments to literate practice, this parent organizes an incredible amount of literacy for her children. Cultural factors in this instance provide a different set of resources (that is, language referents and style of interaction, see Heath, 1980b), but in themselves, they do not appear to be impediments to literacy. This mother pushed her child in rather creative ways to attain literacy and was improving her own skills as well. She was acutely aware of the importance of literacy and of the constraints her limited literacy skills placed on her. She clearly did not want her children to be illiterate. In this mother's efforts to improve her literacy skills, the church became a primary broker for literacy practice, even though the context of this practice was not religious.[4] The child's preparation for school (and, presumably, his subsequent success) was the motivation for much of the mother's literacy interactions with her son. This mother teaches her child what she knows about writing and, as she progresses in her own skills, she teaches the child more. Thus, the mother presents material just outside the child's present realm of understanding and skills in a manner that (for the mother) is the natural developmental sequence for learning to read and write. One would not expect a middle-class variety of parent-directed storybook time in this family, because the mother could not read well enough. However, several interactions around books (such as a wildlife encyclopedia) occurred in which the adult made up stories, attempted to sound out words, and named pictures. Even during play activities in the park, the mother attempted to incorporate literacy by spelling out with sticks any new words she had learned. The mother's own practice with literacy was serving two major purposes at once—the improvement of her own literacy skills and the teaching of these skills (and of the importance of the skills) to her child.

Conclusions

Our observations are especially important in light of some recent trends in assessing the usefulness of literacy for low-income people in our society. There has been a narrow emphasis on one particular set of literacy activities—namely, story-reading and homework. When literacy is equated only with books, the research reports indicate that lower-class families engage much less frequently in literacy activities than do middle-class families. When we turn to studies of other types of literacy events, the little evidence available in the literature also leads to the conclusion that lower-class families are not literate. Except when special constraints are in effect (such as in a civil service examination), people with few or no literacy skills get by by using their general knowledge and social arrangements. Indeed, critics of recent literacy research (Nunberg, 1981) raise the interesting question of the purpose of making people literate if they do not use literacy skills outside narrow technologic realms. Our data suggest that literacy is not a tool used only in narrow technologic realms, but that it is a powerful tool for engaging in many activities in many domains.

The results reported in this chapter suggest a different approach to home intervention. We have observed families engaging in a variety of literate practices with connections to social institutions. Therefore, if we want to reach children in their homes in a manner that will facilitate the development of literacy practice, we would be well advised to focus on the social institutions that serve as the origins of the literate practices they observe. We could introduce interventions through the social institutions where print originates. Thus, we would concentrate on intervening through daily living, entertainment, and religious activities, using the particular organizations and institutions that are the source of these activities in the home.

Notes

1. Research team members include A.B. Anderson, S.J. Stokes, W. Teale, J. Martinez, R. Bennett, B.E. Vaughn, L. Forrest, E. Estrada of the Laboratory of Comparative Human Cognition, the University of California at San Diego.

2. Emic observations are those that attempt to adopt the categories and perspectives of the culture studied [Eds.].

3. The original dependent variable in our study (the literacy event) was differentiated along three major dimensions: the domain of activity in which the event occurred, the participant structure involved in the event, and the lesson structure of those events specifically characterizable as "literacy lessons." Of these three dimensions, only the domains analysis will be presented in detail here. Detailed analyses of participant structure and lesson structure of the events in our sample will be presented in detail in forthcoming papers.

4. A sister from the mother's church visits the mother twice weekly to teach her how to write. On one occasion, the mother showed the observer her assignment. The sister (tutor) had written the alphabet, identified consonants and vowels, and made some words by combination. The mother's homework assignment was to write a word for each letter of the alphabet.

3. FAMILIES AS ENVIRONMENTS FOR LITERACY

Hope Jensen Leichter

Study of the ways in which preschool children become literate necessarily entails consideration of the family environments in which early experiences with literacy take place. And this raises broader questions of how families educate their members and how education within families can best be understood.

In this chapter, I argue that an understanding of education within families needs to be formulated in *family* terms and not on the basis of its similarity or dissimilarity to education in schools. This implies that educational processes within families must be studied on a day-to-day basis in their natural environment. The kinds of conceptual frameworks that can contribute to such an undertaking and the methodological issues inherent in observational and ethnographic approaches will also be considered.[1]

Examinations of Families as Educators

Research efforts to understand the family's contribution to the education of its members, as well as intervention efforts designed to assist families in improving their educational effectiveness, often rest on the assumption that education within families can best be understood and evaluated in terms of models derived from schooling, or even in terms of narrowly conceived outcome measures of school achievement (Leichter, 1974, 1–43; Brim, 1959; Harman and Brim, 1980). Yet a crucial feature of families as educators is that much education takes place on a moment-to-moment basis, including both those processes that are "deliberate, systematic, and sustained" (Cremin, 1976, 1977) and those fleeting actions that take place at the margins of awareness (Leichter, 1974). While it may be argued that an educational curriculum or an educational agenda exists within families (Leichter, 1979, 3–94), this curriculum is structured differently from that in schools in terms of both time and space, and it should be understood in its own terms. At best, formal instruction accounts for only a fraction of the education that takes place in families. Informal instruction in the course of other activities— instruction that is often not even recognized as such—is essential for education within families, including the learning of literacy. Moreover, there are "profound ironies" in educational transactions whereby "what is taught is not always what is desired, and vice versa. What is taught is not always what is learned, and vice versa" (Cremin, 1976, 43).

As I have discussed in more detail elsewhere (Leichter, 1974, 1979), an adequate understanding of education within families is complex indeed. It should include education as it takes place among the various family members—children, parents, grandparents, and others—taking into account differences among these individuals. The relation of familial education to that in other institutions, including neighborhoods, museums, the media, health institutions, and schools, must also be considered. Such an understanding needs to be mindful of changes in the family over the life cycle, and it needs to be fully grounded in the various forms that families take in different social and cultural settings.[2]

One of the basic reasons for emphasizing intensive, observational studies of families derives from the assumption that the categories through which educational encounters are understood are culturally variable, both across larger societies and among families of different ethnic and class backgrounds, so that substantial efforts may be required to achieve an understanding of the symbols, categories, and concepts that organize the everyday life of a family. This is true both when the underlying assumptions of the family are different from those of the researcher and, in different ways, when the underlying assumptions are difficult to uncover because they are shared by the researcher and the family.[3]

Although a number of recent efforts have been made to understand familial education in natural settings, this kind of research is comparatively new. I shall therefore consider methods for approaching education as naturally occurring processes within families, with the hope that this may point toward features of family environments that are particularly important in advancing our understanding of the ways in which preschool children become literate.

The materials on which I am drawing come from a number of studies, recently completed or currently in progress, at the Elbenwood Center for the Study of the Family as Educator, Teachers College, Columbia University.[4] All these studies entail examinations of families in their natural environments that are intensive enough to allow exposure to many layers of communication and to shifts from moment to moment and mood to mood. The studies were designed so that, after a reasonable period of exposure to the family, *grounded theory* could be developed (Glazer and Strauss, 1967). While all these studies were regarded as ethnographic, some were formally designated as interview and observation research. The term *ethnography* has recently achieved the status of a near fad, and within so-called ethnographic research there are a variety of forms and persuasions. For present purposes, I prefer to skirt the debate over what constitutes ethnography and to consider, rather, the forms of data-gathering that are possible within families and that are appropriate for considering questions about families as environments for literacy.[5]

Although none of these studies dealt specifically with preschool literacy, all were concerned with families as educators, and one specifically with the family's role in the acquisition of literacy for learning, so implications may be drawn for preschool literacy. My intention in this chapter is not to report in detail data from any of these studies, but rather to reflect broadly on the experience of studying family environments with educational questions uppermost in mind.

Approaches to Families as Environments for Literacy

Conceptions about the ways in which family environments condition the child's experience with literacy can be clustered into three broad categories,[6] as follows:

Physical environment: The level of economic and educational resources, the types of visual stimulation, and the physical arrangements of the family set the stage for the child's experience with literacy.

Interpersonal interaction: The child's literacy opportunities are conditioned by moment-to-moment interpersonal interaction with parents, siblings, and others in the household with respect to informal corrections, explanations, and other feedback for the child's experiments with literacy.

Emotional and motivational climates: The emotional relationships within the home, parental recollections of their experiences with literacy, and the aspirations of family members condition the child's experience with literacy.

Observational and ethnographic research into one aspect of each of these three areas will now be examined, using examples from our field materials to illustrate the complexities that arise. To some extent, different kinds of data are required in each of these areas. Observations of the physical environment are, for example, different from interviews with parents about their childhood experiences with literacy.

Describing the Visual Forms in the Home

When we set out to obtain a picture of the literacy resources available in the homes of the families being studied, it soon became evident that, in a literate society, even those families that rely to a large extent on conversation rather than reading and writing for communication are inundated by print, both in the home and in the community outside the home. Noting, describing, cataloging, and tracking the forms of print within a home was a substantial task, apart from any analysis of the ways in which print is embedded in and serves to organize family activities. Kitchens proved particularly problematic, since print is so pervasive on packaging. Print also is inescapable in medicine cabinets, in supermarkets, and on television, particularly in commercials. Wastebaskets proved a particularly useful source of literacy materials,[7] reminding us that print does not merely reside in a household but rather flows through it. One example of the continuous processing of print is the junk mail with which many families are barraged.

In addition to the print that comes into the home from outside, there is the writing created in the home, which ranges from neatly organized messages to scrawls found on scraps of paper, pieces of cardboard, or napkins. These can be found in places specifically designated for notes or casually placed almost anywhere. Such communications tend to be elliptical and often contain drawings and idiosyncratic shorthand abbreviations, demonstrating that the line between print and other visual forms is not clear-cut.

We were therefore led to broaden our conception to include other aspects of visual environments (for example, geometric designs and nonphonetic symbols such as logos), with the presumption that one part of the process of becoming literate involves developing the ability to selectively perceive and abstract visual forms, whether or not particular symbolic meanings are attached to them. Although, as we often reminded ourselves, "the grocery list is not the same as Shakespeare," we endeavored to describe as comprehensively as possible the print and other visual forms found in the home. Some examples from the field notes of several observers indicate the variety of artifacts that were relevant to this endeavor:

> Books; dictionaries; atlases and maps; encyclopedias; school workbooks, reports, and tests; letters to and from school; newspapers; magazines; television guides; comic books; junk mail; notes from one family member to another; greeting cards; children's drawings; building directories; appointment books; captioned religious pictures; merit awards; personal letters; kitchen canisters; labels on food, jars, cans, and medicine and bathroom products; postcards; political fliers; coupons; laundry slips; cookbooks; wall plaques; games; name plates; shopping lists; postage stamps; coloring books; sport catalogs; diaries; Christmas cards; gift lists; record albums; sewing patterns; baseball cards; sweatshirts; photograph albums; identification cards; and tickets.

The researchers (primarily graduate students in education) kept extensive day-to-day field notes, yet even with the mandate to describe print broadly, there were certain noticeable gaps resulting from implicit concepts about the research endeavor. The study of the family's role in the acquisition of literacy for learning was distinct from a study concerned with the mediation of television by the family. During the analysis of field notes for the two studies, it became clear that much of the print displayed on television had been overlooked by the researchers on the literacy study. These researchers evidently categorized certain kinds of events and materials as unlikely to relate to literacy, and this seems to have narrowed the area of observation.

In attempting to survey artifacts in homes to determine which literacy resources were available, it became evident that no clear boundary could be drawn between an artifact that served such a purpose and one that did not. Indeed, we seemed to rely on implicit assumptions that certain artifacts were educational while others were not, and that those artifacts containing print were potential resources for learning literacy while those without print were not. Yet these assumptions were unwarranted. Sewing patterns, for instance, are not in the home for the purpose of literacy instruction, but they have potential as an educational resource not merely in the teaching of sewing and the use of patterns but in developing spatial concepts and the ability to recognize visual forms, intellectual skills that may well be underpinnings for literacy. Clearly, whether something is thought of as an educational resource derives more from human attitudes than from its physical characteristics.

From our assessment of individual artifacts, we were led to consider how varying arrangements of artifacts in the home might lead children to develop different visual propensities. In visiting different homes, one cannot help noticing how much families differ in the ways they arrange furniture, decorate walls, array objects on tables, and use cupboards and cabinets. Ways of organizing the visual environment may also have shifted significantly over time. In her autobiography, Margaret Mead describes how clearly she remembers the few treasured objects on her mother's dressing table and their precise arrangement (Mead, 1972). The analogous visual experience for many of today's children might be a jumble of plastic toys that have few distinguishing or memorable characteristics.

There has been a corresponding shift in the experience of print. It has already been noted how the lives of today's children are deluged with print, but we have not considered how often this print differs from the comparatively consistent print of former times. On television, especially in commercials, print is protean: It comes in constantly varying sizes and styles. It moves around, grows larger, shrinks, changes colors, and disappears in rhythms that often are combined with music, speech, and sound effects. It typically appears in constantly varying relations to representations of people, objects, and landscapes, as well as abstract images. How can we characterize this experience? Does it lead to mastery, or is it perhaps overwhelming and ultimately confusing?

Given that the extensive exposure of today's child to print and other visual forms may be counterproductive in some respects, one may wonder how much environmental print is ideal for the acquisition of literacy. Again, a comparison with former times may offer some insights. In colonial America, the child's exposure to print was certainly sparse by today's standards, yet a high rate of literacy was attained, fostered, to a large extent, by family instruction. It was expected, both legally and informally, that reading be taught at home, and even when teaching was somewhat formalized in schoollike groupings, it remained a household activity. In addition to the Bible, the materials of instruction included primers, ABCs, and prayer books, which typically contained such familiar texts as the Lord's Prayer, the Apostle's Creed, the Decalogue, and the catechism. However, this relatively sparse material was used in an intensive way. According to Lawrence Cremin:

> It was read and reread, often in groups, and almost always aloud; much of it was memorized and thus passed into the oral tradition, where it influenced many who could not themselves read; and ultimately it provided a world view and a system of values that families held in common and that communities could therefore assume as a basis of law and expectation. (Cremin, 1970, 31; see also pp. 128–139)

Thus, instruction in literacy was embedded in activities that were meaningful in their own right. The texts used had great cultural significance and were firmly tied to an oral tradition. Moreover, the extensive use of oral instructional techniques tended to stress the social relevance of literacy.

This brief consideration of the colonial experience with literacy brings us to questions about how print is used in the everyday life of families, how reading and writing are combined with other kinds of communication, and how one may best proceed in studying these uses of literacy.

Locating Literacy in the Stream of Family Activities

Locating literacy events in the stream of everyday family activities is a substantial task, especially if one wishes to avoid defining literacy events in terms of previously held conceptions (Barker and Wright, 1971). Yet a full verbal description, even one combined with other kinds of recording (such as photographing, audiotaping, or videotaping), only enables one to know what went on during the period of observation. Researchers often neglect the obvious point that what they did not see may or may not have taken place at another time or in another location.

On entering a home with the intention of learning how the family handles literacy, the observer is immediately faced with such practical problems as where to sit or stand, what areas of the home to attempt to observe, and which family members to watch and talk with. Even with a focus as definite as television-viewing, the observer is faced with numerous decisions about how to focus observations. Sitting beside family members while they watch television, for example, makes it impossible to observe their eye-gaze direction.[8] Since more than one activity is generally going on simultaneously in most households, the observer must continually face the question of where to focus his or her attention. These decisions are made more difficult by the realization that watching one activity frequently means missing another. Even when there is a clearly specified set of activities to observe, the observer cannot be sure when a crucial moment will arrive (for example, when a decision to shift television programs will occur, or when a preschool child will engage in spontaneous drawing or writing). In all the homes, we found a wide range of learning activities that parents engage in with their children. The following are examples which were recorded on initial data sheets:

> Writing notes, asking questions, helping with homework, instructing a child to look something up, instructing a child to use books, doing homework with a child, giving answers to a child, giving explanations to a child during cooking, showing a child how lists are made, allowing a child to make decisions, attempting not to criticize a child, preaching, scolding, punishing, checking to see if homework is finished, instructing a child to be independent, going over picture albums with children, teaching liturgy for Holy Communion, making up children for a school play, making a label for a mailbox, making signs, helping a child read instructions, listening to children's recitations, and carrying out feminist political activities.

There was variation in the duration, frequency, regularity of occurrence, and formality of these activities. Family members and observers did not necessarily characterize an activity in the same way. Indeed, sometimes one participant thought of an activity as educational while another did not. These differences make it complicated to establish a criterion for what constitutes an educational activity.

Attempting to observe and systematically record literacy activities that would be comparable from one family to another led us, at one point, to focus on videotaping children doing homework with the assistance of parents. We selected homework partly because it was readily definable—that is, it was possible to obtain a consensus among family members and observers that an event constituted homework. The focus may also have reflected an unwitting assumption that school-related activities are prototypically educational. Through the videotaped data on homework sessions, it was possible to analyze in detail such interactional features as the beginnings and endings of events and sequences of interaction in homework assistance, such as question-answer-evaluation and question-answer-checking.[9] In this analysis, it became apparent that some simultaneously occurring activities such as the ringing of the telephone were organized so that they became intrusions that interrupted the homework activity, while others were not. Many of these insights would have been missed without a method of recording that allows repeated examinations of the data.

The problem of locating literacy within the stream of family activities may be solved by focusing on interaction with print during such formal moments as homework sessions and reading to children. If, however, one assumes that many occasions for literacy take place in the course of other family activities, then one is presented with the broader problem of tracking and observing an exceedingly wide variety of activities that are potential settings for literacy or that provide context for understanding more formally defined literacy events.

A crucial feature of familial organization is the fitting together of multiple simultaneous activities. Analyzing these parallel activities raises the broader questions of how literacy is embedded in activities that are carried out for purposes other than instruction, and how reading and writing are combined with other modes of communication. A wide range of ways in which literacy was embedded in everyday activity was observed. In all of the families in the literacy study, such daily activities as shopping, selecting programs from television guides, and paying bills were organized on the basis of literacy or required its use. Writing was used for communicating when family members were apart, keeping appointment calendars, writing shopping lists, writing charts for household chores, keeping budgets, and keeping photograph albums and other family records, including those in family Bibles.

The bulletin board kept by one family illustrates the kinds of data that are useful for analyzing the ways in which literacy is embedded in other familial activities.[10] The family was of Irish-American background, and the household at the time of the initial observation consisted of the father (a truck driver), the mother, and two daughters, aged 10 years and 1 year. Their bulletin board, largely maintained by the mother, used print to organize the family's life in terms of its basic concerns. An ERA (Equal Rights Amendment) button, newspaper clippings, and cartoons were reflections and reminders of the mother's newly acquired political and feminist beliefs. A green plastic shamrock and some St. Patrick's Day cards were a display and reminder of the family's ethnic identity. Cards for other holidays served to organize and reinforce other ceremonial events within the calendar year. An envelope for coupons and an unemployment book were reminders of the economic realities of the family's life. An appointment card for visits to the pediatrician and dry-cleaning slips helped to organize memory. The eldest daughter's successful school report and her scores in a bowling tournament in which she did particularly well attested to special achievements of the family members. Notes of apology or notes saying "I love you" reinforced relationships or attempted to ease interpersonal problems. Wedding pictures, pictures of family friends, and a card that the daughter had drawn for her mother served to commemorate special occasions. Fliers, posters, pamphlets, leaflets, and notes telling of school board elections, plays, athletic events, and children's entertainment helped the family keep track of community events. The bulletin board contained print generated outside the home as well as materials written by family members. It combined print with decorations and drawings, pictures, diagrams, and other forms of visual shorthand, and it included texts that were self-explanatory as well as those that were elliptical and dependent on prior understandings or oral communication for comprehensibility.

Placing the coupons on the bulletin board was part of a highly organized process in which the mother and eldest daughter clipped coupons from newspapers and magazines and organized them for the most effective use. They were sorted first by type of store and then into categories that corresponded to categories within stores. Mail-order coupons were separated from the others and periodically were sent for redemption. Thus, literacy was fused into a series of activities that required organizational and cognitive functioning that went beyond the literacy skills required to collect and sort coupons. Most important, literacy was embedded in activities that were meaningful not only in their own right but because they related to the family's economic well-being.

While the bulletin board, which was consciously used by the mother as an educational as well as an organizing tool, exemplifies literacy as it is embedded in family activities, observations of homework sessions within this same family illustrate concerns with literacy that are tied more closely to school evaluations than to events within the home. It is difficult to compare the literacy skills involved in clipping, organizing, and placing coupons on a bulletin board, or in designing a poster to celebrate a family event, with those involved in filling in blanks in a vocabulary notebook. But it is clear that researchers should be alert not only to differences in the family's control over activities but also to the different ways that evaluation and feedback are structured. As we analyze the extent to which literacy in families is embedded in other meaningful activities, we should also attend to the ways in which the emotions and motivations generated under these different conditions vary.

Uncovering Emotional and Motivational Climates Within Families

Investigation of the emotional and motivational climate of a family requires still other kinds of data and analysis. Despite the manifold difficulties of inferring emotions and motivations from external observations, useful data on such matters can often be obtained from interviews.

An essential aspect of motivational climate is the reward system (Bruner, 1960, especially Chap. 5). Although it is difficult to connect an observed reward with its subjective meaning to an individual, it is still possible to make useful distinctions among the types of rewards involved in literacy events. In the previous section, for example, the parent-child interaction in connection with the family bulletin board was contrasted to that connected with completing homework. The bulletin board activities tended to be rewarded intrinsically, while the rewards associated with homework, since they were dependent to a considerable degree on the outside evaluation of the school, tended to be extrinsic.

It is also important to consider the part that literacy skills play in evaluations of individuals, both self-evaluation and evaluations of others. Whether or not they intend to, families often evaluate children in terms of how they are reported to do in literacy tasks in school. Beyond this, the skill that a child shows at home often becomes a focus of familial evaluations, ranging from passing remarks, glances, and gestures to stories that are repeated in varying forms on one occasion after another, sometimes to neighbors, friends, and relatives.

A parent who has experienced problems with literacy and school failure is likely to bring these experiences to evaluations of the child's literacy exploration and skill. Interview material from the literacy study contains numerous examples of traumatic early experiences with reading and writing. A few excerpts from a tape-recorded interview with one father concerning his experiences in a school in Ireland will illustrate the flavor of such recollections:

> The teachers were rough. I mean the discipline back then, they'd sock it to you. . . . We had a fear of the teacher, and when you have a fear of the teacher, you don't like going to

school. . . . In fact, I remember jumping in the river to avoid going to school. . . . I pretended to be sick and I was forced to go so I accidentally fell into the river. I was brought back and I got a spanking and I was sent to school anyway.

I remember trying to read . . . with the scene . . . the family on the beach . . . the beach balls, building the castles and all that sort of stuff. I guess I was 7 or 8. [If you didn't read well] you got whipped. . . . Basically, it was the punishment idea. . . . You used to have to hold your hand and you would get it, maybe six wallops across the hand with a stick . . . and your hand would start bleeding. . . . Your ears would be beaten with a bamboo cane, and you couldn't do anything with your hands. . . . Some kids used to freeze up there [at the blackboard], you know, you'd go blank and you'd get slaughtered again. . . . You couldn't complain at home; you didn't open your mouth; you had no recourse. [The kids that could never read] got beat up more than anybody. . . . We had dummies. . . . They got more stupid by every day.[11]

Such recollections are reconstructions and may be embellished. However, they constitute understandings that the parent brings to the child's explorations of literacy. This is not to presume that there is a direct connection; parents commonly attempt to counteract or compensate for their own unpleasant experiences by creating different ones for their children.[12] Such examples serve as reminders that parental anxiety with respect to children's literacy is omnipresent. It may be that children can learn to become literate on their own without formal instruction, but when experiences with literacy take place in family environments, the emotional reactions of the parents can affect the child's progress significantly.

In examining emotional and motivational climates in families, it is important that the researcher maintain a balance between the somber and the playful. A tendency undoubtedly exists, in research on families as educators, to emphasize the serious side of family life, especially when the research involves questions about achievement in schools and careers. Yet in some respects the greatest intellectual fluency in conversation, reading, and writing occurs during playful, joking, and humorous interactions. At such times, words are given multiple meanings: Puns, both verbal and visual, are made, and thoughts connect freely with one another. Humorous, often elliptical notes from one family member to another frequently allude to a wealth of family history, prior conversations, and shared meanings. Such playful uses of literacy may have a salutary detachment from the formalities of school-related literacy and the dire evaluations that often accompany it. A consideration of the playful side of family life can be especially helpful in achieving an understanding of families as environments for literacy that is formulated in *family* terms.

Issues in the Use of Intensive Studies

Through examples from several studies of families as educators, I have attempted to illustrate modes of inquiry that are basic to an understanding of families as environments for literacy. In each of the areas illustrated, an intensive study that includes many different kinds of data is required even to begin to obtain a picture of the complexity of family environments. To describe visual forms in the home, observation must go beyond narrowly defined literacy resources such as print to include a broad range of forms; to locate literacy in the stream of family activities, a broad range of activities carried out for a variety of purposes must be observed, not merely those explicitly done for the purpose of literacy acquisition; and to uncover emotional and motivational climates, data are needed on a range of family motivations and emotions, from the embarrassing and traumatic to the playful and amusing. To obtain a variety of data, a number of data-gathering and data-recording procedures are required, including photographing physical arrangements, videotaping nonverbal interactions, and tape-recording personal history interviews. Beyond this, as others in the symposium have also observed, data on the family's cultural beliefs and on its place in the society at large are essential for an adequate examination of the understandings that family members bring to particular literacy events.

It is difficult, in carrying out this kind of intensive and extensive research, to achieve a balance between observations so broad that they become diffuse and examinations so narrow that they miss the context within which a particular experience with literacy takes place. However, if one accepts the argument that an adequate understanding of educational transactions within families should be formulated in family terms rather than in terms derived from schooling, a strong case can be made for this kind of research, which is particularly well suited to gaining insights into the complications of family life.

Intensive study is also useful for ensuring the objectivity of the observer. Any research on the family inevitably activates strong emotional reactions and beliefs that the researcher brings from his or her own family experiences. The painstaking kind of research recommended here helps researchers unlearn the biases that they bring to their tasks.

Thus far I have not discussed issues of access, but families are, to some extent, private domains. Even if one gains entry into this domain as a guest, visitor, or researcher (and permission may be extremely difficult to obtain as a researcher), one has access only to certain layers of the family's experience. The glimpses that an observer obtains of a family's life may shift dramatically from one time to another. This supports the argument that observers must be patient enough over a period of time to get beyond the most public behavior of the family, but it also indicates the need for them to remain aware that they can rarely enter a family beyond certain layers of communication and awareness. Since research into the family is necessarily intrusive to some extent, anyone wishing to conduct such research should ask himself or herself the following questions: Under what conditions would I, personally, be willing to have a researcher enter my home? What areas of my family life would I be willing to have a researcher see, analyze, and report on?

Establishing roles for the researcher may require extensive negotiation, since all research must be carried out at the convenience of the family and not at the convenience of the researcher nor solely in terms of some a priori research design. Potential participants may sincerely and justifiably challenge proposals on the grounds that past research has not benefited the subjects of the study or on the basis of a general suspicion of university-based researchers. It should also be remembered that portrayals in the media of what is presumed to be family research often establish images of exposure and exploitation that must be dispelled. On the other hand, with careful negotiation, extraordinary interest in and cooperation with research efforts can be obtained from families. Experience has shown that these issues of access and observer roles should be thoroughly discussed in advance with the sponsor of the research.

Since the intensive examination of families in their natural environments is so difficult, it is essential to be clear about the conditions under which it is the method of choice for a particular research question. I would urge that this costly and seemingly inefficient method is appropriate only when at least the following conditions apply:

1. When social or cultural categories that are essential to the research are not known by the researcher and time is required to learn the culture of the family (for example, when the family's beliefs about competence in literacy are not known to the researcher)
2. When the natural setting is presumed to have characteristics different from specially arranged laboratory or experimental settings (for example, when the allocation of attention to a particular task as it is carried out in the course of multiple simultaneous family activities may be presumed to differ from attention in specially arranged settings in which distractions have been minimized)
3. When natural settings can be presumed to have features that cannot be conveyed by report, or when the level of data in which the researcher is interested cannot be conveyed by report (for example, when the features of microinteraction or the visual and spatial arrangements in the home cannot be conveyed by report)
4. When the data in which the researcher is interested can be presumed to surface only with special kinds of rapport and only at times that are difficult to anticipate, so that waiting is required (for example, when it is impossible to anticipate the time at which a child will imitate the writing of an older child in spontaneous play)
5. When research is theory-discovering and the questions are not entirely specified in advance (for example, when attempts are made to unravel the mystery of the physiological, intellectual, and social processes by which children learn to speak and to become literate)

Despite these cautions, I wish to urge that our present understanding of families as educators can indeed be advanced by intensive examination. Such methods are particularly suited to studying the complexities of life within families: the multiple perspectives of the family members, the multiple layers of current experience, the multiple strands of communication, and the multiple strata of shared history. Such complexities must be encompassed if we are to achieve an understanding of families as environments for literacy.

Notes

I wish to express my appreciation to Eric Larsen for his many insightful comments and helpful suggestions. I also thank Madeline Flannery for her able assistance.
  1. Since I generally concur with the assumptions about literacy that have been set forth elsewhere in this book, I will not discuss my own assumptions here.
  2. Since authors of other chapters in this book discuss the importance of social and cultural conditions, this chapter will concentrate on the kinds of conceptual formulations and research methods that can increase our understanding of families as environments for literacy.
  3. For an analysis of concepts underlying culture in the United States that reveals the perspective of a nonnative, a French anthropologist, see Varenne (1977).

4. These studies include the following: (1) "The Family's Role in the Acquisition of Literacy for Learning" (National Institute of Education Contract R-400-79-0046) is a study of the family's role in helping children to move from the early acquisition of literacy skills to the use of literacy in other kinds of learning. Hope Jensen Leichter was principal investigator and Vera Hamid-Buglione was project coordinator. Other members of the project staff included Professors Raymond P. McDermott and Hervé Varenne with the collaboration of Professors Paul Byers and Spencer H. Jameson. In addition to Professor Hamid-Buglione, the main fieldworkers were Theresa Hsu, Melanie Lewis, Mary Madigan, Ann Morison, and Sybil Stevenson, as well as John Cacace and Verna Denny. Information about the project is available through the Elbenwood Center for the Study of the Family as Educator, Teachers College, Columbia University. Some of the analysis of project materials has been reported in *"I teach him everything he learns in school"*: *The Acquisition of Literacy for Learning in Working Class Families,* by Hervé Varenne, Vera Hamid-Buglione, Raymond P. McDermott, and Ann Morison, Report to the National Institute of Education, 1982; and in Ann Morison's unpublished doctoral dissertation, "Getting Reading and Writing: Literacy Patterns in Three Urban Families," Teachers College, Columbia University, 1982. An analysis that was useful as background in the initial formulation of the project was the doctoral dissertation of Taylor (1983). Discussions of earlier stages of the research can be found in Hope Jensen Leichter's "Final Report of First-Year Activities," prepared for the National Institute of Education, November, 1980. (2) "An Examination of Cognitive Processes in Everyday Family Life," (National Institute of Education Grant G-79-0177) is a study of the intellectual processes inherent in everyday family activities. Hope Jensen Leichter served as principal investigator and Vera Hamid-Buglione was project coordinator. The final report by Hope Jensen Leichter and Vera Hamid-Buglione with Bruce R. Buglione, Spenser H. Jameson, Royce M. Phillips, and Carmen Rodriguez is available through the National Institute of Education. (3) "The Mediation of Television by the Family," a study sponsored by the Spencer Foundation, investigated the ways in which families mediate the television experiences of their members. Hope Jensen Leichter was principal investigator and Jennifer W. Bryce was project associate and principal fieldworker. Reports of this research are contained in Jennifer W. Bryce's unpublished doctoral dissertation, "Families and Television: An Ethnographic Approach," Teachers College, Columbia University, 1980; and in "The Family and Television: Forms of Mediation," by Jennifer W. Bryce and Hope Jensen Leichter, soon to be published in the *Journal of Family Issues.* A comparative study of families and television in Pakistan is described in Durre-Sameen Ahmed's unpublished doctoral dissertation, "Television in Pakistan: An Ethnographic Study," Teachers College, Columbia University, 1983. (4) "Social Networks and Educative Styles," a study sponsored by the Spencer Foundation, examined the ways in which teenagers move through, engage in, and combine educative experiences in a variety of settings from family to school to neighborhood. Hope Jensen Leichter was the principal investigator and Vera Hamid-Buglione was project associate. One report is available in Vera Hamid's unpublished doctoral dissertation, "Social Class Variations in 'Educative Style': Two Case Studies," Teachers College, Columbia University, 1979. For a discussion of the conceptual framework of the study, see Leichter, 1973. (5) "The Role of Memory Within the Family" is a study of memory as social interaction within families. It is being conducted by Hope Jensen Leichter and was supported by a Guggenheim Fellowship.

5. For other discussions of ethnographic and related methods, see McDermott et al. (1978) and Bryce (1980), Bryce and Leichter (forthcoming), and Ahmed (1983) in the preceding footnote.

6. These categories are not exhaustive and do not preclude other factors such as the nature of language usage or stages of individual maturation. A related but different set of factors

influencing parent behavior and therefore family environments, has been proposed by Harman and Brim (1980, 49–65). Included are ability factors, unconscious factors, cultural antecedents, interpersonal and social controls, group structural determinants, and ecological and physical factors.

7. Denny Talyor has suggested the importance of wastebaskets based on her own research (see Taylor [1983]).
8. See Bryce (1980) in footnote 4.
9. Videotaping was done by Paul Byers. Raymond P. McDermott was principally responsible for this portion of the analysis.
10. Discussion of the bulletin board is based on field notes and analysis by Vera Hamid-Buglione.
11. Transcription of a tape-recorded interview, from the field materials of the literacy project.
12. For a discussion of parental recollections of early experiences with literacy, see Taylor (1983).

4. The Achievement of Preschool Literacy for Mother and Child

Shirley Brice Heath with Charlene Thomas

Since the second decade of the twentieth century, parent education has become a common phenomenon in those nations that provide 10 to 12 years of schooling for the majority of the national youth. Initially, the major emphasis was on the physical health and development of the child. In the 1960s, the focus shifted to the parent-child interaction and its effects on the social and cognitive development of the child (Brocher, 1980). Professionals in child welfare began to assert that parents needed to be "socialized" in child-rearing skills and "developed" in their abilities to smooth children's entrance to school and transition into secure and capable adults. Subsequently, parent socialization has focused on specific types of interactions to increase the "effectiveness" of parents and enable them to "improve" the quality of their relations with their children (Fantini, 1980).

Parent-Child Book-Reading

Book-reading with preschoolers or "reading before school" (Smethurst, 1975) is a popular form of interaction highlighted in parent education programs. Numerous parent-academicians have written accounts of their personal experiences with early readers and writers (see Chap. 6 for a bibliographic listing of such reports). Almost all these studies report the early reading of mainstream middle-class children, and their focus is on what the child learns about the uses of literacy and gains from being an early reader. The caregiver's interactions with the young child and the artifacts of literacy (children's books, crayons, pencils, and paper) in the literacy event[1] of book-reading receive little attention, but instead seem to be considered givens or somehow "natural" to parenthood.

By the mid-1970s, however, psychologists, linguists, and anthropologists began to detail the negotiated social construction of such parent-child interactions. Ninio and Bruner (1978) describe one middle-class mother and her preschooler reading a book, with the mother focusing the child's attention, requesting labels, and providing opportunities for the child to move forward in knowledge about the contents and uses of the book. Scollon and Scollon (1981) describe mother and child engaged in book-reading as exhibitor-questioner and spectator-respondent. The mother displays the book, points to, and names items upon which the child is to focus attention; she then asks questions about the names of items, their features and location in the book; the child watches, listens, waits, and responds. In many ways, these book-reading episodes are similar to descriptions of mainstream middle-class caregivers talking to their children (Snow and Ferguson, 1977; Gleason and Weintraub, 1978; Snow, 1979). Scollon and Scollon (1981) and Heath (1982b, 1983) call attention to the intricate ways in which oral language learning patterns are related to literacy habits that focus on naming, retelling, and paying close attention to features of the environment chosen for emphasis by the adult.

These accounts of book-reading illustrate the bundle of collectively sustained symbolic structures that embody overlapping and reinforcing ideas of what it means to acquire literacy skills and to become literate in mainstream school-oriented society. In the classroom, students encounter similar literacy activities in reading circles, social studies lessons, and language arts classes. There, as in mainstream homes, adults select the story or book, focus the child's attention on particular objects, and expect the child to respond as spectator and respondent (see Chap. 1 for an account of book-reading in a school setting). Studies of mainstream middle-class children at home and of literacy activities in classrooms have shown that what is being transmitted in preschool book-reading is much more than how to read and write. The children learn a set of master patterns of language use, which serves as a basis for the subsequent acquisition of other patterns of language and thought. Heath (1983) details the multiple ways in which mainstream parents immerse their children in an environment of repetitive, redundant, and internally consistent habits which enable their children not only to read and write but also to use book knowledge in other contexts. These children learn to link items in one setting to items in their books, to name their points of similarity and their attributes, uses, and functions. Moreover, as these children enter school, their parents continue to stress the early pattern of individual display and achievement lessoned first in bedtime story-like events (Heath, 1982b). All these studies provide support for Bourdieu's (1967, 1973) notion that the transmission of cultural capital by the middle class involves much more than the provision of books and leisure time for book-reading; it implies also a host of sustained institutional and routine mechanisms that work together harmoniously to integrate children from such homes into learning with literacy.

What set of associated habits and multiple minute adjustments of verbal and nonverbal behavior accompany book-reading with a preschooler? If, into a home in which parent-child book-reading has not been a habit, we introduce children's books as literacy artifacts and provide minimal guidance in the literacy event of a caregiver reading with a preschooler, what behavioral changes, if any, will occur along with this innovation? For the anthropologist, this question is no different in principle from that which asks about the behavioral changes that followed the introduction of the fork in Europe in the fourteenth century. The possibility of spearing chunks of meat rather than gnawing flesh from the bone brought changes in menus, requirements for foodstuffs, and types of utensils for cooking and serving food (Kroeber, 1948). Many of these changes seemed unrelated to the fork itself; moreover, many could not have been predicted, for they seemed to occur spontane-ously and in patterns linking habits not consciously related to eating as it is understood by humans.

In this chapter, we trace the behaviors that occurred simultaneously with the innovation of book-reading for an unemployed, high school dropout, black mother of two preschool children. Aside from the financial difficulties caused by the unemployment of the mother and several members of her family (in a period of widespread joblessness), the mother seemed to have ways of living similar to those of the residents of Trackton, a black Piedmont community of the Carolinas de-scribed in Heath (1983).

A Review of Trackton

All adults in Trackton could read and write, but they did not consciously model, demonstrate, or tutor reading and writing for their children. There were no special children's books, and the only materials written especially for children were Sunday school pamphlets or leaflets brought home from church. There were no special times for reading and no routine reading activities such as bedtime stories. At an early age, Trackton children began to tell stories modeled on oral tales they heard adults exchange in their everyday banter, in which a good story was the best way to win an argunent, smooth over a disagreement, or prove a point. Adults did not question children about bits and pieces of the stories the children told. In addition, in their interactions with young children, they did not pick out sounds the youngsters made and respond to them as though they were labels of items in the environment. They also did not ask preschoolers the common teaching questions, such as "What is this?" or "What color is this?" Instead, adults talked about items and events in the environment without simplified speech or special types of questions addressed to young children. Questions asked of young children with the greatest frequency were of the type "What's that like?" "Where'd you get that?" In short, Trackton parents did not exhibit the routines and patterns of talking, reading, and writing with their young children that were described in the research literature on mainstream school-oriented families. Nonetheless, their children did learn to talk, and they went to school with certain expectations of print and were able to recognize such reading materials in their environment as the names of cars and motorcycles, brand names of products, and T-shirt slogans.

In Trackton, I collected these details of the forms and functions of written and spoken language through my participation as an ethnographer in the community for nearly a decade. I did not attempt to introduce any artifacts or events that were not native to the community. However, some years later in another community, in my work with the mother described here, both her ninth-grade English teacher and I did make efforts, though minimal, to introduce into this mother's ways of living a new literacy artifact (children's books) and a new literacy event (reading those books with her preschool child). Furthermore, throughout the year described here, her English teacher and I encouraged this mother to keep a record of her own activities and her 2-year-old's uses of language. As the full record began to develop, the mother agreed to be a research associate and to work with me to provide a published report of her achievement of preschool literacy with her son.

The Story Behind This Story

The conditions and goals of the work which led to the description given here are unusual and merit explanation. The mother described here is Charlene Thomas, (T), a 16-year-old who dropped out of the ninth grade early in the 1981 school term. She was repeating the ninth grade because she missed most of the previous school year when her mother had an extensive illness and died. She had a son born in September of 1980, and another was born in 1982. In September of 1981, T was enrolled in a ninth-grade Basic English class in a high school in a town of 30,000 in the deep South of the United States. The school provided two academic tracks: a general track for students who planned to attend college or technical school, and a "basic" track for those who scored below the fifth-grade level in reading and language arts skills.

The teacher of T's English class was Amanda Branscombe, (B), with whom I worked in a teacher-researcher relationship during 1981 and 1982.[2] B's emphasis in her classes was on writing and reading. As a teaching strategy, she set up letter-writing teams, each composed of one student in her basic English class and one student in her eleventh-grade general English class. The school was large enough and sufficiently socially segregated by the two-track system that it was highly unlikely that students in the two classes would meet. The eleventh graders studied English only in the first semester (from September through December). Therefore, to ensure that the ninth graders had an audience and a reason for writing beyond December, I began corresponding with them as a class in the fall and continued throughout the spring.

In addition, I asked the ninth graders to become associates with me in my interests as an anthropologist in oral language and reading and writing in communities around the world. They began taking field notes on topics such as the types of questions used in their homes and communities. They interviewed family members about recollections of themselves learning to read and write and memories of their children's early language development. To the students, my goal was explained as the comparison of these habits with the research I had conducted in the Southeastern part of the United States, which was being prepared for publication as a book (Heath, 1983). The teacher read portions of the book's manuscript to the class so the students would have some idea of the final product created from field notes. Approximately every 2 weeks during the fall term, B sent me copies of the ninth-grade class's writings and her own field notes describing what she did in class and how the students were responding to their reading and writing. In turn, I provided feedback on developments I saw in the individual students' writing, and B and I discussed research in writing and its implications for classroom teaching in bi-monthly phone conversations.

In late November, B told me that T had missed 15 days of school, which, according to school policy, exceeded the number of absences allowed to a student in one semester. She would have to repeat the grade. I suggested that we encourage T to continue writing letters to the eleventh grader, and B and I also agreed to write to T. I suggested that I ask T to take field notes of her toddler's activities, especially his talking, and I would send some books and ask her to read to her toddler. B agreed and suggested she visit T and take her books, audiotapes, and a tape recorder. The purpose of the tape recorder was to give T an "easy" way to stay in touch with us and to tell us what she was doing with Davaris (nicknamed De), her preschooler, in case she did not continue writing.

The dual goals of this "project" were then to create what might perhaps be some motivation for a school dropout to read and write with her preschool child, and to continue her membership in the community of writers and researchers B had created in her ninth-grade class. The field notes and audiotapes the students had made on their reading, writing, and talking habits and those of their families had legitimated this activity for the ninth graders; moreover, the class had accepted the fact that I was exceptionally curious about how, when, where, and with whom they talked, wrote, and read. The description reported in this chapter, then, does not come from a preplanned "research project" but is an accidental by-product of a pedagogic activity initiated for a high school dropout mother by a teacher and a researcher.

Some background on T's writing in the months between September and November will provide an idea of the literacy skills and habits T had when she quit school. At the beginning of the academic term, B paired the ninth-grade and eleventh-grade students on the basis of their interests as indicated in brief self-introductory letters written by each student. One class period each week was used for the letter exchange: students read the letters they received and answered them. T entered B's class 10 days late and was paired for the letter-writing with a senior girl (L) who was a serious student, walked with a limp, rode horses, and was the daughter of a teacher-minister. The teacher paired the two girls because they both said in their introductory letters that they were interested in riding, although the girls' letters soon revealed that L meant horseback riding whereas T meant riding in a car. To T's first letter (Fig. 4-1), L responded with sympathy for the difficulties of entering school 10 days late and answered the questions T had raised in her letter. In her second letter, T included a salutation and closing and had begun to develop a dialogue with L. By the fifth letter, she told L that she had few friends at school, was

Figure 4-1. Charlene's letter of introduction to L., September 11, 1981.

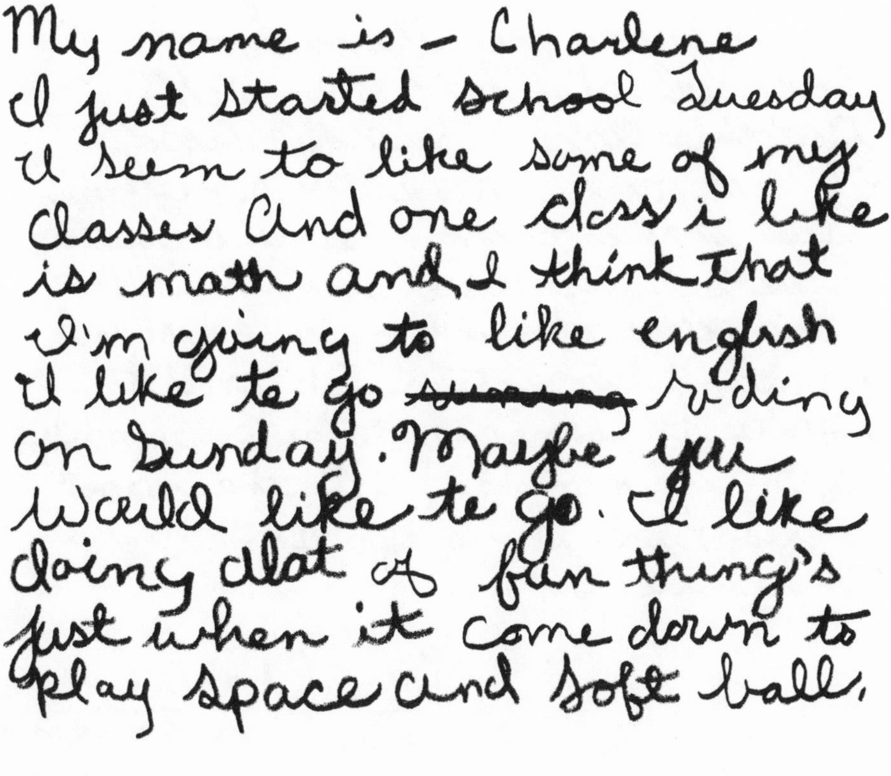

My name is - Charlene
I just started school Tuesday
I seem to like some of my
classes And one class i like
is math and I think that
I'm going to like english
I like te go ~~swimming~~ riding
on Sunday. Maybe you
would like te go. I like
doing alot of fun thing's
just when it come down to
play space and soft ball,

the mother of a son, and had lost her own mother the previous year. L responded by telling T about her limp and her own frequent absences from school because of sickness.

In early November, after only eight letter exchanges, the teacher asked the students to write a brief paragraph about what the letter exchange had meant to them. T's note (Fig. 4-2) indicates that prior to the ninth grade, she had not written a letter.

By mid November, T had missed 16 days, and she quit school. L wrote to her within the week expressing dismay that her own nightmare of missing 16 days in 1 year had become a reality for her friend. Two weeks later, T wrote a letter to L in which she explained: "Well, as you know, I have quit school. I didn't really want to quit. But it just came to point I know I had to do." She asked L to keep writing to her and closed her letter with this postscript: "I wished I could have know who you was." One week later, she wrote to her teacher, explaining that she had quit school because she was expecting another baby in April and she did not believe she should be another girl making "black's look bad" by "walking around the school with a stomach."

Figure 4-2. Charlene's essay on the meaning of the letter exchange, November 6, 1981.

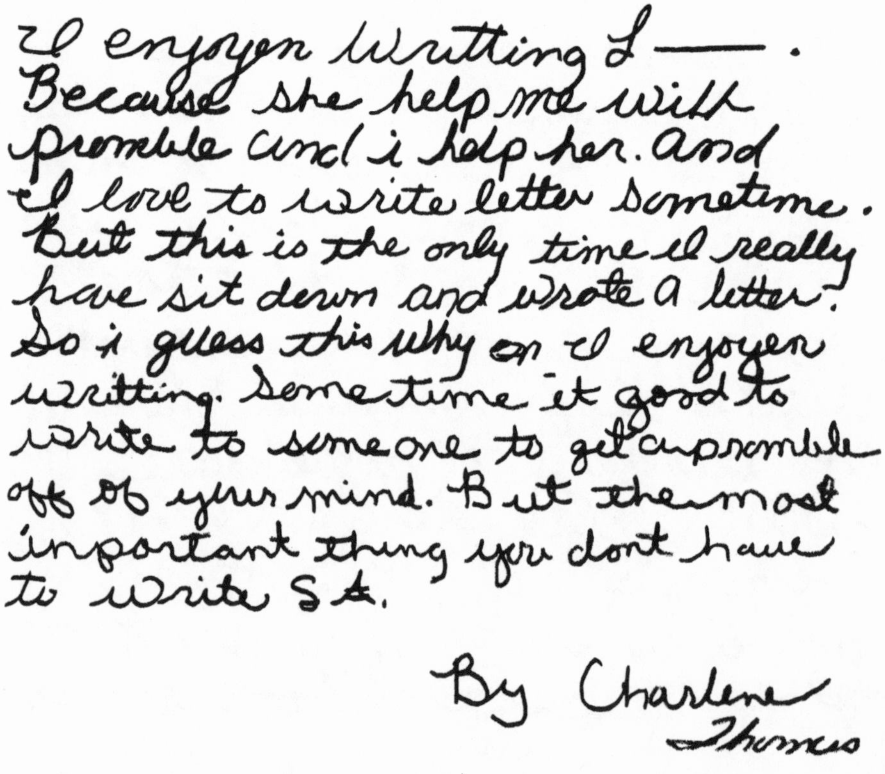

I enjoyen Writting L——.
Because she help me with
promble and i help her. and
I love to write letter sometime.
But this is the only time I really
have sit down and wrote a letter.
So i guess this why en I enjoyen
writting. Sometime it good to
write to some one to get a promble
off of your mind. But the most
important thing you dont have
to write S A.

By Charlene
Thomas

Achieving Literacy

Both B and I wrote T, and B visited, encouraging her to try to obtain her high school diploma through night school. In a letter to T, I asked if she would be willing, now that she was at home all the time, to take field notes on her son's language learning and his daily activities. She responded in late February with three pages of field notes (printed here as they appeared in the original).

Fieldnote   Feb 27, 82

Kid's in my community is in school. And I don't be around many of them that's not in school. But I have a 17 months old son. And his name is Davaris. He is walking and talking a little bit. Well when he started talking it was baby talk. But now I have got that I can understand him. I sit an teach him different thing's. As who people is. And what not to do. And what to do. Kid that he do be around they teach him things. Such as Know' no, and try to teach him what thing's is. Like Dog & cat's. And now he can tell me pot pot. And he mean's he got to use the bathroom. And like when he want something to drink he go and get his cup. And I open up the refrigerator and he point to what he want. But mostly I believe that they learn more from beening around grow up. They watch everything that goes on. And they try it. The way he tell me he wont to go somewhere. He say come go. And he get my hand and take me where he wont to go. It just amazing how kid learn to talk. Because when we came up we didnt know different thing. As these kid's now day is faster than we is. He do talking to himself but mostly is baby talk. And some is when he here me say to him. Like get and what. no' no. Mama, Dada. He does read the only thing he do is look at picture. And say what they are. I teach him how to count. He say one, two, five, six, He cant say the rest of the number yet. But he is learning. I think the more him be around me and other adult He will be smart. He sit A watch TV. Cut it off. Stand up in chair's pick up the phone. And do baby talk sometime he say what. Somebody knot on the door he use to say who. But now he don't say nothing. He will come an get me or somebody. He go outside by hisself when the door is open. Put his cup in the sink. Pull the chair up to the sink and try to wash dish. pull it up to the table. It just so much that he do. So I'm going to let this be it. He stay busy all the time. I hope that this can be a help.

Your friend
Charlene

In these field notes, T terms De's early language "baby talk," and she emphasizes her own priorities for his learning: that he should know who people are, respond to commands, be independent, and learn by watching others and trying. She notes that the children around teach him commands and "what thing's is."

The new baby was due in April 1982. T was the sole housekeeper in a household in which she, the new baby, De, the children's father, her teenage brother Mike, her father, and two other adult males lived. Realizing she had limited time for writing field notes and anxious to give her a specific task, I wrote asking her to read to De for 10 minutes each day and to tape-record (on a recorder borrowed from B) the reading sessions with him and the time when he played alone in his room immediately following the reading. In early May, B reinforced my request by taking children's books, audiotapes, and a new tape recorder as a gift for T. Within the week, T recorded an oral account of what she could remember of De's language development. She reported that De weighed 8 lb. 2 oz. at birth, and within the first week he was holding up his head. By 9 months, he "walked and talked." Her account continues:[3]

Then, really, when he started to talking, he was about 7 months old; that's when he start doing kinda like with baby talk. I really couldn't understand 'im. Then when he was 9 months old, he got two teeth; then he was talkin' and walkin', and then he start to saying things like "dada" and "mama" and "bye bye." Mostly that was all he could say then, 'cause the rest of it was baby talk. Then when he got older, he started to pick up things, like when I would say "no," he would learn that word, that when I was saying "no," he know what it mean. And then when I would tell him, I would say "don't do that," he would say "don't" but he couldn't say "do." and then when I would tell him, I would say "stop" and he would say "stop." Now when I tell him things, like I'll say "juice," he'll say "juice," and things like that. And then he started to, he get to know to where he say "Mike". He can call mostly all of my sisters' and brothers' names. Mostly he can say things now like, he can say "baby," he say "ball," he say [unintelligible]. And sometime like when he wants to go outdoors, he say "door," else when he want something to drink, he say "juice," and then like when he get ready to eat, he will tell you, he will say "eat." And then, like, when something in the refrigerator he want, he got where he could go and open up refrigerator 'n' get whatever he want out of it. You tell him, like when his little cousin come down here, you tell him to play, they don't like to play together, but they fight most all the time when they play and things, so they fuss and carry on and tell each other "shut up" and "no," and don't do things, like "don't do that." And then he's get where he run around outdoors and go up the road [unintelligible]. I tell him to get outta road, 'cause he don't know how to get outta road when the cars come, and he'll say "no, no." Now he's beginning to try to potty train, I tell him to go to his pot, and I say 'sit on the pot,' and then like when he got to pot, he be saying "water, water," he be telling me he gotta use his pot. . . . But mostly, my little brother, he sit down and teach him, he say "one," and he say "one," and he'll tell him to call "daddy," and he say "daddy," and you tell 'im to say "mama," he say "mama," and you tell him to go get something, he'll go get it. And then like when you're trying to get him to count, he'll say "one," and "two," and "three." Then I'll say "Davaris, how old are you?" and he'll show you one finger; he be saying "one."

In this record, made 3 months after T's written field notes, she included specific details of both De's speech and that of others around him. She pointed out that he was independent, obeyed some commands, repeated words after adults, called household members, and was tutored by adults to call family members and to respond to a range of situational circumstances in the busy household in which many people regularly came and went. The remainder of this tape was a recording of T's efforts "just to get De to talk." In several sessions, T said she held one of the children's books in her lap, but on the tape she cannot be heard talking about the book; instead she asked De to name objects in the room and to call members of the family. She named body parts for him, and during this naming, she put her face very close to his. For this and all other labeling, she neither held up nor pointed to the objects or people being named.

On May 28, B returned to T's house and they listened to the tape together as the teacher wrote an account of T's talk about the nonverbal details and general context at the time of the taping. This procedure was followed on each subsequent visit. On this visit, B took with her several books, including an "alphabet book," (groups of items beginning with the same letter on each page), and *The Gingerbread Man*. Proudly, T said she had ordered a set of Walt Disney books for De and had put them away on a high shelf in the bedroom. She did not report having read to him from them. During the visit, T opened the alphabet book, pointed to an item, and told De "say cat." She sat on the sofa; De stood in front of her looking into the book momentarily, but he focused his attention on only the tape recorder. B left, discouraged, reminding T to try to read to De 10 minutes daily.

On June 2, the teacher returned and listened to the tapes made since May 28. T reported that during these sessions, she sat on the sofa, while De stood in front of her and looked into the book or continued to play. In each of the five sessions recorded on the tape, T began the reading by focusing on the objects in the alphabet book and saying, "Say ____." After only several such directives, the requests shifted to people and objects: "Say mama, say daddy." After each request, she waited for De to repeat. Often he made no response; on other occasions he repeated the name, and at other times, his repetitions were indistinct in pronunciation but clearly imitative in rhythm and intonation. T reported that she had not "started reading" to De because she could not get him to sit still long enough. B suggested bedtime, and T replied "He be sleep before I go to bed." The teacher proposed that T read to De at *his* bedtime or whenever he seemed sleepy, tired, and willing to settle down on the bed or sofa sitting close to his mother and looking at the book with her.

During this visit, T, in an effort to get De to read with B, forcefully made him sit down, after which the teacher asked her to follow only two rules when reading with De: never to hit him or force him to read or write with her, and to leave the books available for him to play with whenever he wished. While the tape was being replayed and B and T were visiting, the television was on, and often as many as a dozen people passed through the living room from outside or other parts of the house.

Tape recordings made between May 24 and June 2 indicated that T tried to "read" with De, but in these attempts, she usually told De to "say ____," and she often focused for less than 1 minute on the items pictured in the book. She then moved on to tell him to repeat after her the names of objects and persons in his immediate environment. At one time or another, all members of the household could be heard on the tape, instructing De to "say ____" and repeat after them commands to others (for example, "open it"). Several people tried to get De to call members of the family or to call the dog. In one period, when T left the recorder on while De was playing alone, the child repeated names he had just been asked to say in a session with his mother. He used a sharp staccato tone in the repeating exercise: "cat (pause) dog. . . ."

In T's field notes and oral account of De's language development, she did not mention that she asked him questions such as "what is this?" or interpreted any of his self-initiated utterances as labels of objects. Neither on the tapes nor in person did B hear an adult address such talk to the new baby or to other preschoolers who were visiting. Thus until June, T and others around De seemed to follow many of the patterns of interaction with young children that were described for Trackton residents (Heath, 1983). In Trackton, adults did not talk to infants or young children as though they expected them to be communicative partners, although they talked about children in their presences and surrounded them with verbal and nonverbal communication. The cooing and babbling sounds of children were referred to as *noise* (or in T's terms *baby talk*). The focus in Tracton and in T's account of De's language development was not on the children's language productions but primarily on their exhibitions of how they come to know—that is, how they respond to the language of others.

In her account of De's language development, T indicated how De learned to make language work for him in a variety of functions (see Halliday, 1975). He moved from interactional language, engaging those around him ("dada," "mama"), to instrumental language which, when combined with nonverbal cues (such as standing by the refrigerator), met his desires for juice or food or attention to his toilet needs. Once he began to try to control the actions of those around him, De used language for both regulatory and personal functions. By 8 to 9 months of age, he used pointing as a way of referring to or identifying objects, and he had some utterances that apparently were isolable and bounded by pauses, since T reported that he referred to objects in the environment with sounds she could not understand.

In her account, T placed almost no emphasis on her role or that of other adults in teaching De to talk, and she indicated no special efforts on the part of adults to try to interpret, expand, or repeat De's utterances. Once again, this behavior parallels that of Trackton adults who did not speak of *teaching* children to talk. Nonetheless, during the initial weeks of trying to read with De, T and other family members seemed to equate reading with saying the names of things. At this stage, the adults extended this practice from repeating names of objects to requesting that De call people or the dog, say "no" to others, and repeat specific commands to others. Neither B nor I suggested this approach, and the source of this behavior is not clear. The format of the alphabet book may have been a factor. An even more important source may have been T's sister, a high school graduate who visited T often and "read" with her daughter Eureka, who is 6 months older than De, by saying words and waiting for her to repeat them. Once the project had begun, she spent several hours weekly at T's home. Early tape recordings contain sessions in which she asked her daughter to repeat all the letters of the alphabet, each one after her mother, and to say names of items and people in the room.

Between June 2 and 24, T began what she called *reading* with De, for she was able to get him to sit still beside her while they both focused on the book. She tape-recorded a total of 3 hours in these weeks, but most of the taping was done between June 21 and June 24, the day of B's visit. T estimated that she or another member of the family had read to De approximately a dozen times, but she had not recorded all these sessions. Therefore, we do not know whether all sessions were focused on books or on requests for repetitions of words unrelated to the book but seemingly prompted by an initial session with a book.

Figure 4-3 is transcript of what T regarded as her first successful reading session with De.[4] It was T's first attempt to read to De by holding him beside her on the bed at his bedtime. She began with the alphabet book, reading and occasionally asking De to look when she pointed to items in the book. De began his participation by offering a repetition of her pronunciation of the letter *A* after she had moved on to *B*. When T shifted from the names of letters to object names, De vigorously repeated after her "cow" and "cake," and then fastened on "cake" for several repetitions. The time between T's offering of the stimulus and De's repetition decreased significantly once T switched to names of objects. When De fastened on "cake," T shifted to the letter *G* (for reasons which she could not explain, except that she kept turning pages in the book, trying to keep De's interest). At this point, after only three object names, De focused his attention on the pictures of the boy with a hat and did not

Figure 4-3. Transcript of a taped reading session, recorded between June 21 and 24, 1982.

T reading from text of alphabet book	T talking about text	De's responses
1	this book right here? say A, A.	
2	look	
A (pause) B//		//A
B, C, C, C,		(2 sec.) C (softly)
cow		(7 sec.) *cow*
cake		(3 sec.) *cake*
cook		(3 sec.) cake
cook		(2 sec.) cake
3	say G	
4 G, G	say G	(1 sec.) hat
5 (De's attention here seems	look, say *boy*	hat
6 to be focused on a picture	boy, say *boy*	look, look,
7 of a boy with a hat on the	boy	look
8 page illustrating the	say girl	look
9 letter *G*)	look, lemme read this book	
(De tries to get down)		
10 (T picks up *The Ginger-*	wanna read the gingerbread	
bread Man)	man?	
11	look	
Once upon a time. . .		look (repeated four times
(continual reading for		during reading)
40 sec.)		
12	look at the pig, see that pig?	(2 sec.) pig
13	the gingerbread man	(1 sec.) bread
14	yeah	
(resumes reading for 25 sec.)		look (repeated three times)
		see that pig
		cow, cow
15	look at that cow, cow	cow
16 (book pictures cow beside	*water*	duck
17 pond with ducks)	cow=	=duck
18	the cow ran	cow, cow
19	look, look at this cow	
20	sittin' down, she tired	sh (unintelligible)
But she couldn't catch the		
21 gingerbread man	see the house	(4 sec. unintelligible)
22	gingerbread man	(2 sec.) gingerbread
23 (resumes reading for 20 sec.)		
(book pictures two bears		
24 having a picnic)	look at the bear	(2 sec. two unintelligible
		squeals)
25	say bear, look at the bear,	hat
	say bear	
26	yeah, hat, see that hat on	
	that bear head	
27	hat	(1 sec.) hat
28	yeah, hat	(1 sec.) hat

29		yeah, you see the bear=	=hat
30		yeah, but they can't catch the gingerbread man	
31	(turning pages to end of	look, De, look at this fox	
32	book)	say fox	(3 sec., unintelligible
	(resumes reading for 25 sec.)		utterance repeated four times)
33		look at dat fox, say fox	
34		fox, look, De	
	(resumes reading for 23 sec.)		(two unintelligible utterances repeated one after the other)
35		see the fox	
36	(resumes reading for 25 sec.)	look	
	(resumes reading for 10 sec., in which fox snaps up		
37	gingerbread man)	look	
	(reads final statement) and that was the end of the		
38	gingerbread man.	look, see that fox	(2 sec.) um?
39		fox=	=fox, fox
40		yeah, fox, look	
41		look at my alphabet	
	(session with alphabet book continues for 1 min. more, until baby cries; just as baby cries, De asks:)		what that?

repeat *G* but instead labeled the object "hat." Following this, he tried to take over the task of attention-focusing from T, saying repeatedly, "Look," but his mother reasserted her central role in choosing the focus of attention (line 9, Fig. 4-3) and introduced *The Gingerbread Man*. While she read for 40 seconds, De repeated "look." T stopped after the fifth utterance of "look" to point out an object in the book. When De repeated after her, she offered no confirmation until he said "bread" for gingerbread man, to which she responded "yeah" and resumed reading. De once again repeated "look" during the reading and later pointed out a pig ("See that pig,") and then a cow (a term noted in the alphabet book several minutes earlier). T then responded to him and offered another word for repetition. However, De had already focused on the duck in the water and he labeled the duck. In trying to focus attention on the cow, T offered the first topic comment on the book's pictures or content (lines 19 and 20, Fig. 4-3). She resumed reading only briefly and then pointed out other objects, but she did not do so with question intonation or a direct request for repetition. When T reached the pictures of two bears having a picnic, she broke away from the text (lines 25 through 30, Fig. 4-3), asking for labels, but once again De had focused on the hat of one of the bears, and his mother expanded his response into a well-formed sentence and commented on the picture and the relation of what was happening in the picture to the book's purpose. She then flipped to the end of the book and focused De's attention on the fox. Here, her tone was heightened, and she said "look" more insistently than earlier, as she urged

De to focus his attention on the fox. The child listened and watched the book, saying nothing until his mother had finished the story. She repeated her request that he look at the fox, and he immediately repeated "fox" so that his repetition was connected without pause to her second request. T returned to the alphabet book, but the baby cried. At the sound of the baby's cry, De tried to engage his mother's attention, using language heuristically to ask "What that?" while pointing to something in the book.

Between this session and the next recorded session, transcribed in Figure 4-4, T or her brother Mike read *The Little Red Hen* to De once or twice, but T did not record those readings. The sessions transcribed in Figures 4-3 and 4-4 probably took place within 24 hours of each other. The reading of *The Little Red Hen* that took place during the Figure 4-4 session, then, was either the second or third time De had heard this story. T began with a request for him to focus on the hen. De interrupted her with "hen" and then said "red" when she was saying "hen." T's reading segments throughout this session lasted less than 10 seconds each and she stopped often to focus on objects in the pictures, to ask for repetitions, or to make topic comments. De readily said "chick" when she offered "chicken," and later (line 6, Fig. 4-4), he anticipated what the text said just before his mother read "cluck cluck." He emphasized the second syllable, and his timing clearly indicates that he was following the text so closely that he knew the sentence "then she said to her baby chicks . . ." would end with "cluck cluck." T offered no confirmation or reinforcement of this participation until De interrupted again with "chick." Later in the session, when he focused on the duck in the picture, she again offered no confirmation. At line 15 (Fig. 4-4), T wanted her son to focus on a picture of the hen with many baby chickens, but instead De fixed on the hat in the pictures, and T expanded his word into a well-formed sentence and added a tag question. Her talk about the book continued (lines 15 through 33) until she decided to have De read by repeating the exact words of the text: "They walked. . . ." He repeated "they" and she then asked him to say "walk" and "cluck cluck," but De said only the latter. At this point, he tried to get off the bed and move away. T then commented on the story-reading episode as a "nightnight story." De repeated this entire phrase after her with clear imitation of the rhythm and intonation. They tried to continue with the alphabet book, but the baby cried and T left the room, leaving the tape recorder on.

T reported, in her account to B on later hearing this portion of the tape, that when she walked by the room, De was holding and throwing the books, talking to himself. During this period, much of his talk was unintelligible, but on three occasions on the tape, he said something that clearly related to the books. The first time he said, in rapid succession in sharp, stacatto style, "Look, look, look." On the second occasion, he began by saying "lemme look," and he named "cat, dog." In the third segment, he apparently was "reading" *The Little Red Hen*, and he said "chick chick" several times through a series of utterances that were imitative in rhythm and voice quality of his mother's reading of the text.

In T's next session of reading with De, she began with the alphabet book. Many people were in the living room, where the recording took place, and there were many distractions. She began with the letter *A* and moved through *B*, *C*, and *D*. When she reached *D*, she said several times, "Say *D*," and then asked, "Where's

Figure 4-4. Transcript of a taped reading session, recorded between June 21 and 24, 1982.

T reading from *The Little Red Hen*	T talking about text	De's responses
1 the little red hen	you see that little red//	//hen
2	hen?//	//red
Once upon a time there		
3 lived a mother hen	see that hen?	(2 sec.) um?
4	chicken	(1 sec.) chick
(resumes reading for 7 sec.)		chick
5	see that chickchick	(1 sec.) um chick
6	chickchick	(1 sec.) chickchick
(resumes reading for 4 sec.)		
. . . then she said to her		
baby//		//cluck*cluck*
chicks, cluckcluckcluckcluck,		
we will take a walk=(pause)		=*chick*
		chick
7	yeah, chicken	(3 sec.) chick
(resumes reading for 10 sec.)		look
8	look, *look*, look	
(resumes reading for 7 sec.)		chick
9	look at the chick=	=pig
10	look at the pig, pig=	=pig
11	duck	(2 sec.) duck
12	chicken	(1 sec.) chicken
13	bird, biddy, say biddy	(2 sec.) duck
14 (Mike, T's brother, may have	say Mike	(2 sec.) Mike, ike
entered the room, or she		
may have understood		
duck as *Mike* in De's		
15 previous utterance)	look, look at that picture, whoeeee	
16	look at that picture, see that chicken 'n' them biddies	(2 sec.) chickchick
17	yeah, that chicken 'n' them biddies	(1 sec.) chick
18	yeah, chick (pause) hat	(1 sec.) hat
19	yeah, that hat on that chicken, ain't it?=	=hat
20	yeah	
21	lets see what else in here	
22	um see, lookahere, look at that man	(2 sec.) wh
23	whoeee, look at that man, you see	(2 sec.) man
24 (turning pages of book)	yeah, that man 'n' that chicken look	
25	you look at that, De, say bread	(3 sec.) yeah, chick
26	chicken eat bread	

27		you see them chicken at the table?	
28		look, say chicken	
29		you see hat chair, lookahere	
30		chair, see that chair, look here, look	
31		look at the pig 'n' the duck	
32		see that pig 'n' the duck?	
33		read the book	
34		let's see can you read?	
35		say *they*, De, say they	(2 sec.)
36		walk=	=they (with a shout)
37		say walk, say cluckcluck	(1 sec.) cluckcluck (softly)
38		say cluckcluck, cluckcluck, cluckcluck⹀	(3 sec.) cluckcluck=
39	(De seems to want to take	say pig	
40	the book and move away)	you ain't gonna let me finish reading?	
41		let mama read you a story	
42		let read you a nightnight story	
43		wanna read nightnight story?	(5 sec.) nightnight story um?
44			
45		yeah	(3 sec.) um

(Charlene tries to continue
with the alphabet book for
approximately 30 sec.
more; then she leaves De
alone in the room for
16 min. He plays with the
books she has just read:
the alphabet book first,
and then *The Little Red
Hen*)

D?" Because De did not respond, she repeated, and he said, "Um?" She said "De, say *D*, where's *D*?" shifting the meaning of the sound from the name of an alphabet letter to his nickname. He softly offered an unintelligible reply and she shifted to asking, "Where Mike?" and naming other members of the family who were present. This was the only evidence on the tapes of a phenomenon Scollon and Scollon (1981) emphasize in their characterization of "incipient literacy," a focus on playing with language and its similarities and differences in written and oral uses.

In a session taped on June 24 and described to B when she came to pick up the tapes, De and Eureka (his female cousin) were playing together in the living room, where several adults were visiting. The books were scattered about on the floor, and Eureka wanted to play with them. De screamed in protest, captured a book, and climbed into a chair with his legs straight in front of him, holding the book on his lap. Eureka retook the book, and T asked De to let the cousin read, but De pulled the book away from her and said, "Where chick, chick, chick?" He repeated this question several times, each time more shrilly. Adults finally intervened and started the children on the routine of counting. Adults said the number, and one or both of the children repeated immediately afterward. During this episode, they soon turned to the alphabet. At the letter *D*, De repeated "*D*" first with the intonation he usually gave it in the alphabet repetition game but then shouting "De, De," with a different intonation, he danced around the room seemingly recognizing his own language play.

During the month of July, T and her children moved out of the house to live with another relative, and T began temporary work. By mid-August, she was back in her earlier household, and she made two tape recordings, one summarizing De's language progress over the past 2 months and another including readings and a session in which she introduced De to writing. She gave De crayons and paper at the kitchen table and offered no instructions other than for him to use the crayons rather than the pencil he wanted. Near the end of the writing episode, she asked, "You gonna write your name?" His writing fits Platt's (1977) description of the first level of writing—scribbling that has no isolable parts or recognizable repeated designs, or which are not identified by the child as writing which represents something else. After De's scribbling, T wrote at the top left corner of his paper "Davaris Thomas as Dede."

In late August, B noticed that De held his baby brother (now 4 months old) and read to him. The baby was able to follow when De pointed to objects in the book. B suggested to T that, whenever possible, she read with the baby in her left arm and De on her right, letting De hold the book. De also had a new friend who was a few months younger than he and he read to his friend as she sat by him and tried to imitate his pointing to and naming of objects in the book. T reported that De sometimes did not want her to read to him, but instead he wanted to take the book, turn pages, and read to himself by labeling the items in the book's pictures.

On September 8, T recorded another update on De's activities. She reported that he was completely toilet-trained, could give the baby his bottle, went to bed upon direction, got his own water from the kitchen sink, and enjoyed playing with Mike's electronic games. She also reported:

> He calls hisself readin'—tryin' to read, but the only thing he's done is readin' the picture book. After a while, he can soon learn how. And now he gets where he had learned to count a little bit, but he can't put 'em in order. He will just say the numbers just out of order. But then you sit down and teach him how to say his ABCs, he'll mock you 'n' stuff like that.

She reported that De talked to the baby:

> And then he'll get to talkin' to him, he'll say "hey, babe." You know how the way little kids talk to another baby, the way is mighty strange; they just learn each 'n' every day from their parents. You know when they parents teachin' 'em how to talk to a child and now he just beginnin' to learn how to talk to the baby like he should.

On a tape made on September 19, 2 days before De's second birthday, T told him, "Talk to baby. Tell baby, 'Hey, babe'" (with exaggerated intonation). On this tape, she sang "The Little Drummer Boy" to De while showing him the pictures in the book. The first time through he listened without a sound, but in later sessions recorded on this tape, he picked up the song at the ends of the bars and hummed the tune after his mother. Also, a story-reading episode on this tape was interrupted by T's pointing to a sore on De and saying, "Sore, say 'sore,' 'hurt,' and 'sore hurt.'"

She said this several times, and each time De repeated her words. After a long pause, T stopped repeating, followed by De's saying 'sore hurt' several times. This was the only tape-recorded occasion in which T built a proposition with De about objects that were not pictured in books. She did not, however, expand the proposition into a well-formed sentence, such as "your sore hurts." However, later on this tape, in a long exchange with De's cousin Eureka, T picked up an utterance made by Eureka and then built propositons with her and expanded the child's statements into well-formed statements. This conversation was one of the rare occasions when T and a child were alone together and dialogue occurred without the stimulus of a book. Mike had gone to bed, and Eureka spontaneously said, "Gotta go to school, Mike." T responded, "Yea, Mike gotta go to bed 'n' go to school." She then asked Eureka a series of real questions, beginning with "you wanna go to school?" This conversation follows the pattern of those described for mainstream adults who build from the utterances of the child a set of intentions and restate the child's utterances into well-formed sentences. T did not simplify her talk to Eureka, and the two acted as conversational equals building cooperative propositions in response to utterances initiated by the child.

Retaining Literacy

T's progress in her own literacy skills in the year between September 1981 and September 1982 was considerable. Outside stimulation was minimal. I wrote her six brief letters but never saw her; our communication has been entirely through letters, audiotapes, and B's field notes of her ten visits to T's home. We had provided T with books, tapes, and a tape recorder. She was never given any direction other than to read with her child, record the reading and his play immediately following the reading, and to listen to the tapes with B during her visits and summarize the activities that had surrounded the recording.

A comparison of T's first letter to L. (Fig. 4-1) and her later letters and field notes written in February indicates her increased confidence in expressing herself, some improvement in her command of the mechanics of writing, and development of an ability to write a well-formed friendly letter and to summarize facts in a narrative style. Following the first history of De's early language development, made at my request, T decided when to provide summary updates of his language progress, and she initiated the recording of each of the five subsequent summaries over the year. Her reading had not been restricted to De's books; she has read my letters and drafts of this chapter. In reviewing the latter with B, she clarified facts, discussed interpretations, and added assessment of her own and De's achievements. T's keen observational skills (demonstrated in her first tape about De's language development) have improved with each recounting of the details surrounding tape-recorded events and De's subsequent language progress.

With regard to the specific reading and writing sessions with De, T has found her own way to numerous literacy socialization strategies. She has learned when and where to read with him, how to hold him and the book, and how to focus his attention on the book. She makes some use of attentional vocatives; she waits and lets De make his contribution to the reading. She tends to use vocatives primarily at those points in the reading when De is restless, and she then also moves from a strict reading of the text to topic-comment structures and attention-focusing commands. She has mastered the basic components of a dialogue with De about a book's content. De repeats her entire utterance, selects segments for repetition, or offers topic comments. T has provided him with crayons, pencils, and paper, and she supervises his drawing and writes his name on his drawings. In short, she has achieved preschool literacy with De.

What cannot now be known is whether T will retain and extend these skills with De and his younger brother. During the past year, T has initiated activities and talk that call attention to language itself. However, the tape recordings do not indicate that, as yet, she engages in the common mainstream ways of extending the functions and uses of literacy—providing narratives on items and events in books and real life, asking De a wide range of teaching questions, and carrying on extended dyadic conversations with him. T does not yet link objects or events in books to their real-world counterparts. Neither she nor other adults in the household do more than minimal reading and writing, and these activities consist primarily of reading the daily newspaper and filling out job applications. In the final months of the summer of 1982, Mike began to buy and read sports magazines. Either the television or the radio is on at all times, and as many as a dozen people often are in the busy, noisy household. In T's busy schedule of caring for an infant and maintaining a large household, she has little time to be alone with De. The reading and writing events are almost the only times in which her involvement with him is not focused on physical caregiving or disciplining. However, the motivation for reading and writing with De is high, since both T and the father of her children remember they were not successful in Head Start and had to repeat their year. Both are now high school dropouts, and they believe that failing Head Start was the beginning of their academic downfall. Both compare De to themselves before Head Start; they say of themselves, "We were fast, but Head Start slowed us down." De's parents want him to "pass" Head Start "so he can finish high school." As a dropout, T sometimes expresses despair over her lack of choices, points to her daily routine, and asks, "Do you realize I be doing this the rest of my life?" (recorded August 16, 1982).

Historical and cross-national studies of literacy have reexamined traditional claims that for both the society and the individual, literacy brings certain changes: e.g., benevolence (Lockridge, 1974), improved socioeconomic status (Graff, 1979), increased reasoning abilities (Creesy, 1980) (for a comprehensive review of these studies see Graff, 1983). In spite of all the claims about consequences of literacy, recent research has shown that the changes which have come with literacy across societies and historical periods have been neither consistent nor predictable. We cannot yet make generalizations about literacy as a causal factor, nor indeed as a necessary accompaniment of specific features of a society. The prior conditions and co-occurring contexts of literacy in each society determine its forms, values, and functions.

A recent survey of societies into which literacy had recently been introduced suggests that certain specific factors are critical to the *maintenance* of literacy by any group that achieves basic literacy (Heath, forthcoming). What is needed are certain ways of talking about language and repeated occasions for using talk in institutions. The extension of literacy within a society depends on opportunities for new literates to participate in redundant, multiple, and reinforcing occasions for oral construction of the shared background needed to interpret written materials. Some societies seem to carry within their habits of talking about language and using talk in institutions the precursors of the development of extended literacy, whereas other groups seem to have to acquire, along with literacy, new ways of viewing language and new occasions for interpreting written materials.

We suggest here that the two conditions necessary for the maintenance of literacy by a group are also essential to an individual's retention of literacy. Thus, for T to sustain her newly achieved preschool literacy habits with De and his younger brother, she will continue to need occasions for talking about what she and De have learned from their jointly achieved literacy, and she will need opportunities to see that this literacy can extend to institutions outside her home. At present, she has acquired some aspects of the first condition for literacy retention, new ways of talking about language as such (see Chap. 14).

The case of T's development of preschool literacy gives overwhelming evidence that an individual's ways of using talk about language are highly interdependent with patterns of acquiring literacy. In her home, before she began reading with De, T did not exhibit the patterns of talking to children that were described in the mainstream literature. She did not simplify her talk, adapt situations to the child, and structure times and places for dyadic interactions with him. Rather, she seemed to expect De to adapt to the multiple visitors and shifting situations of his everyday environment.

Ochs and Schieffelin (in press) compare their fieldwork in Western Samoa and Papua New Guinea with reports of mainstream language development and suggest two orientations of caregivers toward children and two corresponding patterns of talking to children. They point out that mainstream parents adapt situations to children, simplify their talk, and negotiate meaning through expansions and paraphrase. These adults build propositions cooperatively with young children, and they respond to topics children initiate. In contrast, caregivers in Western Samoa and Papua New Guinea adapt the children to the situation, engage children in a wide variety of multiparty speech acts that are not simplified, and continually direct children to notice others. Talk arises from a wide range of situations to which the caregivers want the children to respond. Heath (1983) details other orientations toward children and corresponding caregiver speech patterns and suggests that certain relationships obtain between sociocultural characteristics of the society and the types of language addressed to children.

All indications from T's reports and from the recordings in the early weeks of the project suggest that the adults in T's household did not focus De's attention in redundant and multiple nonverbal and verbal ways on objects. They did not provide labels or talk to De in short sentences with simplified verb forms. Instead, they directed him to notice others, to call them by name, to greet them, and to give them orders (for example, "go home"). Adults modeled these and other unsimplified utterances for De to repeat to third parties, asking De to "Say ____" or "tell [someone else] ____."

The introduction of literacy artifacts and the literacy event of book-reading seemed to bring with it simplified language input focusing on labels of objects and requests for repetition. Book-reading provided opportunities for dyadic interactions between mother and child outside nurturing occasions. During these literacy-focused sessions, T spontaneously began using some teaching questions and topic-comment structures. T's evaluations of De also appear to have changed as the reading and writing continued. In the early tapes, T spoke positively of both De's independence and his willingness to fight and be boisterous with other children. In tapes recorded in September 1982, she described De as "wise," and she talked to both De and Eureka about their going to school in the future. When De carried his books under his arm, she asked: "De, are you going to school?"

In this household, mother-child book-reading was the first occasion of extensive labeling, and the link between reading and labeling was made not only by T, but also by other members of the household. The act of book-reading shifted the family's orientation toward the child from enabling him to learn to needing to teach him, at least in some circumstances. Adults (and De) now point to objects in the environment and name them and talk about them for De's younger brother. This behavior contrasts with earlier nonfocused requests for De to repeat a given term. Both T and others in the household are now heard talking *to* the infant and attempting to engage him as a participant in pointing out and labeling activities.

Sutton-Smith (1979) has pointed out the powerful orientation of middle-class parents to objects in their interactions with young children. Snow (1979) has emphasized the link between object orientation and the semantic content of speech addressed to young children—a focus on the present tense, concrete nouns, and events in the here and now. Heath (1983) demonstrates, however, how mainstream caregivers shift from a focus on present items and events to the future in interactions as the toddler grows older. Actions of the present are repeatedly linked to the future.

More than a decade ago, Geertz characterized the culture of a people as an "ensemble of texts, themselves ensembles, which the anthropologist strains to read over the shoulders of those to whom they properly belong" (1972, 129). In this chapter, we have looked over T's shoulder to discover what happened when she initiated, with minimal guidance, a new form of parent-child interaction (book-reading) with De, her preschool child. Introduced with almost no direction from B, the on-the-spot intermediary, this innovative behavior gave rise to other new forms of behavior. Book-reading seemed to bring with it new ways of talking to the toddler, changed perceptions of the child and of caregiver roles, an increased consciousness of the child's language development, and altered patterns of talking about language.

T may be a unique individual, and the behaviors that occurred simultaneously with book-reading for her may not follow for other individuals in the same cultural conditions. Other fine-grained analyses of different individuals in the same cultural conditions are needed to allow generalizations about the interdependence of patterns of oral and written language use under this innovation. In addition, we need to know what caregivers in other social and cultural contexts do with their children when new literacy artifacts and events are adopted. The majority of writings on the consequences of literacy speak only of very general behavior shifts, such as increased socio-economic mobility. It is extremely difficult to speak of literacy as a causal condition for the host of behavioral changes which may come with such an abstract shift. The case of T suggests that we must more closely examine fine details of behaviors which are concomitant with specific literacy events. Only with more of such "close readings" (Geertz, 1972) of human behaviors will we be able to speak with confidence about ways in which uses of oral and written language are related and to identify prior conditions and consequences of literacy. Moreover, this type of research may enable us to recognize the sociocultural conditions under which literacy may not only be achieved but also sustained and extended. In short, we need more and different kinds of literacy research before we can identify the habits of perception and conceptualization which are the unconscious supports behind the collectively sustained symbolic structures of literacy in varied societal contexts.

To accomplish these goals, we may also need new and different research strategies. Cooperative work between teachers and researchers has here been extended to a student-parent. The productivity of this research method, as shown by the present study, suggests that it could be added to the present inventory of parent education techniques. Professionals in parent education help parents to care for their children and to provide them with access to information and skills necessary in order for them to take their places as adults in the community. Traditionally parent educators have focused on issues of physical and mental health and school achievement. With respect to the latter, the goal of parent educators' programs has been to help parents prepare their children for reading and writing tasks as performed in schools. It is common to sponsor "books for tots" programs and to encourage parents to read to their children at home; often such programs contain explicit attempts by professionals to help parents teach, discipline, and interact with their children in ways which will help prepare them for school. Despite a growing awareness on the part of parent educators of cultural differences in parenting, they often have no answer to the question of how to enable parents, in settings rarely experienced or even imagined by teachers, to act as partners with teachers to improve their children's academic achievement (Hess, 1980). At present, many parent educators acknowledge that their programs have been planned without parent input and without evidence from child language or psycholinguistic research, and many have had as a common base the presumed incompetence of parents. Presented in this chapter is a possible new model of parent education, a model based on the parent as researcher. In this study, the parent identified a problem she considered important and relevant to her concerns, and she plans to continue as a partner with a teacher and professional researcher.[5] The power of decision-making has rested primarily with the parent, and the teacher and researcher have supported her in the collection, analysis, and interpretation of data. Thus, in this project, the parent has been playing an active role as a researcher of literacy socialization, while at the same time she has been acquiring and transmitting some of the skills of reading and writing involved in the achievement of preschool literacy for herself and her children.

Notes

1. A *literacy event* is any occasion in which a piece of writing is integral to the nature of participants' interactions and their interpretive processes (Heath, 1982a). See also Chapter 2 and Anderson et al. (1980) for illustrations of literacy events. Following Hymes (1972), these researchers contend that there are rules for the occurrence and internal construction of literacy events, just as there are for speech events.

2. See Goswami (forthcoming) for case studies of teachers as researchers. Branscombe (forthcoming) describes her activities as a teacher working with Heath in a cooperative search for answers to questions raised by Branscombe about what was happening in her classroom. This relationship and the participation of Branscombe and Heath as "real researchers" legitimated for students in Branscombe's class numerous extended reading and writing activities.

3. T is a speaker of Black English, who shifts toward some standard English features in some registers. No attempt is made to represent the exact sounds of her speech. The modified spellings are used here to represent the natural flow of her speech and in full awareness that all natural English speech differs from what the standard orthography seems to indicate.

4. The following conventions are used in Figures 4-3 and 4-4: underlining represents heightening of primary stress by vowel-lengthening and raising of pitch; double virgules (//) represent interruption and overlap; a question mark represents rising intonation and pause; a period indicates end-of-sentence falling intonation and a full pause; and an equals sign (=) indicates continuous utterances.

5. The identification of the subjects of this research has been done with the full written consent of Charlene Thomas and her father. We expect to continue to work together to follow the progress of De and his brother through 1983. Throughout this year, Charlene has played a role similar to that of graduate students who compile data, provide summary reports, discuss and interpret their professors' write-up of the material, and provide suggestions for revision and additions to drafts of the article. With the students in Branscombe's ninth-grade class, I made an agreement that they were to be acknowledged research associates to the fullest extent possible. I also frequently reminded them that with this role came responsibilities for gathering and reporting data carefully, discussing on tape or in person my questions and challenges of their data, and allowing their writing and their oral discussions of the research to be reported in any publication that resulted. The goal of this policy was to make research, reading, and writing as meaningful as possible to the ninth graders and to motivate them to see themselves as becoming writer-researchers. Several other articles are currently being prepared with students who were in Branscombe's ninth-grade class in 1981 through 1982.

5. Learning Literacy Through Play: Puerto Rican Kindergarten Children

Evelyn Jacob

Understanding the nature of children's experiences at home that contribute to their learning of literacy is an important focus of current research. Learners need information and models (Yinger and Hill, 1982). Some researchers (see Chap. 2) have documented adult literacy activities that might serve as models for children. For experiences to result in learning, children need opportunities to practice; they must internalize new information and then incorporate it into their behavior (Yinger and Hill, 1982).

Play is a particularly productive context for learning by young children because (1) there is voluntary elaboration and complication of activities, (2) the consequences of failure are reduced, (3) it affords a temporary moratorium on frustration, and (4) it is voluntary (Garvey, 1977; S. Miller, 1973; Sylva et al., 1976). Much research within this framework has dealt with mastery or practice play with tools or objects (Bruner et al., 1976). Other researchers have focused on the role of symbolic play in learning social behaviors to be used later in nonplay settings (Fortes, 1970; Swartzman, 1976). Still others have examined games as a means of teaching children the conventions of a culture (Roberts et al., 1959). Previous studies of children's literacy activities have focused primarily on those occurring in nonplay contexts (Anderson, 1980; Jacob, 1982; P. Miller, 1981), although some researchers (Calkins, 1980; Clay, 1975) have commented, in studies with different focuses, that children's early writing activities resemble play.

Literacy is a complex activity. It involves a variety of cognitive skills, motor skills, and social behaviors (Gibson and Levin, 1975; Mason, 1981; Scollon and Scollon, 1981; Scribner and Cole, 1981; Vukelich, 1981). Literacy is not a unitary construct; the skills and social behaviors employed vary depending on the task to be performed (Gibson and Levin, 1975; Scribner and Cole, 1981).

This chapter describes Puerto Rican children's literacy activities during play and examines the role of these activities in children's learning of skills and social behaviors associated with literacy. The primary data are previously collected observations and audiorecordings of the home activities of kindergarten children in the town of Utuado, Puerto Rico.

Setting

The town of Utuado, with a population of approximately 12,000, is located in the western highland region of Puerto Rico. Literacy is an important and visible part of life in the town. There are signs on the streets and in shop windows. Newspapers are sold on street corners and magazines are offered in many stores. Most goods and products have labels or directions on them. In a more direct way, literacy is a part of the work lives of many *Utuadeño* adults. Approximately 45 percent of those who are employed work in white-collar jobs that we can assume involve daily literacy activities (U.S. Bureau of the Census, 1972, Table 93). School and its accompanying literacy activities are an important part of the lives of most *Utuadeño* children.

Procedure

This study is part of a larger investigation of the relationships between the culture, behavior, and cognition of Puerto Rican children. Data were collected between November 1974 and September 1975. I was a participant-observer in the town during the entire 10 months and collected detailed data on a sample of twenty-nine kindergarten children. The focus of the current analyses is the observations of these children's activities at home. The methods used in collecting and analyzing these observations are summarized here (see Jacob [1977, 1982] for more detailed discussions).

Sample

Four Puerto Rican assistants and I observed a random sample (stratified by sex) of twenty-nine children—ten middle-class boys, four middle-class girls, seven lower-class boys, and eight lower-class girls. The mean age of the children was 6 years 3 months, with a range of 5 years 7 months to 6 years 8 months. There were no statistically significant differences in age by gender or social class.

Data Collection

The children were observed in their homes between 9 A.M. and 6 P.M. during their vacation between kindergarten and first grade (June and July 1975). The Puerto Rican observers were one male and three female *Utuadeños* in their late teens and early twenties. Only one observer was present during each observation.

Before beginning the observations, I visited the children's female caregivers, explained the procedures to be followed, and stressed that the children should be allowed to do what they normally do. Observers tried to maintain the role of "a friendly, nonevaluating, nondirective, and nonparticipating person who is interested in what people do" (Barker and Wright, 1971, 211). The observers delayed beginning their observations for a few minutes after their arrival each day to allow for an adjustment period. Then they sat near the child they were to observe and placed a small tape recorder near the child. During the observations, the children were free to go anywhere or do anything they wanted. The observers made running notes describing what the child did and said and what others did and said to the child.

At the conclusion of the assigned observation period, each observer expanded the notes and transcribed the tape that had been made. The observers then integrated their expanded descriptions with the transcriptions of the audiotapes in the form of continuous narratives. To maintain comparability across observers, I read and checked the observations of all observers before they were typed.

We conducted four home observations for each child; two were approximately 15 minutes long and two were approximately 30 minutes long. The time spent observing all children in the sample totaled more than 48 hours. Observations were distributed systematically over daily time slots, observers, and the entire 2-month period.

I interviewed each of the children's primary female caregivers twice. The first interview was conducted before the detailed observations and focused on the home environment, demographic characteristics of the household, and the caregivers' attitudes about certain aspects of child training. After the observations were completed, I conducted a second open-ended interview that focused on the experiences of the children and on the child training practices and attitudes of the caregivers.

Analysis of Observations

For purposes of this study, I defined *literacy* broadly to include reading, writing, and counting (see Anderson et al., 1981, and P. Miller, 1981, for similar approaches). *Reading* is defined as the use of printed materials with attention to the symbolic aspects of the materials. Thus, a child looking at a book, even if we were not sure the child was reading, is treated as reading here; but a child carrying the book from one location to another is not. *Writing* is defined as the production of printed materials. This includes activities such as printing letters or words and placing blocks with letters printed on them to form words. *Counting* includes activities in which number or frequency are determined. Thus, a child who says aloud a series of numbers in ordinal sequence to determine the number of objects present is considered to be counting.

After conducting the observations, I developed units of analysis to identify all segments of behavior during which children have explicit opportunities to learn skills and social behaviors associated with literacy. The first unit of analysis (termed *literacy skill activities*) identifies children's activities that offer opportunities to learn the cognitive and motor skills involved in literacy.[1] Our general rule was to include all instances when a child performed an activity related to literacy, explicitly watched or imitated another person involved in such an activity, or was the object of verbal or nonverbal instruction in literacy. The second unit of analysis (termed *literacy behavior activities*) identifies activities in which children have the opportunity to learn social behaviors associated with specific functions of literacy. We reviewed the observations to identify all instances when the children acted out social behaviors associated with literacy, whether or not actual literacy artifacts were used. We also developed operational rules for identifying the beginning and end of each literacy acitivity, for interruptions in the children's behavior, and for overlaps between units of analysis.

I then established criteria for distinguishing play from nonplay. A definition of *play* cannot be based on the specific activities that occur but must focus on the structure of the activities (S. Miller, 1973). Piaget (1962) distinguishes three kinds of play: practice play, symbolic play, and games. *Practice play* is the exercise of a group of activities merely for the pleasure of these activities. An example is a child repeatedly jumping back and forth across a stream. Although many practice play activities are primarily sensorimotor functions, children may also engage in practice play with more complex activities (for example, by asking questions merely for the fun of asking, without interest in the specific answers). *Symbolic play* implies "representation of an absent object . . . [and] make-believe representation" (Piaget, 1962, 111). A child pretending that a stick is an airplane or a group of children playing house are examples of symbolic play. In *games*, the "rules are a regulation imposed by the group and their violation carries a sanction" (Piaget, 1962, 112–113). Games include activities such as tag, baseball, and dominoes. We used Piaget's approach to identify instances of literacy activities occurring during play.

We coded literacy activities according to a variety of variables including the following:

Kind of activity (observing, imitating, or performing a behavior)
Content of the literacy activity (reading, writing, or counting)
Kind of symbol involved (alphabetic or numeric)
Social character of the activity (alone or with others)
Age of the child
Gender of the child
Relationship of the child to persons participating in the literacy activity
Duration of the literacy activity
Initiation of the activity (by the child or by another)
Initiation of the child's participation in the activity (by the child or by another)

Three research assistants helped identify and code the literacy activities. I conducted initial training and periodically checked data reduction and coding sheets to maintain high reliability.

Background on Children's Literacy Activities

All the children in the sample had attended kindergarten in the school year preceding the summer during which we conducted the observations. Five items on the children's annual evaluations relate directly to their literacy development:

1. Recognizes differences and similarities in sounds and words
2. Recognizes his or her name
3. Writes his or her name
4. Knows how to count with meaning to 10
5. Recognizes numbers to 10

The three rating categories for each item were: "on the way to progress" (*en vías de progreso*), "progress" (*progreso*), and "rapid progress" (*progreso rápidamente*). More than three-fourths of the children received the highest rating for items 2 through 5. One-fourth of the children received the highest rating for item 1; another half received the middle rating.

A variety of literacy artifacts were present in the children's homes. The female caregivers' replies to being asked how many books they have in their homes ranged between 0 and 300, with a median of 10 and a mean of 42. In middle-class homes, the median number of books reported was 63 (mean, 78); in lower-class homes the median was 5 (mean, 11). Approximately half of the caregivers mentioned the types of books they have, including fiction, encyclopedias, dictionaries, religious books, magazines, schoolbooks, sports books, newspapers, car repair books, and books related to work.

In a previous analysis of the same children (Jacob, 1982), I identified fifty-two literacy skill activities. Twenty-four of the twenty-nine children studied participated in these activities. There were both gender and social class differences in the frequency with which they engaged in them. Middle-class children were more likely to engage in them than lower-class children, and girls were slightly more likely than boys to participate.

Literacy skill activities involved a wide range of behaviors including reading comic books and other printed materials alone, reading aloud with other people from school notebooks, counting the number of objects in front of oneself, counting as part of games, and copying words in a school notebook.

Ethnographic data (see Jacob, 1977) indicate that *Utuadeño* mothers believed that there are no universal laws of development for children, that children learn at their own pace, and that they learn gradually as they develop an expanding capacity (*capacidad*) for new information and skills. These attitudes seemed to be manifested in the caregivers' interactions with children during literacy skill activities. The caregivers were more likely to respond to the children's behavior and expressions of interest rather than to initiate literacy instruction for the children. In fact, children initiated approximately 75 percent of the literacy skill activities, and they played an even greater role in initiating their own participation in these activities.

Literacy Activities During Play

Learning Skills

Fourteen (48 percent) of the children engaged in literacy skill activities during play. These children represented approximately 50 percent of each of the gender and social class groups. They produced a total of twenty-five literacy skill activities in play contexts, accounting for almost half of all literacy skill activities.

Very few of the literacy skill activities in play settings involve observation or imitation; most (92 percent) involve actually performing an activity related to literacy. Three different kinds of literacy activities occurred: counting occurred most frequently, then reading, and finally writing. In most of these literacy play activities, the children do only one of these activities during a segment.

Counting

Ten literacy activities that involve counting occurred during practice play. The most frequent type (50 percent) is one in which a child alone counts aloud the number of objects in his or her presence. Example 1 is characteristic. María had been playing with a toy piano on the floor in the living room. María's sister Luz started crying in her bedroom and María went to the room. Then María returned to the living room and sat on the floor.

Example 1.

María: *Uno, dos, tres, cuatro, cinco, seis, siete, ocho* (one, two, three, four, five, six, seven, eight) [counting the keys on the piano]. *Estas que tienen puntitos, yo no lo sé* (these that have little dots, I don't know).

Brother: [Walks close to María.]

María: [Continues counting the piano keys.] *Uno, dos, tres, cuatro, cinco, seis, siete, ocho, nueve, diez . . . problemas* (one, two, three, four, five, six, seven, eight, nine, ten . . . problems).[2]

María then stood up and shifted her attention to the doll she had nearby. In Example 1, the child elaborated her counting by repeating and extending it; in the other four instances of this type of activity, the child only counted once. All children counted ten objects or fewer. These were very short activities, lasting less than 1 minute, and occurred as brief isolated activities. Many kinds of objects were counted, including fruits, markers from a game, pages in a book, flowers, and piano keys.

In two other instances, children (one middle-class boy and one lower-class girl) counted the number of objects present, and an adult or older sibling participated in the activity and offered instruction. One of the cases is presented in Example 2. Before the activity began, Martín was moving chair cushions around, putting them one on top of the other; then he began to count them:

Example 2.

Martín:　　　　　*Uno, dos, tres, cuatro* (one, two, three, four) [touching the cushions as he counts them from bottom to top].

Grandfather:　　⎡　*Uno, dos, tres, cuatro, cinco* (one, two, three, four, five).　　⎤
Martín:　　　　　⎢　[Touches the cushions while his grandfather counts them.] *Cinco*⎢
　　　　　　　　⎣　(five).　　　　　　　　　　　　　　　　　　　　　　　　　　　⎦

Grandfather:　　*Ah* (oh).

In the instruction occurring in Example 2, the instructor (grandfather) did not initiate the interaction but responded to the child's error in counting. Martín participated in the instruction by touching the cushions as his grandfather re-counted them.

Three other instances of counting occurred during practice play. In one instance, a child counted from 1 to 3 alone without any objects present. In two other cases, a child counted aloud alone the number of times he or she hit something. These activities were all very brief, involved counting to less than 10, and occurred as isolated activities.

Nine children produced the ten instances of counting during practice play. Fifty percent of the middle-class and lower-class girls, 20 percent of the middle-class boys, and 14 percent of the lower-class boys were involved, suggesting that girls are more likely to engage in these kinds of activities than boys.

One child (a middle-class boy) performed a counting activity during symbolic play. The boy counted and recounted the number of toy cowboys and Indians he and his playmate each had (to make sure they had equal numbers) before they began playing with them in a play fort. This counting activity lasted approximately 4 minutes during a 15-minute period of play; the boy was joined in his counting by his playmate.

There were seven instances in which children (three middle-class boys and two lower-class boys) counted as part of games. Three involved counting out spaces so the child could move his marker while playing either Monopoly or Parcheesi. In three other cases, a child counted (and recounted) the number of pieces he and another player had to make sure they had the correct number of pieces before beginning to play. Example 3 is characteristic. In Example 3, Roberto and his sister Cláribel (who is 4 years old) prepare to play a game in which the two players each start with ten toy figures in a line and each takes a turn at rolling a marble and trying to knock over the other player's cowboys. Roberto and Cláribel had brought a cup of marbles and a bag holding toy cowboys, soldiers, and horses. Roberto explained to Cláribel that they would each get ten cowboys and were going to try to hit them with the marbles. Then Roberto began to count out the cowboys:

Example 3.

Roberto: *Dos, tres* (two, three) [while he stands three cowboys on their feet, putting them in a line side by side]. *Cuatro* (four) [adding another cowboy to the line].

Cláribel: [To her mother, while putting four horses in a line:] *Mami, mira, dos en—dos* (mom, look, two on—two). [She continues to line up some cowboys and horses in a line.]

Roberto: [Picks up a cowboy from the floor and stands it beside the other four he has.] *Cinco* (five). [Then he picks up another cowboy and puts it beside the others.] *Seis* (six). [He picks up another cowboy and puts it beside the others.] *Siete* (seven). [He knocks down four cowboys. Then he picks up a cowboy and puts it beside the three that remain standing.] *Cuatro* (four). [He knocks all four down.] *No* (no). [He picks up some cowboys from the floor and says to himself:] *Uno más* (one more).

Cláribel: [Continues putting horses side by side in a line.]

Roberto: ¿. . . . *qué falta?*—*Diez, robé uno* (what's missing?—Ten, I stole one). [He counts Cláribel's horses, pointing to each one as he counts it.] *Uno, dos, tres, cuatro, cinco, seis, siete, ocho* (one, two, three, four, five, six, seven, eight).

After this segment the two children continued getting ready to play the game for approximately another 2 minutes, during which time Roberto counted and recounted the toy cowboys and horses. In the remaining case that involved counting during a game, the boy counted the number of billiard balls while playing a loosely structured game of billiards.

Middle-class and lower-class boys participated in games that involved counting. In all instances, the children did not play alone; in five instances (71 percent), people older than the children participated in the games. Some instruction occurred during these literacy skill activities. In one example, the boy said aloud (incorrectly) that there were two white billiard balls on the table. His friend (a neighbor, 8 years old) corrected him by saying that there were three. They then continued to play. The games lasted between 2 and 18 minutes; counting activities within the games lasted for less than 1 minute up to $3\frac{1}{2}$ minutes.

Reading

Three children (two middle-class girls and one lower-class boy) read numbers aloud as practice play. The girls read numbers from a book. The playful nature of one girl's activities is evident in that she read some of the numbers printed on a page (9 through 15) in a songlike register and she added "tu tu tusi" (nonsense syllables) at the end. The girls engaged in these activities alone, each for approximately $\frac{1}{2}$ minute. In the third instance, the boy held a deck of cards and turned them over one by one, looking at them and then placing them face up on the table. He did this alone for approximately 20 minutes.

One child (a lower-class girl) read during symbolic play. She looked at food stamps that were being used as play money for pretending to go shopping. She performed this activity alone, and it lasted less than 1 minute.

On four occasions, two boys (one middle-class boy in three cases and a lower-class boy in one case) read numbers as part of card or board games. Twice the boys played card games and twice they played Monopoly. "War" *(guerra)* is a card game in which all the cards are divided between the two players who turn their cards over one at a time; the player with the card of higher value wins the opponent's card. Example 4 presents part of a 5-minute segment during which Roberto and his older brother Jaime play War while seated at the dining table.

Example 4.

Roberto:	[Takes a card from the top of his pack of cards and puts it on the table.]
Jaime:	*Diez* (ten) [referring to Roberto's card]. [Takes a card from his pack and puts it on the table. It is an ace.] *Ah, gané* (ha, I won). [Picks up both cards from the table and puts them in his pack of cards. Then he takes a card from the top of his pack and lays it face up on the table.] *Cuatro* (four).
Roberto:	*Cuatro* (four). [Then he takes a card from the top of his pack and lays it face up on the table.]
Jaime:	*Tú ganaste* (you won).
Roberto:	[Picks up the two cards from the table and puts them in his pack.]

In Example 4, the child is able to read the numbers on the cards and his brother lets him do that. In other instances, older siblings or adults compensated for a child's lack of certain literacy-related skills by reading for them. The games the children played lasted between 2 and 16 minutes; the time they spent on reading numbers ranged from less than 1 minute up to 5 minutes. In all cases, people older than the children studied participated in the games.

Writing

One child (a lower-class girl) explicitly observed another girl writing. Luz watched her older sister Sandra (12 years old), write on a slip of paper to make play money for use in pretending to go shopping. Before the literacy activity started, Luz, Sandra, and Luz's friend Zulmarie (6 years old) had been getting ready to pretend that they were going shopping. After Luz and Sandra began to play, Sandra pretended to sell Luz some items, and Luz pretended to pay for them. Then Sandra began to write in a notebook to make play money while Luz observed her. After this literacy skill activity, Luz and Sandra changed the focus of their pretending. They decided to play doctors, pretending that the pieces of paper on which Sandra wrote were prescriptions instead of money.

During play, Puerto Rican kindergarten children have a variety of experiences associated with learning literacy skills. They take an active role during play to practice and elaborate these skills, and they are exposed to instruction about and models of literacy skills.

Learning Social Behaviors

Children can also learn social behaviors associated with specific uses of literacy through what I call *literacy behavior activities*. In five instances, three girls (a lower-class girl in three cases and two middle-class girls in one case each) engaged in these activities, but none of the activities involved actual printed materials. In four cases, the girls pretended to go shopping, and in another a girl pretended to use slips of paper as prescriptions while playing doctors. Example 5 is interesting because it involves the pretend use of a shopping list and money. Marie and her older brother Ivan (9 years old) had been playing together with Ken and Barbie dolls in the living room. Marie picked up the Barbie doll and said that today they had to buy food. She then indicated where the supermarket would be and told Ivan to make her a shopping list.

Example 5.

Marie: . . . *Házme la nota, amigo* (make the shopping list, friend). [Then she sits down.] *Ya yo comí, por fin terminé de comer* (Now I'm done, I finally finished eating). [She puts Barbie on the toy bicycle.] *Oh, amigo, te tiró* . . . (oh, friend, I knocked you over . . .).

Ivan: [Pointing to a chair:] . . . *la nota. Toma la nota, Marie* (. . . the list. Take the list, Marie).

Marie: *Pues, mire, dámela* (well, look, give it to me).

Ivan: [Pointing to the back of the chair:] *Toda ésta es la nota; todo eso que hay escrito* (all this is the list; all that which is written).

Marie: [Picks up the chair.] *Pues dáme; yo la cogeré. Me la llevaré.* (Well, give it to me; I'll take it. I'll carry it with me.) [Then she looks at the chair.] *La nota era de mentira, nene* (the list was pretend, little boy).

Ivan: [Points to the chair.] . . . *está la nota. Mírala ahí, está escrita* (. . . the list is right here. Look at it here, it's written).

Marie: *Yo voy. Tenga la nota, señor* (I'm going. Take the list, sir). [Moves the bicycle toward the front of the house.] *Yin, yin, yin, yin, yin* [making the sound of a bicycle. Then she stands up and puts the bicycle and Barbie on the floor near the toy store.] *Ya, ya, se la compraré. Tenga, tenga el peso, me sobraron cinco.* (Now, now I'll buy the food. Take, take the dollar, I have five left.) [The last sentence is said as if addressed to the storekeeper. She smiles and then takes Barbie and the chair back to where Ivan is sitting.]

Ivan: *La nota, ¿ la trajiste?* (The list, did you bring back the list?)

Marie: *No, se quedaron con ella; sí, la traje, tenga* [she hands the chair to Ivan] (no, they stayed with her; yes, I brought it, take it).

Ivan: [Looks at the back of the chair as if reading:] *Ya, la* . . . *dice-e arroz, lentejas, sopa* . . . (now, it says-s rice, lentils, soup . . .).

Marie: *Por eso me cobraron—este* (that's why it cost me—this much). [Puts the bicycle on the side of the sofa.] *Bueno,* . . . *me cobraron—cinco pesos* (well, . . . they cost me—five dollars).

Ivan: *¿ Qué?* (What?)

Marie: *Cinco pesos, están las cosas caras, amigo, porque yo no sé* (five dollars, things are expensive, friend, I don't know why).

Marie then shifted the focus of their pretending and suggested that they prepare to go out to eat supper that evening. Later in the observation period, they resumed pretending to go shopping. Although the child being studied did not interact with any actual literacy artifacts during the observation period, she indicated her knowledge that literacy can be used to construct and use shopping lists and acted out social behaviors associated with shopping lists at home and in the store. She also acted out paying for goods with money, another literacy artifact.

Literacy behavior activities all involved children other than the child being studied and lasted between 1 and 3 minutes. Only girls performed these literacy behavior activities; there did not seem to be any differences in structure based on social class.

Clearly, during pretend play activities, Puerto Rican children act out social behaviors associated with using literacy in nonplay settings. In the data examined here, girls demonstrated knowledge of behaviors involved in using shopping lists, prescriptions, and money.

Discussion

Play is an important context for literacy skill and literacy behavior activities of young Puerto Rican children. Approximately half of their literacy skill activities occurred during play. Most involved the children actually performing an activity related to literacy rather than observing or imitating another, and most literacy skill activities occurred during practice play or games. Children also acted out social behaviors associated with literacy during symbolic play.

Some investigators (Garvey, 1977; S. Miller, 1973; Sylva et al., 1976) have suggested that play can be a productive context for learning in young children. In this study, Puerto Rican children used some play activities as an opportunity to practice and elaborate literacy skills. Several girls also acted out social behaviors associated with specific uses of literacy. They pretended to construct and use shopping lists, buy goods with food stamps, and get prescriptions from a doctor. Children also are exposed to instruction about and models of literacy skills in play settings.

S. Miller (1973) has suggested that practice play with new skills occurs after some initial competence with the skill has been acquired. Hutt (1976) reports a similar pattern for young children's play with a novel object. She found that after an initial period of exploration, the children then played with the object. This play involved repetition, transformation of function, and incorporation of the object into games. Based on these studies, we would expect that skills in which children have the most familiarity (but not complete mastery) will occur most frequently during practice play.

The findings on literacy skill behaviors support these suggestions. Counting behaviors involving numbers between 1 and 10 occur most frequently during practice play. School records indicate that more than 80 percent of the children can count to 10. Reading behaviors are the next most frequently encountered literacy skill behavior in practice play. Although more than 75 percent of the children can recognize their names and numbers to 10, most have limited reading ability beyond that (that is, only 25 percent can recognize similarities and differences in words).

Cultures may vary in the degree to which they encourage and support play as a context for learning literacy skills and social behaviors, as well as in the types of play they encourage for subgroups of children. Although there are not sufficient data to test the statistical significance of within-culture differences here, there are some trends worth noting. Girls performed more literacy skill activities during practice play than boys, and only boys engaged in literacy skill activities during games. Only girls acted out social roles associated with literacy during symbolic play. Social class seems to be related to the kind of games in which boys participate and use literacy skills. Middle-class boys played board games, such as Monopoly and Parcheesi, which involve using more than one literacy skill, whereas lower-class boys played dominoes, card games, and a game in which players try to knock over their opponents' toy figures with marbles.

The findings reported here raise many questions. How do these literacy activities during play contribute to children's literacy development? At what stage in children's literacy development are literacy activities incorporated into play? What is the relationship between their play and nonplay literacy activities? What is the relationship between learning literacy skills and learning literacy social behaviors? Moreover, what is the significance of the subgroup differences?

To answer these questions, time-sampled data for a group of children are not sufficient (see Erickson, 1982). Future studies are needed that focus on a specific skill and document in detail the changes over time in individual children's behavior. These studies need to examine closely the children's interactions with their environment, their incorporation of skills into play, and the relationship between their play and nonplay activities. Variation in these patterns both within and across cultures must be documented, including descriptions of values, attitudes, and institutions that support these types of activities.

Notes

The data collection and preliminary analyses of the corpus were supported by the National Science Foundation, Social Science Research Council, and the American Association of University Women. Further analyses were completed with a grant from the National Institute of Education. I would like to thank Bruce Davis, Joan Isenberg, Marie Wilson Nelson, and the editors of this book for their comments on earlier drafts of this chapter.
1. In a previous analysis of these data (Jacob, 1982), literacy skill activities were included with chore and game activities, and together they were called *potential learning activities.*
2. Examples present complete segments unless otherwise indicated. Nonverbal behavior and explanatory comments by the observer are presented within brackets. Translations of the Spanish are in parentheses immediately following the Spanish text. I attempted to translate colloquially to preserve in English the style of the speech rather than to translate strictly literally. Pauses are represented by a dash (—), and unintelligible words by ellipses (. . .). Large brackets enclosing speech or behavior of more than one individual indicate overlapping behavior or speech.

PART II. LEARNING TO BE LITERATE

6. The Child as Teacher

Glenda L. Bissex

In conversation with my 9-year-old son Paul, I once spoke of his having read aloud when he was very young so that I could tell him if his reading was correct. I was wrong, he explained to me: Rather, he had read aloud so *he* could hear and judge himself. How presumptuous I felt. But I was a teacher and I "knew" that learners— especially those just starting out—needed adult feedback to keep them on course. Reflecting on his first-grade year, Paul remarked, "I taught myself how to read in my head. I remember a lot of the kids couldn't do it." Since that conversation I have seen more of children's abilities to manage their own learning. Not all children are as conscious of or as outspoken about this self-teaching as Paul, but they have demonstrated it again and again.

Anthony Weir was $2\frac{1}{2}$ years old when his mother recorded his language in the crib (Weir, 1962). Alone in bed, he clearly was not speaking for the ears of any adult when he corrected his own pronunciation and grammar or when he practiced minimal phonetic pairs and made substitutions in his own sentence frames. Holdaway (1979) has shown us children as young as $2\frac{1}{2}$ years making self-corrections while they reconstruct texts, page by page, from familiar books. Harste et al. (1981, 143–144) found that "whether in the midst of writing their names or forming certain letters children often as young as 3 would say, 'No,' hesitate, and then cross out, proceed along or change to another communication system. They knew not only what they knew, but what they did not know and needed to work on." The researchers comment:

> We found this phenomenon particularly interesting in that it flies in the face of current pedagogy, which assumes that corrective feedback must come from an obliging adult; that errors, if not immediately corrected by an outsider, become reinforced habits of some consequence to the acquisition of literacy. Children in our study seemed well aware of their literacy decisions, changed their perceived errors and capably self-selected a set of things upon which they knew they needed work. (Harste et al., 1981, 144)

This chapter considers the role of the child as his or her own teacher, particularly with respect to the development of writing. I will argue that children mediate between the structures of their minds and the information available in their environments, that they carry on several kinds of dialogue with both outer and inner voices, and that this teaching-learning process is guided by certain principles (very possibly innate) that organize human learning. Finally, I will reflect on the relationship between such a view of "child mind" and some assumptions and practices of traditional classrooms.

Two Children

Paul and Scott are two self-teaching children. Paul is a preschooler I observed in his home, and Scott is a first grader I observed in his classroom. Paul comes from a middle-class, highly educated family, and Scott from a working-class, modestly educated family. Compared with others his age, Paul was advanced in his literacy skills while Scott was behind. Paul did much of his early reading and writing in a very quiet home environment, where he worked undisturbed for stretches of time. Scott, on the other hand, worked in the midst of his classmates, with whom he talked a great deal, and he concentrated on his work for briefer periods. Both boys were in the early stages of learning literacy and both were teaching themselves, organizing and monitoring their own learning.

Paul

Before he was much of a reader, Paul was a writer, inventing his spellings according to the principles that Read's research (1971) has illuminated for us. Read argued that children, without instruction in sound-letter relationships, taught themselves a spelling system based on using letters to represent their letter names (as in DA for *day*), on abstracting sounds from letter names (as "duh" from the letter *d* or "ch" from *h*), and on categorizations of sounds in terms of place of articulation. Representations of short vowel sounds are not evident from the letter names children know. The spellings that Read found among preschoolers for short vowels—unconventional but consistent across children—seemed to be derived from letter names closest in place of articulation to the short vowel sounds.

Like other inventive spellers, Paul at 5 years old represented the short *e* sound with the letter *a* as in TADE for *Teddy*, his dog. When he changed the spelling to TEDE, he pointed out the change to his father. In the same piece of writing, however, Paul had spelled *fetches* with an *a*, so the *e* spelling was not yet generalized despite Paul's awareness of his shift. A week later, as he read the print on a red raspberry yogurt container, he observed that he had spelled *red* RAD, which he now understood was not right because, as he explained, RAD said *raid.*" Thus, at 5 years old Paul was aware of his own learning, was able to note differences between his own and the conventional spelling systems, and was able to explain why his was incorrect.

In a case where the conventional spelling did not make sense to him—the spelling of the *-tion* ending—Paul did not master the spelling for 3 years, despite direct instruction. The evolution of Paul's spelling of *directions* shows the evolution of his understanding of our spelling system:
DRAKTHENS (5 years 7 months)
DRAKSHINS (5 years 8 months)
DIREKSHONS (7 years 5 months)
DIRECTOINS or DIRECTIONS (8 years 1 month)
DIRECTIONS (8 years 7 months)
That particular word, or any word, could have been corrected earlier but might have stood as an isolated item to be memorized. When Paul finally mastered *directions*, he wrote lists of what he titled "hard words," including many ending with *-tion*. His spelling reflects the learning of a principle, not merely a word.

In Paul's spelling of *Teddy*, the modification of his letter name strategy for spelling the long *e* sound was gradual. Paul started, mostly with proper names, to use *y* rather than *e* for a final long *e* sound. After his friend Toby corrected Paul's spelling of her name (TOBE), he had written KANDYS but also TADE. The next day he questioned the spelling of his father's name, Henry. "Is it an *e* at the end?" he asked. Two weeks later he wrote TEDY. Twice he overgeneralized the *y* for a final long *e* spelling, writing FRY for *free* and SEY for *see*. Paul's ability to generalize and even overgeneralize such spellings reveals his search for principles rather than isolated correct words.

As he finished writing a song about Teddy, TEDY O.TEDY WIL.U.KAM BAK. O.PLES.WIL.YOU KAM BAK.SUN (Teddy, oh Teddy, will you come back. Oh please will you come back soon), Paul observed that SUN, intended for *soon*, said *sun* instead. He had not been taught to read *sun* (that is, he was not taught to decode or to recognize the word on sight), yet here he was applying to his own spelling the knowledge he had gained through reading and he was noting discrepancies between the two systems. Three weeks earlier, his reading knowledge had called another of his own spellings into question. While writing a friend's last name, Potter, which Paul had written PATR, he realized, "p-a-t spells *pat*. So what would that be?" he asked me.

Thus Paul was able to keep taking in information about our writing system from the world around him and to modify his system accordingly. He did not take in at once all the information that was present in the world around him—that is, all the words he read that were spelled differently from his invented spellings. Often the new information was not fully incorporated into his system until several confirmations had established that something, such as *e* to represent "eh," was indeed part of the conventional system. Paul's spelling, like his language acquisition, was a process of active learning and experimentation, hypothesis-making and -testing, and incorporation of new information from his environment through the processes of assimilation and accommodation, as described by Piaget. In doing this, Paul was not unique. He is simply one carefully observed example of a preschool literacy learner. As Söderbergh (1971, 15–16) has argued:

> Now if a child learns to talk at a certain age without formal instruction, solely by being exposed to language, and if written language is to be considered as an independent system, why cannot a child learn to read *at the same age and in the same way* as he is learning to talk, solely by being exposed to written language? He would then be supposed to attack the written material, forming hypotheses, building models, all by himself discovering the code of the written language.

Söderbergh's study documents this in detail, revealing her daughter's spontaneous induction of word analysis—first morphemes, then phonemes—from words learned by sight. Literacy learning, like language learning, is not merely imitative but systematic and creative, in the sense that the child constructs (or reconstructs) the rules for himself or herself.

Reflection

Schools appear to assume that children do not learn from direct interaction with their environments but that this interaction must be initiated and mediated by the teacher. The teacher selects, organizes, and calls children's attention to information the child needs to learn. As we have seen, children's search for the rules governing the systems of spoken and written language powerfully organizes their learning. Children also have been seen to structure their learning in ways strikingly like textbook or workbook exercises. Weir's son Anthony, at $2\frac{1}{2}$ years old, practiced making substitutions in his own sentence frames: "What color. What color blanket. What color mop. What color glass." Paul at 5 years old, devised his own phonics exercises. "You spell *book* 'b-o-o-k'," he commented after writing one day. "To write *look*, you just change one letter—take away the *b* and add an *l*." While lying in bed one evening he mused, "If you took the *l* out of *glass* and pushed it all together, you'd have *gas*. After a conversation about Daedalus and Icarus, Paul observed, "If you put an *l* in front of *Icarus*, you get *licorice*, and "if you take the *t* and *r* off of *trike* and put a *b* in front, you have *bike*." Yet Paul had a difficult time completing workbook exercises the next year when he was in first grade. The playfulness and sense of discovery were gone, and he was not interested in merely demonstrating what he already knew.

In addition to selecting and organizing information for children and giving them corrective feedback, the teacher's role includes asking questions. Usually, however, these are questions to test children's knowledge rather than questions to which the teacher is truly seeking an answer. Sometimes teachers' questions are designed to help children think further about a topic. In any event, the classroom is seen as a place where teachers generally ask the questions and children answer them. Yet children are full of questions, about written language as well as about many other aspects of their world.

When Paul started to spell inventively, he asked questions about how to represent sounds: "What letter makes the 'uh' sound?" "How do you spell 'sh'?" The questions reflected his concept of writing as the transcription of speech sounds. Only later did he come to ask for the spellings of *words*. At the start of his invented spelling, Paul asked a great many questions. Several months later, when he had incorporated this information into his system, he wrote independently. When he needed instruction, he sought it, and then he learned it by practicing because it was information he needed.

Torrey (1973, 156) has reported the case of an unlikely self-taught early reader—a child who, on the basis of currently accepted predictors of reading success, might have been expected to fail:

> John has no more than average tested verbal ability and perhaps even less than average cultural stimulation in the direction of reading. The key factor in reading therefore must be something else. Large vocabulary, sophisticated thinking, accurate articulation of standard English, active encouragement and instruction in reading skills, may very well help a child to learn to read. However, even a single case like John's shows us that they are not indispensable.

What Torrey sees as crucial was John's ability as a learner: "He appears to have asked just the right questions in his own mind about the relation between language and print and thus to have been able to bridge the gap between his own language and the printed form" (Torrey, 1973, 157).

Children's attention may be focused on specific information they want rather than on the broader questions that guide their search for specific facts. Ferreiro's research (1979–1980; see also Chap. 12) has shown us the fascinating journey children take in their search for understanding the relationship between print and meaning or speech, questions the children did not articulate but demonstrated in their responses to print by selecting, for example, a longer word to represent a larger object.

Paul reflected on the relationship between reading and writing. When he started spelling inventively, he announced, "Once you know how to spell something, you know how to read it." However, as his reading advanced and he became more aware of conventional spellings, he commented on words he could read but not spell. At 6 years old, he commented, "*Hate* is about the only word I can read but can't spell. I always spell it *hat*." Three months later, Paul observed that "sometimes you can read a word and you can't spell it—like *dinosaur*. I can read but I can't spell that." *Spelling* now meant to Paul conventional spelling, which he did not see as preceding or enabling reading. He articulated a broader question at about this time, a question he compared to the chicken-and-egg riddle: "Which came first, reading or writing?" He decided that writing came first because you had to have letters, or even a picture, before you could read it.

The dialogue of question and answer and of reflection seems to be a natural part of the learning process. Dialogue is carried on between children and the sources of information in their environments, and it is carried on within children's minds as they hypothesize and reflect. Dialogue is essential to learning but the classroom is not essential for the creation of dialogue. Perhaps more genuine dialogue occurs outside classrooms than within.

Scott

Scott was another self-teacher, a child I knew in his first-grade classroom, where he was given space and support to explore writing. Each morning the children had up to 1 hour, as they needed it, to write and/or draw on topics of their own choosing. After the children finished a piece, they took it to their teacher and read to her what they had written or told about what they had drawn. In the first week of school, Scott drew roughly representational pictures, dictated action-packed stories that accompanied them, and wrote only his name, copied from a placard on his desk, and the date, copied from the blackboard. In the third week of school, Scott started what was to become a series of shark drawings and stories. Focused as I was on his writing development at the time, I overlooked what these drawings showed about Scott as a learner. Only later, when reviewing his writing folder for the year, did I see them as remarkable evidence of Scott's ability to teach himself and as forerunners of the approach he was to take in working on his own literacy skills.

Scott made his series of six shark drawings (see Fig. 6-1A through F) within a 2-week period. Although he was not receiving instruction in drawing or, as far as I know, referring to other pictures of sharks, his shark evolved from what looked like a grinning, bobbing toy to a huge, fierce creature emerging from the ocean depths.

(In the picture reproductions, other objects Scott drew on the page have been excluded to concentrate on the shark's evolution.) Without instruction or immediate models, how did Scott learn to draw a shark? Possibly, he received some comments from peers that led to changes, since the first graders wrote at tables and often talked and commented on one another's work. More compelling, the stories Scott dictated after drawing each shark indicated his clear intention from the start to portray a fierce creature:

Figure 6-1. Scott's six drawings of a shark.

Figure 6-1A
The ship shark comes and the ship goes away because the shark was too slow for it and finally the shark bited into him. Inside it was cold so the man put the heat on.

Figure 6-1B
The sailboat was floating for days and days and this old shark come and it was heading right for the boat and it got mad and it was getting sunny. It was all clouds He was going to Hawaii.

Figure 6-1C
The shark was gonna attack the boat.

Figure 6-1D
The sun was coming out. Then the clouds were getting shady. Pretty soon a shark came. Then the boat was heading for it. Then the shark was looking at the clouds.

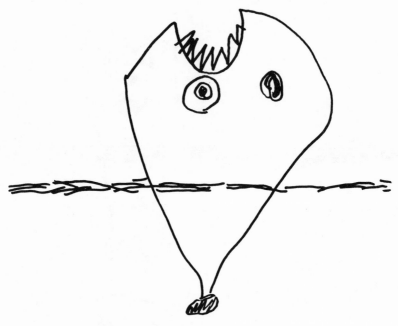

Figure 6-1E
The shark's gots to get to the sun. The shark's trying to get something. The shark's trying. . . . [The rest of the story is lost.]

Figure 6-1F
Once a time there was a shark and a whale fighting. And the shark stopped 'cause he saw some boats coming down from the sky. He ate them.

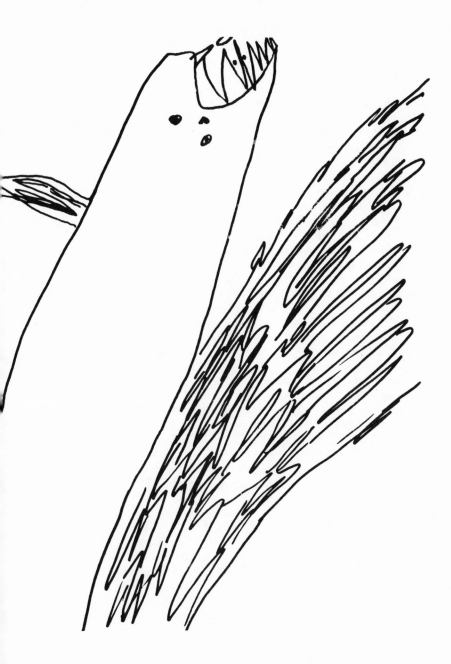

Scott's revisions of his shark drawing move steadily in the direction of expressing this intended fierceness or "sharkness," and the story itself becomes more coherent and focused as he reworks it. His most important teacher must have been his own eyes—his ability to measure the work he had produced against what he intended, to clarify that intention to himself, and gradually to find the means of realizing it. Art educator Schaefer-Simmern (1948, 198) has documented many such cases of artistic unfolding among untutored adolescents and adults, arguing that "the ability to create artistic form by means of visual conceiving is a natural attribute of the mental existence of man."

Although Scott did not work on his drawings and writings for extended periods on any one day, his writing folder shows how many different times he worked further on a particular thing, such as his shark, by starting it again and again, not to repeat but to learn and improve. In November, he began a series of tracings of his hand that also involved spelling and numbering. I have selected for discussion only certain tracings from this series, which was made over several months' time, to illustrate Scott's approach to his own literacy instruction.

In his first piece on the hand, Scott wrote a string of letters ("KinHeL") not corresponding phonetically to what he said aloud about the piece ("This is my fingerprint"). Approximately 2 weeks later, he wrote above the tracing of his hand another letter string ("ASFA"), but on the palm he wrote "hhb" (intended to be "hnd"), corresponding to his oral statement "this is my handprint." In January, Scott was able to represent *handprint* much more completely as "hdprit," and in another month he wrote a full message: "ImaDafgrprnt/it is mIfig print/afigrrint" (I made a fingerprint. It is my fingerprint. A fingerprint). His spelling was not entirely conventional but would be readable if his letter formations and use of space were more conventional. He had come a long distance from the letter strings that did not represent sounds to a phonetically, if not yet conventionally, spelled-out message.

In another similar example, in April, Scott worked on elaborating both his drawing and his message and on making them correspond more accurately (see Figs. 6-2A through C). The first piece in this series shows a person with kites flying up from each arm. Scott wrote, "I am fiingg a Kite" (I am flying a kite) (Fig. 6-2A). In the second drawing, the person is more completely represented and the kites have faces and ears. "I am flin A Kite," Scott wrote, and then, more accurately, "I am Flin 2(?) kites" (Fig. 6-2B). In the final piece (Fig. 6-2C), Scott includes more information in his writing: "A em fline A Kite in the Felb it is A mikemas Kite" (I am flying a kite in the field. It is a Mickey Mouse kite). His drawing focuses on the juncture between himself and the kite, detailing the fingers of his hand as it holds the kite string.

Scott persistently rotated letters, sometimes continued his writing on the line above rather than below what he had just written, and was in the lowest-level reading group in his room. Having these difficulties, Scott might, in a different school, have been removed from his writing time to do special exercises so he would be "ready" to write later. Instead, Scott directed his own learning. He gave himself his own exercises, he learned a great deal about written language, and by the end of second grade he was reported to be reading at grade level. As his shark drawings demonstrated, Scott was both a learner and a teacher.

Figure 6-2. Scott's kite drawings.
Figure 6-2A

Reflection

Scott learned from many teachers in his classroom: from his own self-criticism and persistence, from the talk and writings of his classmates, from the books he read, and from the instruction and support he received from his first-grade teacher. Learning is part of what the human mind *does*; it is hard to stop it from learning. We do not need to go to school to learn, except to learn those things we cannot learn through association with the people and world around us. In a literate society, literacy is not one of the things for which we need schooling. As Smethurst (1975, 3), who surveyed the history of teaching young children to read at home, stated:

A first grade classroom is by no means the only place for a child to begin reading—and maybe it is not even the best place to begin. Throughout the five thousand years or so that people have been reading, many children have been taught to read at home. Their teachers have been parents, siblings, relatives, servants, masters, governesses, tutors, or playmates. In some societies this sort of teaching has even been commonplace. Perhaps reading is, as Margaret Mead suggests, an apprenticeship skill.

The same argument could be made, of course, about learning to write.

We have *chosen* schools as the places to teach literacy, a decision that is more political than educational. This being the case, research on preschool literacy learning may have as little impact on teaching as has research showing that instruction in formal grammar does not significantly affect the language use of students. The issue may not be how children learn but why schools teach as they do.

Until fairly recently, research on learning to read and write focused on school settings, reinforcing our society's identification of literacy learning with schooling. However, during the past 15 years, beginning with Durkin's (1966) study of children who read early, preschool literacy also has received some research attention. Steinberg and Steinberg (1975), having taught their son to identify letters and words before he could speak, argued that *readiness* meant readiness only for formal instruction in a school setting, and not necessarily readiness to begin the process of

Figure 6-2B

Figure 6-2C

reading in itself. Based on her study of early fluent readers, Clark (1976, ix) remarked that "certain characteristics may appear crucial because of the particular approach used in learning to read and the fact that learning to read normally takes place in a group situation—in school." Early readers often were discovered to be early writers as well (Durkin, 1966; Clay, 1975). Read's (1971) study of preschool inventive spellers dramatically revealed the power of child mind, as have the subsequent studies of children's encounters with print by Harste et al. (1981). And yet schools still operate as though children were empty vessels to be poured full of information about literacy.

Child mind asks questions, seeks order, and monitors and corrects its own learning. These are natural functions of human mind. However, these are also functions that teachers have regarded as their own special domain, functions that teachers have so preempted that children often abandon them when in classrooms. Such distrust of child mind in the classroom is but one manifestation of the school system's distrust of the learning ability inherent in human mind. It is further manifest in the increasing control of curriculum and teaching methods by the "outside experts" in publishing companies, which Smith (1981c) has decried, and in the proliferation of administrators in proportion to the teachers they supervise and make decisions for.

To look closely at child mind is to take it seriously. Children are small; their minds are not. Child mind is human mind. Its contents are different from adult mind because it has had less time to gather information, to gain knowledge from experience, to develop certain kinds of thinking and means of expression. And, probably because it is not yet completely acculturated, it is more of a world mind in the sense that it is open to trying options that other cultures have developed, for example, in their writing systems (Ferreiro, 1979–1980; Harste et al., 1981; Bissex, 1980). Although these options, whether conventions used in writing (such as dots rather than spaces between words) or principles (such as letters representing syllables rather than sounds), are discarded as part of the child's literacy learning in his or her own culture's system, exploring them may function to define for the child the characteristics of the system he or she eventually adopts. They not only reflect the scope of the child's intellectual explorations but enable those explorations and the asking of those unarticulated but overarching questions about the nature of written language.

Children reconstruct their language systems, both spoken and written. You cannot reconstruct a system by accumulating bits and pieces of information; you reconstruct it by discovering, through all the specific information you know about it, what its principles are—the rules by which it works. Children, in searching for order, assume order exists in the world. *Independently* they all invent virtually the *same* systems—for syntax, for example, or invented spelling—which bespeaks something more at work than immature minds in isolation. The immediate context in which learning takes place has been attended to in recent ethnographic research, but there exists also a broader context of historical and universal dimensions, which somehow is internalized. Or let us say that child mind possesses structures isomorphic with historical and universal ones. This is not surprising, since human intellectual history has been shaped by the same human mind in which child mind participates, and because language universals *are* universal by virtue of their greater cognitive simplicity.

Slobin (1977, 194) has formulated such a principle about language: "Forms which are late to be acquired by children are presumably also relatively difficult for adults to process, and should be especially vulnerable to change." We find this to be true for spelling acquisition in the greater regularity and stability of consonant sound-letter correspondences than of vowel sound-letter correspondences. It is the consonant representations that preschool inventive spellers master first; the vowels remain a problem for many of us into adulthood. The salience of consonants for representing the language can be seen in the development of Speedwriting, a shorthand system that essentially omits vowel representations yet remains readable. Historically, the greatest shifts in spelling and pronunciation surround the vowels.

In describing the acquisition of phonology, Jakobson (1968) stated that at the beginning of language development the child possesses only those sounds that are common to all the languages of the world. The last sounds to be acquired are those occurring comparatively rarely in the languages of the world. Pointing to studies of phonological development in children of many different countries, Jakobson observed that "the relative chronological order of phonological acquisitions remains everywhere and at all times the same" (Jakobson, 1968, 46).

In all parallels between child language (or aphasia) and the languages of the world, what is most conclusive is the identity of the structural laws which determines always and everywhere what does or will exist in the language of the individual and in the language of society. In other words, the same hierarchy of values always underlies every increase and loss within any given phonological system. (Jakobson, 1968, 66)

Thus, it appears that there is a force outside a society's educational institutions, including the family, which guides the language learning of children.

To understand child mind in its engagement with written language, we need to be not only psycholinguists but comparative and historical linguists and cultural anthropologists. Harste, et al. (1981, 137), in their study of 3- to 6-year-olds, noted the range of conventions the children explored:

It is as if, among the 48 children studied, every convention that has been adopted by written language users worldwide was being reinvented and tested by this group of very young language users. Some tried writing right to left, others bottom to top, and a not surprising majority, given the culture they were in, wrote left-to-right, top-to-bottom. The use of space in relationship to placeholding individual concepts posed difficult problems for these children. Some used space and distance freely about the page, others drew dots between conceptual units, some drew circles around sets of markings, others wrote in columns to preserve order, while still others spaced their concepts using what we would see as the conventional form for this society. . . . The symbol system itself proved no less interesting. Children's markings, while having many English language features, ranged from pictorial graphs to symbol-like strings.

Schaefer-Simmern (1948, 199) has observed a similar phenomenon in the artistic development of children and adults who are permitted to be self-teachers: "In the organic development and realization of visual conceptions, definite corresponding stages of artistic configuration in works of art of various epochs and races are reexperienced." In her analysis of children's self-taught art, Kellogg (1969, 218) argues that "a comprehensive documentation of the Gestalts found in child work and a consideration of the possible bearing they have on the adult art of all times and places would enhance human self-understanding."

When we speak of children's development in writing, we mean development toward those forms selected and refined by our culture. Often we do not appreciate the forms, used in other times and places, that children independently explore but must unlearn as part of their schooling. We tend to see our writing system as a given and children as developing toward it. Yet if we step away to gain a broader perspective in time, we see the writing system itself developing; we see that the child's literacy learning is cut from the same cloth as mankind's written language development.

The child as teacher is child mind interacting with the information and structures provided by its immediate environment, and guided and supported by the enduring structures of human mind and language which, like a great net, protect it from falling into the abyss of nonlearning. Children have demonstrated their power to abstract, hypothesize, construct, and revise. Given this view of children, surely one role of education is to affirm each child's inner teacher.

7. The Development of Initial Literacy

Yetta Goodman

When I first began to study how first graders learn to read, I discovered that even those children who had taken tests which predicted they were not good risks for learning to read provided evidence that they had all kinds of knowledge about written language. All were aware of the alphabetic nature of English print. They knew that the print in books and on other objects in the environment communicated written language messages. They knew how to handle books—which way was up, how and when to turn pages, and which aspects of the print were significant for reading and which were not. They knew that print was read from left to right most of the time. They were already predicting and confirming, using graphophonic, syntactic, and semantic cues with varying degrees of proficiency. They used pencils to write, observed the writing of others, and knew that what they had written could be read. It slowly became obvious to me that children's discoveries about literacy in a literate society such as ours must begin much earlier than at school age. Becoming increasingly aware of the significance of social context and with a developmental view of learning, I hypothesized that children develop notions about literacy in the same way that they develop other significant learnings: That is, children discover and invent literacy as they participate actively in a literate society. I believe that *all* children in our highly literate society become literate, even when they are part of a group within that society that values literacy in ways different from the majority.

In this chapter, I explore the kinds of learnings that all children develop as they become literate, the kinds of personal as well as environmental factors that play a role in literacy development, and the kinds of written language principles young children develop as they interact with their environment (Goodman, 1980; 1982). These explorations are based on research I have been doing with 2- to 6-year-olds since 1973 (Goodman and Altwerger, 1981) and on the research of others who have greatly influenced my work (including many whose work appears in this book).

Generalizations about Literacy

Building on the work of Halliday (1975), K. Goodman and I extended to literacy learning the idea that learning language is learning how to mean. The child learns how to mean through written as well as spoken language. Initially, as children interact with the literacy events and implements in their culture, they grow curious and form hypotheses about their functions and purposes. They discover, as they are immersed in using written language and watching others use it, that *written language makes sense*. It communicates or says something. As this generalization begins to develop, children also become concerned with the organization of written language in terms of *how it makes sense*. They begin to find stability and order in the form of written language in the everyday context of its functional use. As these two generalizations are developing, children discover that *they can make sense through written language* as they use it themselves. They develop control or ownership of the strategies of comprehension and composition similar to those they have used in oral language, making allowances for the different constraints of written language forms and functions. They become more intuitively aware of the transactions among the reader, the writer, and the written text. These three overarching generalizations are driven by and, in turn, drive the development of the roots of literacy as children continue to experience written language.

The Roots of Literacy

Although it may seem obvious, it is important to remember that children's development of literacy grows out of their experiences, and the views and attitudes toward literacy that they encounter as they interact with social groups (the family, the local community, and other socio-economic classes, races, or ethnic groups). The soil in which the roots of literacy grow has significant impact on each child's development (Goodman, 1980). The ingredients in this soil include the amount of functional literacy that children encounter in the environment and the quality of those encounters; the attitudes and values about literacy expressed by other members in the social group; children's intuitive awareness of the symbolic nature of oral language, art, music, and dance; and children's own oral language.

Literacy can be said to have three major roots, each with smaller branches within it. These roots are:

1. The functions and forms that the literacy events serve,
2. The use of oral language about written language, which is part of the literacy event and reflects society's values and attitudes toward literacy,
3. Conscious awareness about literacy, including its functions, forms, and context.

Functions and Forms of Literacy

Children develop both reading and writing as they participate in meaningful literacy events. They develop control over functions and forms of reading. They respond to names, logotypes, and directions that usually occur as one- or two-word items embedded in conventional environmental settings. Their responses show understanding of the symbols' meanings even when the item is not read according to its conventional alphabetic form. For example, a stop sign may be referred to as "stop," "don't go," or "brake car" but, for the child, the meaning is the same. In learning to read environmental print, there seems to be little difference among social class groups.

The ability to read connected discourse, which includes books, newspapers, magazines, and letters, also develops through children's participation in literacy events. In this area, though, there are differences in responses among social classes. Although economically poor children develop ideas about connected discourse and know a good deal about how to handle books, middle-class children seem to develop greater flexibility and adult conventional knowledge about this type of reading. There are wide individual differences within all groups, but all the children who have been studied have some knowledge of book-handling before they come to school.

The functions and forms of productive writing also are developing in all the children we have studied before schooling. They know what purpose writing implements serve and, at a young age, they respond in different ways to "draw a boy" and "write boy." As with reading of connected discourse, productive writing varies a great deal from one household to another.

Using Oral Language about Written Language

Children and other members of society talk about the literacy events in which they participate. Words such as *read, write, pencil, story, letter,* and *book* all relate to concepts that are expressed orally during a literacy event. At 14 months of age, Alice brought her mother a book and said, "Read me, read me." Eduardo, aged $3\frac{1}{2}$ years, pointed to a large *M* on a bulletin board and asked his dad, "Does that say McDonald's?" Children as young as 3 years begin to use *say* as a metaphor for *read.* "What does this say?" and "this says my name" are common expressions used by 3- and 4-year-old children in response to written language.

Children talk not only about written language that relates directly to the literacy event itself, but also about literacy experiences in relation to schooling, job-hunting, books read, or bible use. These interactions all influence children's developing attitudes and values about literacy, including belief in their ability to learn to read and write. Some children as young as 3 years express the fear that learning to read or write will be very hard and can only be learned in school, whereas others are confident that they read already and that no one has to teach them because, as one youngster put it, "the words just fall into my mouth." These attitudes seem to be related to social class differences. Middle-class children tend to respond more confidently to learning to read than do lower-class children.

Conscious Knowledge about Literacy

At the same time that children use written language functionally to read and write and to talk about those experiences, they become aware of written language as an object for study and discussion. This conscious awareness—being analytic about the functions and forms of written language—develops in concert with the use of written language. It has been called, by some researchers, *linguistic* or *metalinguistic awareness.* Although I do not reject these labels, I believe it is important to distinguish a conscious or overt knowledge about language from intuitive awareness that children demonstrate when they use language. Reading, writing, or using oral language in the context of reading and writing is not necessarily conscious knowledge. The child is using linguistic knowledge intuitively just as he or she does when speaking or listening. Likewise, calling written forms by linguistic labels may not demonstrate conscious linguistic knowledge, since the child may at this point know the names of the forms and functions of literacy without consciously analyzing them. Children can appropriately call a dog by its name long before they can explain that it always has four legs and barks and why it is more like a cat than like an elephant or a fish.

There is evidence that children do begin early to develop conscious knowledge about the forms and functions of written language. Quincy, aged 4 years, says as he looks at the word *Ivory* on a card which has had its logotype shape retained: "It says soap, but you know if you put a dot up here (he points to the *i*) that's in my name, and if you put a line down here (he points to the *o*) that's in my name, and this . . . this . . . (he is pointing to the *y*) this is. (Then he points to each finger on his left hand with one of the fingers on his right hand as he continues his analysis.) This is a *q-u-i-n-c-y*. . . That's a *y*." Quincy is an example of the many children who develop conscious knowledge about written language before they receive formal instruction in school.

Principles of Literacy Development

Thus children have many experiences with written language as they grow. For some children, these experiences begin when they are as young as 6 months old, as mothers and some fathers read to their children, enveloping the child and the book together into an emotionally satisfying literacy event. Other children generate written language in other kinds of literacy events (for example, looking for a particular gas station that sells at the lowest price; finding letters or words on highway signs during a family game in the car; or watching for a particular written symbol on television because, when that symbol appears, the child will be allowed to stay up late).

As children participate in literacy events, actively reading and writing, they develop three major principles about written language: The *relational* or *semiotic principles* are the understandings that children have about the ways that meaning is represented in written language, the ways that oral language is represented in written language, and the ways that both oral and written language interrelate to represent meaning. The *functional principles* are the understandings that children have about the reasons and purposes for written language. The *linguistic principles* are the understandings children have about how written language is organized and displayed so that communication can occur, considering the orthographic, graphophonic, syntactic, semantic, and pragmatic systems of language.

During early development, children may construct principles which they later have to discard. Some of these principles may actually interfere with the development of others for a period of time. The principles will overlap and interact, and the children will have to sort out which principles are most significant to meaning and which are not very useful; which operate differently given the constraints on each; and finally, which may be important in the understanding of other symbol systems the child is developing. These principles cannot be taught through traditional structured reading programs. They emerge for all children, but because of the idiosyncratic nature of the use of written language, the times and ways in which these principles emerge will vary extensively.

Relational Principles

Children learn to relate written language to meaning and, where necessary, to oral language. They develop the knowledge that some unit of written language represents some unit of meaning. Although this relationship may include words or letters, it also includes propositions, ideas, concepts, images, signs, symbols, and icons. Many children also know that their drawings represent ideas or things in the real world. They know the picture of a dog is not the dog itself but represents a dog. By the time most children enter school, they are aware that written language represents meaning. The developing writer and reader comes to know the relationships between writing, the object being represented, oral language, and the orthography.

These relational principles can be observed in a number of ways. Ferreiro and Teberosky (1982) suggest that children first believe that written language is a particular way of representing objects. It is not a drawing but acts like a drawing as the children respond to it. Children believe that print related to a picture says the name of the items represented in the picture, not that it is an oral language equivalent to the print. According to this theory, for children at a particular level of understanding, print that reads "the boy plays ball" says "boy" and "ball," although the children may interpret the picture as "the boy is playing ball." Children later develop the idea that there is an equivalence between oral and written language, first treating it as syllabic and finally as alphabetic.

My own research with children in English provides support for these conclusions drawn from research with children in Spanish and French. When told to write his name, 3-year-old Josh wrote what appeared to be a small— ⌍ As he did this he said, "This is a boy." Then, without any further probing, he wrote a much larger character— ⌡ —which resembled the first in form, and he said, "This is a dad." Finally, at the bottom of the paper, he made the same character even larger—

⫛ —adding a second character which looked like an *O* superimposed over the first, and said, "This is the boy and the dad together."

Josh's father's name is Joseph. Although the child was using characters that resembled the first two letters of both his and his father's names, these characters did not represent sounds for him; they represented "the boy" and "the dad." The child was able to represent his meanings in written language, and these meanings signified something in the child's personal experience. After a period of time of using size, shape, and number to invent written language forms, children develop alphabetic principles to relate oral and written language.

Children also show their developing awareness of the relationship between the length of the written string and the oral string. As they read or write, children will elongate their oral response to match their reading or writing. Eric, 4 years old, read "cee-ree-ull," stretching out the sound until he was finished pointing to the words *Kellogg's Raisin Bran*. As Mary wrote her name, she continued voicing the sounds of her name until she was finished writing it. Observation of children pointing with their fingers while an adult reads to them or of children's oral production as they watch an adult take dictation provides evidence of this developing principle.

Additional evidence of the development of the relational principle has been provided by researchers who have shown that children know written stories are represented in books following a particular story format (Doake, 1981; Haussler, 1982). They will repeat almost verbatim a whole story that has been read to them often, showing that they know how to represent the story form as well as its meaning.

Functional Principles

The degree to which literacy events are meaningful and purposeful to the child and the value those events have for the child will influence the development of functional principles. In homes where parents are college students, computer programmers, or authors, children will discover functional principles different from those developed by children whose parents read only the Bible daily or whose parents use writing selectively for shopping lists, filling out forms, and taking phone messages. Negative or positive statements made by adults about schooling and the ability to read and write, and the difficulty with or pleasure derived from reading and writing as shown by adults will also influence how children come to understand the functions of literacy.

Specific functional principles that children develop early include ownership and labeling, extension of memory, sharing information about self and others, invitations and expressions of gratitude, representation of real and imagined events (such as narratives), and control of behavior and information. For example, children will produce their own name as a label or recognize their name in appropriate settings. When children respond to printed items embedded in context, they tend to use nouns for naming items and imperative phrases for direction-giving signs in the environment. Stores and names of products and games usually are called by related names, whereas stop signs and school crossing signs elicit responses such as "don't go" or "watch out for kids." We have samples of children's notes, written a year or two before they enter school, which express a concern, a message, or an invitation for their parents or siblings. These are real uses of spontaneously produced written language.

In addition, the play in which children participate prior to schooling, both at home and in child care centers, demonstrates the development of functional principles. As children pretend to be mothers, gas station attendants, store clerks, doctors, or teachers, they use reading or writing appropriate to those occupations. The impact of home minicomputers and the new computer age in general on the functional principles of literacy that children develop can only be speculated about at this time (see Chap. 10), but that this understanding of literacy will appear in the play and real use of written language by children between the ages of 2 and 6 is unquestionable.

Linguistic Principles

Linguistic principles help young children solve the problems of (1) how the written language system is organized, (2) how the organization of written language changes, depending on its function and its relationship to other symbol systems, (3) what the units of written language are, depending on its functional and relational uses, (4) which features of written language are most significant in which settings, and (5) the stability of the organizational system (that is, which rules are most reliable and which are not very useful).

The evidence shows that children hypothesize about all the linguistic cueing systems needed for written language. The orthographic system, including directionality, spelling, punctuation, and form variations, as well as the graphophonic system, is new to children. The phonologic, syntactic, semantic, and pragmatic systems are developed through oral language use, and children exhibit a growing awareness of how these systems operate differently under the constraints of written language.

Children's early scribbling resembles the writing system used conventionally by adults in a society, but the writing of children in an Arabic literate culture will look different from the writing of children in an English literate culture. Samples of children's writing demonstrate that written language can be represented by single characters as well as in a scriptlike form. Punctuation, spacing, and directionality are used inventively at first and later, more conventionally.

Children seem to work through some of the same problems that the adult inventors of written language historically have had to solve, such as which way to display letters and how to organize the writing into units. Aesthetic issues are evident in children's work as they balance their art with their writing. Children explore these problems, discovering solutions that may be more appropriate for orthographic systems other than their own. For example, Roxanne, a 6-year-old, wrote a story with no spaces between her words, but she made the final letter in each word backwards when possible and underlined the last letter when it was not possible to reverse it. In Hebrew, some of the final letters of words are marked so that they look different from the same letter in medial or initial positions. When Roxanne was asked why she had done this, she said, "So you can read it better."

The work of Charles Read (1975) and others has provided insights into the ways in which children invent a spelling system based on their knowledge of phonology. Their spelling becomes more and more conventionalized, regardless of instruction.

Punctuation is another convention that children begin to develop as they write. Bissex (1980) reports that her son used the exclamation mark before any other form of punctuation. Other children discover the use of the period, sometimes over-generalizing its use as a word boundary marker before they control the use of space to separate words. At age 6 years, Jennifer used dialogue in her first-grade writing, but it was not until she was 7 years old that punctuation related to dialogue appeared in her stories:

January, Grade 1

. . . The mastr yald at hem you onle have two galns of hone he tot to the flor He sed tri to gev me som mor natr. [The master yelled at him, "You only have two gallons of honey." He talked to the flower. He said, "Try to give me some more nectar."]

March, Grade 2

. . . "So he said I will go to the camping stor, and I will ask what I need to go on my trip." . . . So he "said Im going camping"

Children provide evidence that they know about syntactic aspects of written language as well as the semantic and pragmatic aspects. For example, children develop control over the principle that some morphemic endings remain the same regardless of their phonologic composition. At age 4 to 6 years, children spell words such as *walked, jumped,* and *kissed* with the letter *t* at the end. (See Jennifer's spelling of *talked.*) Later, they realize that *ed* is the most common graphic represen-tation of past tense in English. Some young readers overgeneralize this rule, reading or writing *walkted* for *walked*. Two first graders, in spontaneous writing, showed additional evidence of experimenting with morphemic issues. Carol, writing a letter to her grandparents, spelled the ordinal numbers as "firSt," "fourSt," "sixSt," as she was relating what grades she and her brothers were in. However, when she read the letter aloud, she produced the conventional oral English forms. Michael wrote to a friend about his "sidiren" and "bidren," but when he read his letter aloud, he read the words *sisters* and *brothers*. Could his morphemic endings have been overgeneralizations from the spelling of *children*?

Miscue analysis, which compares readers' observed oral responses to the listeners' expected responses, has provided evidence that children control syntax as they read. Miscues result in syntactically and semantically acceptable sentences, and substitution miscues are most often the same part of speech as the expected response. When children even as young as 3 years are reading or writing narrative stories, they usually begin with "once upon a time." We have never collected a child's letter that began with this traditional story starter. Rather, most letters open with "Dear _____," "how are you?" or the like.

There may be certain hierarchical sequences in the development of specific principles of language. For example, it seems that children develop a syllabic principle about written language before notions about alphabetic principles emerge. Also, children do not seem to represent the preconsonantal nasal when they begin to invent spelling in English, although it appears later in their development of literacy skills.

Learning to Become Literate

The development of written language is very complicated. The generalizations about and the roots and developing principles of literacy all interact as children develop control over making sense through written language. With this knowledge, children enter school where, too often, they are placed in a rigid instructional setting that ignores and is incompatible with what they already know. No published instructional program has ever provided the generalizations and concepts that people must develop to learn to read and write. A highly structured instructional system that focuses on mastery of one rule or skill before another loses sight of the complexity of learning written language. It oversimplifies what children really do learn and focuses some insecure children on insignificant and often erroneous principles about language.

In further research, each aspect of written language must be studied in greater depth and over longer periods of time. The focus should be on single subjects and on groups of children from widely different backgrounds who are reading and writing spontaneously. We must have more evidence of how capable the human toddler is of solving his or her personal needs for written language.

School is an important setting for literacy learning. There, the learning of literacy skills can be an exciting and stimulating experience; however, it can also be discouraging and inhibiting. Teaching children literacy through functional use has been advocated for more than 80 years (Iredell, 1898; Huey, 1908). Although there still is much that researchers and teachers must learn about literacy learning and teaching, we currently have the scientific foundation for helping teachers make learning to read and write an exciting literacy curriculum for all children.

8. Reading to Young Children: Its Significance for Literacy Development

William H. Teale

Experience in being read to features prominently in the histories of early readers, those children who become literate before formal schooling (Krippner, 1963; Plessas and Oakes, 1964; Sutton, 1964; Durkin, 1966; Gardner, 1970; Harty, 1975; Clark, 1976; Price, 1976; Cebuliak, 1977; Bissex, 1980; Doake, 1981; Tobin, 1982; Hoffman, 1982; Lamme, n.d.). It also has been found to be positively related to academic readiness and success with beginning reading in school (Almy, 1949; Sheldon and Carrillo, 1952; Durkin, 1974–1975; Harty, 1975; Briggs and Elkind, 1977; Wells and Raban, 1978; Walker and Kuerbitz, 1979; Moon and Wells, 1979; Wells, 1981, 1982).

Significantly, these findings are regarded as reflecting more than mere correlations. Virtually unquestioned by researchers is the premise that reading to children contributes directly to their early literacy development. Specific effects of reading to a child have been described in several studies. Baghban (1979), Holdaway (1979), Doake (1981), Hoffman (1982), and Snow and Goldfield (1982) present numerous examples of children displaying literacy skills, uses of language, and information structures which they had previously encountered in book-reading episodes. On a theoretical level, Smith (1978) argues persuasively that being read to is a basic means by which children come to understand the functions and structures of written language. Clay (1979b) takes a similar stance, saying that being read to is a primary means by which children learn that (1) print can be turned into speech, (2) there is a message recorded in the print, and (3) some language units are more likely to occur than others. Also, ethnographic research conducted with preschool children in their homes (Taylor, 1983) indicates that experience in being read to directly affects literacy development.

Interestingly, the belief that the practice of reading to young children is beneficial is accepted by researchers as well as by the educational community and, to a large degree, by the general public. Statements attesting to the advantages of being read to can be found not only in the educational writings of today (look in any reading methods book) but even in the literature from the turn of the century (Iredell, 1898; Huey, 1908). Over the years, however, surprisingly little research has been conducted on the subject. Recently, we have begun to investigate the practices and effects of reading to children, and our findings are exciting.

In this chapter, selected research on the topic of reading to children is reviewed, and some future directions for work in this area are suggested. Specifically, four questions will be addressed: (1) What is the nature of the activity known as *reading to children*? (2) What beneficial effects does this activity have on preschool children's literacy development, and how or why does it have these effects? (3) Does story (or narrative) play a special role in the informal development of literacy? (4) Just how important is being read to in the process of learning to read and write?

What is the Nature of the Activity Known as *Reading to Children*?

How the activity of reading to children might be characterized has more or less been a nonissue in educational research. Studies, such as those cited earlier, that investigated the correlations between preschool experience in being read to and achievement in literacy have generally paid little attention to defining or describing what constitutes a book-reading episode. For whatever reasons, researchers made no concerted effort to specify what was meant by *read to your child* in questions such as "how often did you read to your child before he or she went to school?" Rather, it seems that, in formulating their questions, researchers relied on a folk notion of what constitutes reading to a child and that parents also adhered to a folk notion (perhaps even a similar one) in formulating their replies. The significance of variation in book-reading episodes may not have been considered by researchers; if it were, the assumption seems to have been that all episodes of reading to a child could, for analytic purposes, be assessed similarly. In other words, researchers were concerned primarily with how many times a parent and a child engaged in interaction involving printed material rather than the particulars of what happened during those interactions.

Comparison of book-reading episodes from several recent studies shows that the social organization and language aspects of these events vary significantly, depending on such factors as the material being used, the age or developmental level of the child, and the sociocultural backgrounds of the participants.

Ninio and Bruner (1978), examining readings of picture books by a mother and her young (8-month- to 1½-year-old) child, found that the events consisted of dialogue cycles and a standard action format. The interaction typically consisted of three elements: attentional vocative, query, and label. Feedback from the mother also was present often in the cycle. An example of such an interactional pattern follows:

Mother:	Look. [Attentional vocative]
Child:	[Attends to picture]
Mother:	What's that? [Query]
Child:	Cow! [Label]
Mother:	Yes, it is. [Feedback]

In her study of the literacy socialization practices in the homes of fifteen middle-class primary school teachers who had preschool children, Heath (1982a) found that book-reading episodes with the young children were played out similarly to the pattern described by Ninio and Bruner. However, she also found that, for older children, the nature of the interaction was different.

> When children are about three years old, adults discourage the highly interactive participative role in bookreading children have hitherto played and children *listen and wait as an audience*. No longer does either adult or child repeatedly break into the story with questions and comments. Instead, children must listen, store what they hear, and on cue from the adult, answer a question. (Heath, 1982, 53)

Moreover, there is evidence that the features of book reading episodes vary not only across age levels but also within these levels. From observations of the literacy socialization practices in a sample of San Diego area homes, I have noticed significant variations in reading events. On one occasion, a mother sat down with her $2\frac{1}{2}$-year-old son, began on page 1 of a storybook, and read it straight through, without pausing for comment, question, or any type of interaction about the story. Only when the child interrupted the mother on two occasions and initiated dialogue about the story did this pattern change. In another family, the following interaction between $2\frac{1}{2}$-year-old Donna (D) and her mother (M) took place. (The actual text of the book is enclosed in quotation marks.)[1]

Mother:	"And when the rain forgets to come down, who cares! We'll just make our own." What are they doing?
Donna:	Umm. They're pouring what?
Mother:	Right! They're pouring what?
Donna:	Pouring water.
Mother:	They are! Oh, do you like that?
Donna:	Yeah.
Mother:	[M. turns the page.] "And suddenly one day our garden is full of delicious vegetables, ripe and ready to eat. Hurry! Hurry! We must pick them now." You turn the page? [D. turns the page.] "Come, look at what we grew! And we have so much, enough for us all and all our friends too!" What are you doing?
Donna:	I'm eating 'em.
Mother:	Are you gobbling them all up?
Donna:	Uh-huh.
Mother:	Can you tell me what some of those vegetables are? Can you show me where the tomatoes are? [D. points to tomatoes.] And where's the lettuce? [D. points to beans.] No, that's not lettuce.
Donna:	[Undecipherable.]
Mother:	Where's the lettuce? Where's the lettuce that we make the salad out of? [D. points to turnips.] Right there? Those are turnips.
Donna:	What is that? [Points to the lettuce.]
Mother:	That's lettuce, and that's cabbage [pointing]. And where are the green beans? [D. hesitates.] Right there! [M. points to the beans.]
Donna:	Right there.
Mother:	And what's the dog doing?
Donna:	He's holding the [unintelligible].
Mother:	He's watching the little boys and girls.

Finally, there is this excerpt from a tape-recorded book-reading episode in a third family. At the time of this event, Anita was 2 years 10 months old. Notice the child's echoing and pretend reading (mumbling) in concert with the mother, features not characteristic of the previous examples.

Mother:	"Baby kittens [love play. . ."]
Anita:	[baby kittens]
Mother:	Okay. "Baby [kittens love playing on the farm."
Anita:	[mumbles] . . . . farm.]
Mother:	"At [night] [the farmer gives them fresh cow's milk and they"
Anita:	[night] [[mumbles] . . . .

Mother:	". . . curl up together in the big red barn."	⎤
Anita:	. . . . big red barn.	⎦
Mother:	Okay.	
Anita:	Lookit Mommy.	
Mother:	Okay. ⎡ "Baby rabbit . . ."	⎤
Anita:	⎣ Baby rabbit	⎦
Mother:	". . . lives in a hutch ⎡ which . . ."	⎤
Anita:	⎣ which	⎦
Mother:	Okay. "Which, in his tiny little house . . ."	
Anita:	Lives in hutch in house . . ."	
Mother:	". . . He sniffs noses ⎡ with . . ."	⎤
Anita:	⎣ sniffs noses	⎦
Mother:	". . . the kittens and puppies ⎡ because they are all friends."	⎤
Anita:	⎣ kittens and puppies	⎦

These examples illustrate differences that occur in social interactional and language features of book-reading episodes involving children of the same age. Other recent or in-progress studies provide additional evidence of variations (Harkness and Miller, 1982; Snow and Goldfield, 1982; Taylor, 1983; DeLoache, personal communication[2]). Overall, the results of these studies indicate that factors such as the type of text, the number of times the book has been read (see Harkness and Miller [1982] for an analysis of changes in interactions over repeated readings of the same story), the number of children involved in the reading, and the temperamental characteristics and sociocultural backgrounds of the participants, as well as the age or developmental level of the child, affect what happens when parents read to their children.

Such findings have important implications for research into the relations between being read to and literacy development, because they indicate that being read to is not the seamless whole that it has been considered in much previous research. Therefore, we should not be content merely to find out how much a child has been read to during his or her preschool years and then to relate the amount, or the presence or absence, of this type of experience to literacy development. We also need to attend carefully to the nature of the activity itself.

Research by Heath (forthcoming) and Ninio (1980) illustrates that the issue of what occurs when parents read to children is a fundamental one. Both studies found that the language and social interactional characteristics of literacy events were linked directly to the emergent literacy abilities and conceptions of the children involved. As well as investigating the storybook-reading practices in fifteen mainstream[3] homes, Heath (1980b) examined the activity in a white working-class community (Roadville) only a few miles from the neighborhoods of the fifteen teachers' homes. She found similarities in storybook time in the two communities, but she also found substantial differences, the most important of which were the degree to which the content and habits of the book-reading were extended beyond the event itself and the degree to which the children were asked for "why" explanations and affective commentaries. Significantly, Heath noted that although Roadville children performed well early on in school and in certain phases of lessons (such as providing "what" explanations), they experienced increasing difficulty as they moved through the grades or were asked in the lessons for "why" explanations or for their evaluation of stories. Heath said, ". . . When they move ahead to . . . activities considered more advanced and requiring more independence, they are stumped" (Heath, 1982a, 63). On the other hand, the mainstream children, because of the way in which their book-reading episodes and other preschool literacy experiences were structured, were much more adept at applying knowledge gained in one context to another context, at answering the types of questions typically asked about stories in reading lessons, and at giving personal comments on stories they heard or read. Thus, they were much more capable of coping with what was asked of them in the classroom.

Ninio (1980) found similar links between literacy socialization practices and children's emerging strategies and abilities. She studied picture book–reading in mother-infant (17 to 22 months old) dyads from two socioeconomic classes and discovered significant differences between high-SES and low-SES mothers in the formats they used for interaction involving books. Furthermore, Ninio found that the productive vocabulary of the high-SES children was greater. She attributed this result to the greater use of "what's that?" questions in the formats of the high-SES mothers.

Thus, we have indications that the nature of book-reading events (as well as other literacy interactions) should be of central concern to us in our attempts to understand early literacy development. Only by describing as completely as possible the dimensions of the activity can we hope to understand fully how such experience influences children's skills in and uses of literacy.

What Beneficial Effects Does Reading to Children Have on Their Literacy Development (and How Does It Have These Effects)?

We cannot hope to draw definitive conclusions about the effects that reading to children has on their literacy development without adequate descriptions of the activity of reading to children and its variations. At the same time, we need not ignore the issue of the effects of the activity while we await such thorough descriptions. Rather, our knowledge about the activity, on the one hand, and its effects, on the other, should develop in an almost synergistic fashion, with information about one giving rise to insights about the other.

Although much remains to be clarified, we have already acquired a great deal of knowledge about how the preschool experience of being read to promotes literacy for the child. As we have just shown, though, the actual effects of this type of experience on an individual child will depend, to a degree, on how the activity is played out in interaction with the parent.

Four Areas of Literacy Development

Growth into literacy is characterized by a child's development of assumptions and knowledges about written language and attitudes toward the reading-writing activity itself. I draw liberally on the work of Clay (1979b), Goodman (1980), Holdaway (1979), Mason (1982), Sulzby (Sulzby, 1982; Sulzby and Otto, 1982) and, no doubt, other scholars in the following description of what might be considered fundamental aspects of the child's development from an essentially nonliterate person to an independent reader. Scollon and Scollon (1981a) employed the notion of an "orientation toward literacy" when they discussed their 2-year-old daughter's emerging abilities to deal with written language. This idea of orientation to literacy shares much with Holdaway's (1979) "literacy set." Each of these authors considers both cognitive and affective aspects of children's development of literacy when describing how young children are ushered into the world of reading and writing. The following list summarizes what seem to be the crucial facets of the initial phases of learning to read and write:

1. Assumptions about the functions and uses of written language, including:
   General function (to communicate meanings)
   More specific functions (for example, mnemonic, recording, or poetic function)
   Mediation (activities related to daily living, interpersonal communication, work, entertainment, religion, and school; informational exchange; and activities related to learning literacy itself)
2. Concepts of print, books, and reading, and the form and structure of written language itself
3. Attitudes toward reading
4. Reading strategies (including "ways of taking" from text)

Only at a general level is it possible to talk about these four areas of literacy development for the child. It is important to remember that development in these areas occurs simultaneously and interdependently. (In fact, these categories are probably more real for adults than for any child.) In the most global sense, the child first must come to understand that print is used to convey meanings. More specifically, the child begins to learn certain functions of print and the ways in which print is used to mediate everyday activities.

The second area mentioned above may be thought of as the skills needed to process written language. Basic concepts of print, books, and reading in English (directionality, orientation of letters, and so on), the way in which our alphabet represents language (for example, orthographic patterns), and the discourse patterns of our culture (especially story structure) must all be learned by the child.

Attitudes toward reading represent a third area of literacy development, but they are by no means separate from the first two areas. There are important cognitive dimensions of attitude (Teale and Lewis, 1981) that relate directly to what children perceive to be the functions and uses of literacy. Also, certain dimensions of attitude correlate highly with the skills discussed in the previous paragraph. However, I consider attitude a separable component of a child's literacy development and, like Holdaway (1979) and others, regard it as a crucial aspect of a child's orientation to literacy.

The fourth area, reading strategies, is closely related to the assumptions, concepts, and attitudes that children are developing as they form orientations to literacy. It also is possible to identify strategies, such as self-monitoring and predicting, that children develop in concert with learning about the form and structure of written language. Also, children must learn how to approach various types of texts so that they will comprehend them appropriately.

The Effects of Reading to Children

Interestingly, reading to children has been found to have beneficial effects for each of these four aspects of preschool children's literacy development. With regard to general function, reading to children helps them develop, as it did Bissex's (1980, 130) son Paul, "some global sense of what reading is all about and what it feels like." It also is one means by which children develop the basic insight that print is meaningful (Smith, 1978; Doake, 1981), and it helps children experience certain functions and uses of written language. For example, reading to children enables them to participate in entertainment activities that are mediated by literacy, and in certain families, the organization of storybook time replicates the structure of school reading lessons, thereby creating a type of match with school literacy practices (Heath, 1982a). Also, listening to stories can constitute the beginnings of using literacy to explore existential or moral issues.

Being read to can also have a significant effect on a child's attitude toward reading. As Hiebert (1981) suggests, role models are important in the process of becoming a reader, and book-reading episodes afford the child an opportunity to see trusted adults engage in and enjoy the experience of reading. In fact, there is almost a pervasive affective aura about the activity of book-reading between parent and child, with a sense of sharing being primary. Speaking of the activity of reading to his children, one father in Taylor's (n.d.) study said, "You don't even have to listen to the words; it's that kind of rapport."

Holdaway (1979) lists motivation first among the factors involved in establishing a literacy set in the child. He states, "Predominant is the personal joy and motivational strength displayed in the behavior (literacy)" (p. 52). Reading to children is one way of helping them realize the special rewards that are offered in written language. As Doake (1981, 553) found in his study of four preschool children who were read to on a regular basis, ". . . Books were able to be associated with the extremely positive, secure, and enjoyable atmosphere which pervaded the shared book experience of the children."

Furthermore, as evidenced by the tendency of children to request that particular books be read to them repeatedly, book-reading experience is one way of building familiarity with certain texts which, in turn, breeds anything but contempt for those texts.

It seems almost self-evident that the experience of being read to is an important means by which preschool children can begin forming concepts of books, print, and reading. Clay's (1979b) theories have outlined certain concepts of directionality and book handling, about what tells the story in books and so forth, that are fundamental for literacy development. The studies of Hoffman (1982), Doake (1981), Taylor (1983), and Baghban (1979) contain numerous examples of children who learn these concepts as a result of their experiences of being read to.

That being read to is extremely beneficial for preschoolers in learning the form and structure of written language is also evident from a review of the literature. A positive correlation between vocabulary development and being read to has been found (Burroughs, 1972; Chomsky, 1972; Fodor, 1966; Irwin, 1960). The research of Ninio and Bruner (1978) and Ninio (1980) convincingly demonstrates that vocabulary development can actually result from book-reading episodes.

Smith (1978) has argued that understanding that written language is different from oral language is one of the two fundamental insights necessary for learning to read. Clark (1976) found that being read to was one way that the early readers in her study had learned of the distinctive nature of written language, and Scollon and

Scollon's (1981a) report shows that their daughter had picked up the prosody of written language (in English) by the time she was 2 years old. Holdaway (1979) studied children's independent reenactments of storybooks that had been read to them several times. His analyses demonstrate convincingly that children learn the vocabulary and syntax of written language as a result of being read to. Numerous anecdotes from the diary studies of Hoffman (1982), Rhodes (1979), Doake (1981), Baghban (1979), and White (1956) support this conclusion.

Many of these same studies also indicate that preschoolers develop metalinguistic awareness about print (Schickedanz, 1981), extend their letter and word recognition abilities, and learn about sound-symbol correspondences from book-reading experiences. Recently, Tobin (1982, 25) found, from her research with forty-seven early readers, that:

> The type of parental assistance that appears to be most conducive to the development of precocious reading skills seems to consist of strategies that (a) direct the child's attention to the relationship between spoken and written words and (b) help promote the child's understanding of the materials that are read aloud to him/her.

A final aspect of the form and structure of written language is text structure. Especially pertinent is what children are learning about the structure, or grammar, of stories. I believe being read to is a crucial facet of developing a story schema, but I also believe that a profitable way to approach the relevance of story-reading to becoming literate is by considering structure and content together. Therefore, we shall discuss this topic in detail in the following section, 'Does Story, or Narrative, Play a Special Role in the Informal Development of Literacy?'

Certainly being read to has been shown to have beneficial effects on preschoolers' reading strategies. Both Holdaway (1979) and Doake (1981) have shown how children's self-monitoring and predictive strategies develop as a result of being read to. However, another sense in which children are learning a reading strategy from their experience in being read to has received less attention, largely, I think, because it has been assumed to be a natural skill. It generally is accepted that comprehension of written discourse results from a transaction between the reader's prior knowledge and the semantic structure of the text (Anderson, 1977; Blachowicz, 1977–1978). However, as Richard Howard (1974, ix), a literary critic, points out in his preface to Roland Barthes' *S/Z*, when it comes to the ways by which we as readers transact with literature, "what we assumed . . . was nature is in fact culture." In other words, readers are provided by their culture with a "way of taking" from text. Just as we learn about the conventions of print and the orthography of the language, we learn a way of taking from books.

Certainly, development of such a strategy is an important aspect of becoming literate. Characteristic ways of taking from text are present in story-reading episodes that occur in both the home and the nursery school. The analyses of Heath (1982a) and Cochran-Smith (1982), especially, have shown that strategies employed by adults in book-reading episodes actually involve children in particular ways of taking from text. One type of verbal interaction described by both Heath and Cochran-Smith is termed *life-to-text interaction*. Such interactions help story-listeners use their knowledge of the world to make sense of the text. Through the types of questions they ask or the responses they encourage, certain parents involve children by bringing their life experiences to bear when attempting to understand text. Thus, a type of higher-order reading strategy is promoted through social interaction when the parent reads to the child.

How Reading to Children Achieves These Effects

We now must consider how reading to children achieves the effects that it does. By no means will this question be answered thoroughly here. However, I find Vygotsky's (1978, 1981) notion of development as a process of internalizing social relationships to be an appropriate theoretical account of learning in general and aptly suited to describing how children informally develop literacy during their preschool years (Teale, 1982).

Essentially, in becoming literate, children are internalizing the structure of activities that involve literacy which are conducted in the world around them. This is not to say that literacy development can be explained as an "outside-in" phenomenon. In an important sense, the child's literacy environment does not have an independent existence; it is constructed in the interactions between children and the people around them. The studies by Ninio and Bruner (1978), Heath (1982), and Scollon and Scollon (1981) demonstrate this process in action. They show that literacy is at first an interpsychological process structured and supported by the parent. With development, this parental scaffolding self-destructs as the child takes over more of the interaction. Eventually, reading and writing become intrapsychological processes, and the child is an independent reader and writer.

Book-reading episodes are one type of social interactional activity from which the child can internalize features necessary for reading and writing. We have evidence that such episodes are mutually negotiated activities. Virtually all analyses of what occurs when parents read to their children (or when teachers read to their students) show that the events are socially interactive ones in which the actual reading of the text and the meaning produced in the reading are constructed through a cooperative negotiation between adult and child. We are beginning to gather evidence that as children develop, they internalize the social interactional and language features of book-reading episodes. This, I think, is a general theory for how informal development of literacy proceeds.

Does Story, or Narrative, Play a Special Role in the Informal Development of Literacy?

There are several senses in which reading stories can promote literacy development. On the one hand, participation in storybook-readings can serve to familiarize the child with the literary heritage[4] of the culture. Coincidental with being introduced to the stories of a culture, the child is socialized into a particular pattern of attitudes and values. These effects are linked closely to schooling. Much as story is a culture's way of remembering, school is an institution for conserving certain stories and the values and attitudes that they embody. Experience with stories during early childhood can make the link between home and classroom a stronger one.

Also, experience with stories can help the child develop a specific way of taking from text. According to Rosenblatt (1980, 388) attending to storybook-readings is a way that the child participates in *aesthetic reading*, which "fuse(s) the cognitive and affective elements of consciousness . . . into a personally lived-through poem or story." In other words, we adopt a certain stance when we read aesthetically, one that does not focus primarily on the referential aspect of text (or the information to be taken away from the reading) but rather stresses the journey experienced through the text.

In addition, participation in storybook-readings familiarizes the child with certain literary conventions and serves to develop the child's schema for stories, or his or her story grammar. Considerable research (for example, Mandler and Johnson, 1977) over the past decade suggests that readers use an internalized story grammar to help them understand and remember new stories and that story grammar structure has a strong influence on comprehension (Mandler, 1978).

Storybook-reading episodes also provide the child with the opportunity to develop his or her response to literature. During the late 1960s and the 1970s, numerous studies on people's response to literature (Purves and Beach [1972] provide one review) showed that response was part of the reading process itself. Additionally, I believe that response is another of the learned parts (not an innate part) of aesthetic reading, a by-product of the social interaction of storybook-readings.

Thus, story plays a special role in early literacy development in that only experience with narratives can initiate the child's familiarization with his or her literary heritage and that participation in story-readings is an almost necessary occurrence if a child is to learn to read aesthetically. Still, there is the broader question of what part stories play in becoming able to read and write in the most global sense.

Hardy (1977) contends that narrative is "a primary act of mind." Gregory (1974) argues that all our lives we are telling ourselves stories about the world and our place in it. Several authors have said that we all are constantly creating our own inner story, our autobiography (Hardy, 1975). These ideas relate closely to Bruner's (Chap. 15) claim that the intention-outcome format of narrative is a fundamental way of imposing structure on the sequence of events in life, in which case story can be seen as an aspect of both daily experience and literacy. The story of literature simply heightens and more self-consciously reflects on life's narratives. As both Smith and Bruner (see Chaps. 11, 15) point out, the stories of books may create new or different worlds. But, because they are still story, the art can relate to life. Developing a sense of story is a basic facet of the child's way of remembering (Applebee, 1978; Harding, 1937). It can serve as "a stimulus for and validation of the child's own story" (Spencer, 1976, 19) in the sense that it provides an opportunity for continuing the planning, remembering, and dreaming of everyday life.

Thus it may be, as Bruner claims, that children are initially attracted to reading by ". . . the opportunity that text provides for penetrating possible worlds" (p. 196). We cannot state with certainty that story is *the* key to or a necessary aspect of informal literacy development in children, but it does seem to be a most felicitous gateway through which young children enter the world of reading.

Just How Important Is Being Read To in the Process of Learning to Read and Write?

We have seen that experience in being read to is characteristic of early readers, that it promotes a child's literacy development in several respects, and that children benefit in particular ways if stories are read regularly. Overall, researchers as well as teachers agree that there are positive correlations and direct causal links between being read to and achievement in reading. Wells (1981, 1982), for example, has very strong convictions about the relations between success in reading in school and experience in being read to. As part of the longitudinal Children Learning to Read Project, he studied the correlation between reading achievement in school and factors such as oral language, parental interest in and help with schoolwork, and early experience with literacy. He found that listening to stories had the most beneficial effects of all of the factors. He maintained that the story-reading situation, because it provides experience with decontextualized language and the opportunity to learn some of the essential characteristics of written language, facilitates the acquisition of literacy and helps the child to cope with the reflective, disembedded thinking that is so necessary for success in school.

On the other hand, there are indications that regular experience in being read to during the preschool years is not a *necessary* condition for successful literacy development in school or even for learning to read before school. During naturalistic observations of the literacy environments in more than fifty homes with young children, we found certain children who had not been read to during their early years who were nevertheless above-average achievers in reading in school (Teale et al., 1981). Also, some early readers in the Durkin (1966) and Clark (1976) studies were not read to regularly, and Torrey (1969) reported that no one had read to the early reader described in her case study.

In summary, then, we can conclude that although it seems that children can learn to read without having been read to by parents or siblings when the children were preschoolers, there is overwhelming evidence that such experience has numerous facilitative effects on literacy development. We still have much to learn about the relations between various patterns of organization and language use in book-reading episodes and the specific effects these have on the child's literacy strategies, knowledge, and attitudes. However, results from research consistently indicate that being read to is one type of experience that delightfully and effectively ushers a child into the world of literacy.

Notes

1. The segments of the transcripts presented here and on page 000 are taken from audio-recordings of the events made by the mothers. No observer was present during the taping. Nonverbal actions were added to the transcript as a result of conferences held after the taping between the mother and the author.
2. In DeLoache's project, videotaped sessions of mothers "reading" picture books to their 18- to 36-month-old children are being analyzed. Dr. DeLoache can be contacted at the School of Human Resources and Family Studies, the University of Illinois at Urbana-Champaign.

3. Heath (1980b, 47) described mainstream families as "school-oriented, aspiring toward upward mobility through formal institutions, and providing enculturation which positively values routines of promptness, linearity, and evaluative and judgmental responses to behaviors which deviate from these norms."
4. By *literary heritage* I do not mean only the "great books." Rather, to use Applebee's (1974, 248) idea, the literary heritage offers "a continuing dialogue on the moral and philosophical questions central to the culture itself."

9. Literacy at Home and at School: Insights from a Study of Young Fluent Readers

Margaret M. Clark

The importance of the preschool years and the contribution of the home to the development of literacy has been stressed increasingly over the past 10 or so years (Smith, 1971; Clay, 1972a, b). There has been, over the same period, evidence of a growing interest in writing by those who have previously published work on reading (Smith, 1983) and also increased interest in a possible reciprocal relationship between reading and writing (Clay, 1980; Bissex, 1980). Since 1970, the process of learning to read rather than the best method of teaching reading has been the focus of much research; likewise there has been growing awareness of the insights that may be gained, even by those working with children who have difficulties in reading and writing, by studying in depth the development of children who make rapid progress toward literacy, including children who already read with fluency, understanding, and interest on entry to school.

I conducted an in-depth study of a small group of children (twenty boys and twelve girls), all of whom were already reading fluently and with understanding on entry to school at approximately 5 years of age (Clark, 1976). The aim of the research was to consider the implications of the strengths of these children and of their homes which had contributed to this early development of literacy. Furthermore, I wanted to identify the weaknesses which, in others, might have been expected to explain failure but in spite of which these children had been successful at such an early age and, in most instances, without formal instruction. It would be dangerous to oversimplify the findings or to minimize the complexity of the factors that appeared to be involved. *Young Fluent Readers* (Clark, 1976) discusses the factors involved in these children's early literacy development and explores their relevance to relationships between home and school. The characteristics of these children and their homes that are significant to the present discussion are as follows:

1. The abilities of these children were widely varied and not confined to the reading situation, although not all scored high on a conventional intelligence test.
2. Although few children had received formal instruction in reading, the support and involvement of adults, usually the parents, in dynamic oral interactions with the children in a variety of settings was impressive.
3. The strengths of these children appeared to be a growing sensitivity to spoken and to written language rather than a high level of visual-motor development.
4. The majority of children studied were boys.

Many of these children showed limited motor coordination and therefore could write or print only with limited success from an aesthetic point of view, but most were showing evidence of a growing awareness of the sequential probabilities of letter arrangements in English words. Already at between 5 and 6 years of age and before formal instruction in spelling, these children generally could (1) spell a number of simple words correctly; (2) provide plausible alternatives to correct spellings within the conventions of English spelling, as evidenced by their errors; and (3) show an awareness of what they did not know and, in some cases, an unwillingness to attempt a word they were sure they did not know.

The parents of these children were interviewed as the children started school and again approximately 2 years later. Information also was obtained on the children's school progress for another 2 years, providing valuable insights into the relationship of their early reading and wide range of reading to their development of competence in written language. A knowledge of the children's home background during that period allowed the identification of ways in which the home had provided, not only at the preschool stage but also later, a supportive and educational environment that was continuing to contribute to the child's growth toward literacy in school. It was tempting to continue the study for a longer period, but it became apparent that there was danger of adversely affecting at least some of these children and their families by such intense observation if continued.

In the intervening years, I have come to believe that another look at some of the evidence gathered in that study, particularly the reports of the parental interviews and the children's attempts at spelling, would be valuable. Some of the observations in this chapter are based on just such a reappraisal. One publication that led to my decision to take a second look was the study by Bissex (1980) of her own son's early attempts at spelling, particularly her reports of the lack of vowels in his earliest attempts to communicate in writing, his use of uppercase rather than lowercase letters, and his early inventive spelling before he began to appreciate that there is a correct way to spell a word.

Another influence was the evidence from two widely different studies I conducted. One study focused on students with learning difficulties in secondary school. Their written work in different contexts was analyzed closely with the hope of helping to develop a policy for such students that would enable them to use literacy for a variety of purposes and thus to have access to a normal school curriculum. The other study had a very different focus: Preschool education and children with special needs, with the major attention directed to oral language interactions in preschool units. Insights from as widely divergent sources as these have made important contributions to my views on growth toward literacy and on the contributions of home and school to this growth.

Some of these insights and many related works, published and unpublished, have been discussed with students in my Master of Education course which is concerned with young children. One student in that course chose for her dissertation to study her own child during the child's fourth year, looking at the reciprocal relationship between spoken language and print and at the meaning of her daughter's early attempts at writing (Payton, 1982). Because *Young Fluent Readers* (Clark, 1976) was based on a retrospective study from the time the children started school, it was not possible to observe the youngsters in their early interactions with print and during their earliest attempts at written communication. Therefore, such additional insights discussed in this chapter are drawn from Payton's recent study of Cecilia Payton (1982). Payton's study provides tangible evidence of the extent to which a child's readiness for reading is developed from a wide variety of experiences in his or her environment. Also significant is the range of qualities Cecilia brings to the school situation even though she, unlike the children in Clark's (1976) study, does not actually read yet. One of the challenges of school is to provide for other children some features of the environment of language that children such as Cecilia have experienced already; another is to assist children who already are developing a sensitivity to print so that they meet experiences in school which match, for stimulation and educational potential, those they have experienced before school.

What Can Be Learned from *Young Fluent Readers*

Home Background

As might have been expected, some of the children in my study (Clark, 1976) who read fluently were from professional homes and an environment providing an extensive and varied range of books. Some had older brothers or sisters who already were experiencing success in school. There was, however, great variety in the children's backgrounds, the size of their families, and their position within the families. One striking feature about all the parents interviewed was their interest in their families and how interesting they themselves were as they discussed, with knowledge and sensitivity, their children's experiences. It was clear that extended and positive interaction with an adult was a feature of the preschool background of all these children, although such interaction did not involve books in all cases and seldom involved any direct formal instruction in reading.

In some homes, siblings had learned to read early, were succeeding in school, and were available as models and even potential teachers of their young brothers or sisters. Some parents contrasted the early reader with his or her siblings in terms of memory and powers of intense concentration.

Many sources and types of print were cited by the parents as arousing their child's interest. In most homes, the local library was included among the sources of printed material. Most parents used the library for themselves and introduced their children to it. For the most part, children chose their own books with encouragement from their parents. Parents reported that these children had many interests, including playing with other children—unless they were too absorbed in something else!

The Parents and Their Insights

A review of the parents' answers to the questions in the structured interview revealed the parents' pleasure in their families and that they could express that pleasure with quality language, regardless of their social class and however limited their schooling. One mother of five young children commented during the interview: "Who would do housework when you could play with children?" Another commented: "I was a latchkey child; I'd never do that to my children." In the parents' comments, the children's memory and power of observation were stressed, as was their ability and desire to concentrate. A father commented, "He always surprises me," and the mother said, "I think it's an enquiring mind that's did it" [caused him to learn to read at an early age].

Most parents had observed significant incidents and could retell them graphically, revealing the quality of the interactions in the family. Their sensitivity was apparent in the specifics of their children's learning which they could recount. One child interested in the Bible was reported to note the use of the word *spake* rather than *spoke*. Another, at a later stage, was interested to know the meaning of a Latin phrase in a novel about school days. From the context, it was clear that in incidents such as these, a dialogue had taken place and extended learning, to the extent that the child could and wished to develop it, had been achieved.

Shared enjoyment also was described by a mother who had left school at any early age but later studied English literature in the evenings: She described with pleasure how her life was enriched by books and how, when her son was approximately 7 years old, they could sit together for up to $1\frac{1}{2}$ hours reading and not speaking.

Television (even the much-maligned advertisements) was clearly a stimulus to many children. One parent commented, "It's amazing what he culls from that" (referring to television advertisements. One parent described her child's "love of learning," and another described his child's breadth of knowledge and early development of literacy as "kind of scarey." Yet another parent described the child's great memory for things that happened, "for seeing and hearing," whereas another said, "He corrected us, not we correcting him; he has a marvelous memory." The shared experiences in which all these comments are embedded are particularly impressive.

The Children and Their Reading

The quality of the children's comprehension of print is perhaps best illustrated by the following two examples: One child was reported to have read a poster in a bus which stated, "Friday night is danger night." His response had been, "It's a good job it's Saturday." The second child, younger than 5 years, was reported by his teacher to have read a letter she had given him to pass on to his mother. In the letter, the teacher mentioned the 7-year period over which they would have contact. The boy had remarked in a tone of utmost concern, "Whew! Seven whole years!"

Although the children had high scores for both accuracy and comprehension in the conventional reading tests, I now realize that such tests failed to capture the quality of their literacy. Isolated passages to be read orally in a formal setting cannot recreate the quality of these children's response to print any more than similarly artificial print is able to develop such literacy in less precocious children. At the time of the study, I questioned the use of such artificial text as that in standard reading tests. I also doubted the value of assessment by *oral* reading tasks of the reading competence of these children, since some of them normally read silently for meaning. Indeed, some had developed reading competence without resorting to any prolonged period of oral reading that the parents could recall.

In light of subsequent studies of young children's responses to elaborate story structure and of their growing awareness of how to predict the ideas and even precise words and sentences of print, my uneasiness with conventional oral reading tasks and conventional artificially created print as a medium for early reading instruction now is even greater. This is discussed in more detail in the case study of Cecilia (see the section, Language Growth Before School and Its Potential for Literacy Development). The range of real-world print from which these children learned and to which they responded is perhaps typified by the examples given at the beginning of this section. To ensure that print becomes a dynamic and significant part of the environment in school is an important challenge if most children are to become literate.

The Children and Their Writing

Even in 1970 and 1971 questions were asked about the children's interest in writing and the extent to which this seemed to have contributed to their reading, but it did not occur to me to ask the parents for samples of the children's written communications from preschool. Thus, at that early stage of the study (Clark, 1976), all I had of the children's writing was the conventional spelling test set as part of the research shortly after they entered school. Most parents reported that their children had some interest in writing, primarily as an extension rather than a precursor of reading. Pens, pencils, crayons, and blackboards had been of interest to most of these children, as had word games. Some parents commented that their children wrote in uppercase letters although they read lowercase letters. One parent whose child used a mixture made the observation, "You need to be very artful to read it." Most parents suggested that lowercase letters were beginning to be used only since the child's entry to school.

In reporting the findings of my earlier study (Clark, 1976), reference was made to the children's spelling on the conventional test, and it was stressed that most children could spell many of the words. They also tended to be sensitive to what they could not spell, and most errors bore some resemblance to the intended word. I recently decided to look again at the attempts at spelling of these thirty-two children in the light of recent literature about the early development of spelling, particularly Bissex's (1980) description of her own son's early spelling attempts. Within this group of thirty-two children, there were some (proportionately more boys than girls, perhaps because of the greater interest of the former in reference books) who used uppercase letters consistently for each word written, and some (relatively few of these and more girls than boys) who used lowercase letters for all words. In addition, there were children who used a capital letter at the beginning of some words or all capital letters for some words. A sizeable number of words, even those spelled correctly, had a mix of uppercase and lowercase letters (for example, "BeG," "friEnd," "womeN," "lOuD"). This variation was apparent even in children with a spelling age of more than 9 years. One child wrote "ARE," "SEEM," "FOR," but "Chop," "Ship," and "who." Another wrote "ANy" and "GReAT." Given the fairly poor coordination of a number of these children, it was difficult to determine whether some letters were uppercase where only the size distinguishes the two forms.

These atypical uses of letter case probably should not be considered errors at this stage of the children's literacy development. Rather, it is more appropriate to consider what they illustrate of these children's awareness of the critical features in letter discrimination. Their spelling attempts show clearly their awareness that *e* and *E* are similar, in terms of reading, in ways that *A* is not, and that *D* and *d* share critical features for reading that *b* and *d* do not.

Most of the children had developed sufficient awareness of spelling patterns to attempt successfully words such as *beg* and even *ship* and *food* as well as common irregular words such as *the* and *are*. However, words such as *who* gave difficulties to a number: It was spelled "Ho," "HWO," "Hoo," or "HOW." When incorrect, the spelling of *date* often was "DAT," and a common incorrect rendering of *done* was "DUN." *Any* was sometimes "ENY" or "EANY." Even a word such as *women* was spelled correctly by eleven of the thirty-two children, whereas eight would not attempt it (possibly knowing their own limitations) and the remainder wrote it as "WOMAN," "WOMIN," "WIMN," "wumen" (a very Scottish rendering), or "WIMEN;" only one gave "Wmn" (without a vowel).

In view of the comments by Bissex (1980) in *GNYS at WRK* it was interesting to observe that these young children were at the stage of being able to spell regular words and common irregular words and that they used vowels as well as consonants in most spelling attempts, often using a vowel which, if wrong, might still have been possible. By their earliest school years, they had an appreciation of critical features of words. The superficial appearance of their attempts at spelling, including large writing, a mixture of uppercase and lowercase letters of varying size, and some variation in alignment, could easily mask the children's increasing mastery of the written features of English. Furthermore, in a situation such as this in which their attention was only on spelling, the children were more likely to show the extent of their potential and grasp of the conventions of English spelling than the quality of their attempts to generate communication in writing, which might well have been equally impressive as a creative act. In such creative situations, it is not likely they would succeed in sustaining the same level of competence in the surface features. Thus, as described by one parent, you would have to be artful to read it.

One dilemma faced by schools receiving children as advanced as these is how to help the children retain sensitivity to their errors and improve their command over the surface features, yet still not destroy their wish to communicate in writing for a variety of purposes. The issue is no less important with children who are less advanced toward literacy on entering school but who also may have developed their own forms of written communication for purposes important to them, even if the spelling is less conventional and the communication less meaningful to others. In recent publications by Bissex (1980) and Smith (1983), the competing claims of these two necessary aspects of written communication are highlighted.

Extending Literacy in These Children at School and at Home

All the children in the young fluent reader study (Clark, 1976) entered school with two things in common: the *ability* and the *desire* to read at a very early age. In few other ways were they similar. Much discussion focuses on the need for children to be ready for school and, even now, on deficiencies in the homes of children who come to school, at whatever age, "not ready" according to the conception of readiness held by the particular school system. Although some allowance is made for individual child differences, it is on a very limited range of the spectrum. From discussions with teachers, parents, and the children themselves, it was clear that the school as a learning environment presented difficulties for some of these children. There were those who found it unchallenging or boring, and others who chose not to display too much of their undoubted talents to avoid appearing very different from their classmates. Some consideration of the needs, abilities, and features in the environment of even exceptional children such as these may provide insights in developing a stimulating environment in school for more children, within which they can learn to read, learn from reading, and enjoy the wide range of shared experiences that could be opened up for them by literacy.

Literacy for these young fluent readers involved a wide range of materials and was used to develop a wide range of interests. As one father reported, "brain books" fascinated one child, and telephone directories, another. Newspapers were a source of information to several children, for events in the outside world and, more immediately, for the times of their favorite television programs. This latter source was likely to be of continuing interest only as long as there was an element of real choice that the youngsters could exercise, with the hope of actually viewing programs of their choice. One child was interested in predicting sports results which he then checked. Some read to themselves stories they had enjoyed previously, and others read stories that would not have been read to them yet. Thus the children's reading was an enjoyable part of their environment for varied purposes, and it was an activity that extended opportunities for learning facts and information they considered relevant to themselves.

On entering school, most children already belonged to the local library, as did other family members. Their views on the books they wished to read were regarded as important. As one father put it when asked about his child's choice, "He is fussy too." Access to the library, advice, and encouragement were all there, but choice to a great extent belonged to the children and was related to and varied with their other interests at a particular time.

Implications for Other Children

The quality of environment and interaction with adults that these study children experienced also was available, in most cases, to their brothers and sisters. Although many of the siblings did not read before entering school, many did so shortly after, and they seemed to make good progress in school. Some would be regarded as successes of the school, of course, but it is clear just how much their readiness and receptiveness had developed from the breadth of experiences in the home. This was highlighted when, some time after the completion of the research, I had occasion to visit the home of one family in which there were four children, the boy in the study being the youngest. When I visited I noted that there was no bookcase full of books in the small living room, but there were a number of books borrowed from the local library by all six members of the family who clearly enjoyed reading and shared their reading experiences with one another. The progress in literacy development by the youngest boy's siblings had been impressive, and although they had learned to read within school, it is important not to underestimate the contribution of their stimulating home environment. On talking to the father, whom I had not met previously, I realized that I had failed to appreciate his contribution to this environment. He had left school early and had an unskilled job. Nonetheless, he was fascinated by books and confessed that he had read fairy stories to the children partly because it gave him an excuse to read them as he enjoyed them. Like the others I had met, he described in amusing terms how his young son had used his early reading skills, in this instance, to help an elderly neighbor to place her bets!

Had it been possible to study over a period of years two children from each of these homes, the child who could read on entering school and another who could not, further valuable insights could have been gained regarding how to stimulate literacy and how to bridge home experience to school experience in the development of literacy.

Language Growth Before School and Its Potential for Literacy Development

The previously discussed study was a retrospective one insofar as the preschool experiences of the children were concerned. It seems valuable to include in the final section of this chapter a discussion of some implications from a prospective study. The study is of a young preschool child as she discovers language in her environment by the reading of others and through her own active participation in the writing process. It is clear that Cecilia's language growth, like that of the children discussed so far, is a product of her active search for meaning and the responsive environment in which she is learning.

In discussing the language development of her daughter Cecilia from approximately 3 to 4 years of age, Payton (1982) claims Cecilia emerges as a hypothesizer, active in her own growth, testing and amending her comprehension of events and spontaneously promoting, with each new insight, knowledge regarding the further possibilities of language. This view is very much in accord with that of Donaldson (Donaldson and Reid, 1982), who refers to children as hypothesis-testers and rule-users by nature and describes them as having a strong drive to make sense of what they encounter and to understand what people mean when they speak, in ways that are more subtle and complex than we once supposed. Payton, with apt examples from the child, explores this increasing power and sensitivity in Cecilia and the interrelatedness of her hypothesis-testing in oral language encounters, in encounters with situational print, in story-reading settings, and in her early attempts at written communication. Payton stresses that the oral language situations may have more obvious impact on young children who are responsive and articulate than does print which is passive. Her approach to this aspect of readiness for literacy is particularly valuable, since the situations of the encounters are related, in such a way as to suggest possible causes of a particular response, including error or overgeneralization by the child. When Cecilia first read the word *co-op*, Payton believed this to be a genuine and legitimate inference from situational print. She suggests that, on a number of occasions, her daughter appeared to be seeking confirmation of those propositions about which she already was fairly certain, as a means of verifying and extending her knowledge. One example of this is the child's comment, "That says 'Boots.' Why does it say 'Boots'? Did you buy them in Boots?"

Payton also provides examples of instances of the child's confusion which she sometimes appreciated only in retrospect from a tape recording. The examples include oral discussions of flower *beds* and car *parks* and story-reading in which "burnt to a *cinder*" caused Cecilia confusion because she related the word *cinder* to a Sindy doll, a misunderstanding that disrupted the whole mood of the story. A similar confusion resulted from Cecilia's lack of understanding of the word *wicked* with reference to the queen in *Snow White and the Seven Dwarfs*, since the term's meaning could not be deduced easily from the illustrations in the book. The value to teachers of subsequent analysis of some interactions with young children should be apparent. Teachers may become aware of children's misunderstandings that could make the subsequent content of a story unintelligible. They might also become aware of instances in which they had responded with a lack of full understanding to questions from children who were seeking clarification or amplification to appreciate the meaning of stories.

Payton also discusses Cecilia's simultaneously growing awareness of the potential of her attempts at written communication. Some of her written messages are understood only by the child herself, acting as a temporary reminder, and are soon forgotten. The author gives examples of interrelated drawing and writing, each serving a specific purpose. In some instances, a guided analysis makes it possible for the reader to identify meaningful writing embedded in drawings. At the age of 3 years 2 months, a letter given to the child's mother seemed a genuine milestone, a confirmation of Cecilia's appreciation that writing serves a real-world purpose. Writing's value as a form of communication was further evidenced in Cecilia's desire to prepare a shopping list and particularly in her response to her mother's query as to whether she would write *sweets*: "It doesn't matter. We won't forget sweets," she said. There are lessons in this example for teachers who do not always ensure that writing required of young children has a real purpose as a communication with others or, alternatively, a function as a reminder to the child. At this stage, Cecilia's writing was not conventional and it did not communicate effectively with others. Although drawing and writing were interactional and her communications often contained some of each, it was apparent from the dialogue that Cecilia was aware of the differences in these forms of communication. Cecilia's awareness of her growing competence was evidenced in her announcement one day at teatime: "I can cut my egg now 'cause I can write my name."

Comments

It is a challenge for schools to provide stimulating environments that are responsive to the search for meaning by the children who attend, particularly those less fortunate than the children discussed here, so that they too can experience the sense of achievement expressed by Cecilia in the preceding example. In their promotion of literacy in an inevitably more formal environment than the home and with competing claims of the various children at different levels of language development, schools need assistance in extending the contexts they provide for the development and practice of literary skills, and there are insights to be gleaned from those children who learn early.

10.]RUN TRILOGY: Can Tommy Read?

Suzanne B.K. Scollon and Ron Scollon

The Language Problem in the West

Much of the current interest in literacy, especially in preschool literacy, is inspired by a concern with teaching children to write. This concern has various motives. Some scholars are interested in the real or apparent decline in literacy skills over the past decades. Others are concerned with the centrality of literacy in achieving access to the controlling bureaucratic institutions of modern society. (This is particularly strong among those who believe political and economic discrimination against members of ethnic minority groups is directly tied to lack of literacy skills in members of those groups.)

Although we share these interests, our work is motivated by what we see as a prior question. There is little doubt that literacy has radically changed the world wherever it has developed as a societal phenomenon. It is not at all clear, however, that the changes which have come about because of literacy have been universally positive. In the West, there has been a growing concern among philosophers and writers with what we might call the negative side of literacy. Writers such as Wittgenstein and Beckett, to name only two, have focused on language as the central problem. One might argue, without stretching the point, that it is not language in general but written language that is the problem of Western literature and philosophy.

George Steiner (1981) has urged us not to cheat in our love of literacy and literature. If we accept that literacy provides us a window on the best thought of mankind throughout the centuries, we must also ask if literacy can do us any harm. If we accept that literacy provides us access to the controlling bureaucratic institutions of our society, we must also ask if that access and those institutions can do us harm.

It has been argued frequently in the recent social scientific literature on literacy that there are at least some connections between literacy, schooling, and ways in which people use their minds. Causality obviously is problematic. Our work is motivated by the necessity we feel of asking the unpopular question: In what ways might the darker sides of our modern experience be tied to the development of literacy and modern Western forms of schooling?

Two Strategies

Two general strategies have been employed in attempting to view ourselves critically. Foucault (1973, 1976, 1980) has taken an historic approach. It has been his strategy to construct an "archaeology" of the present period. Others such as Ong (1967, 1977a) also have worked at understanding our present literacy in the history of such movements as Methodism. Illich (1981) has recently begun the history of what he calls *The 500-Year War on Subsistence*, the war against particularistic, vernacular home values. He has pointed to the crucial connection between the voyages of Columbus and the grammar and dictionary of Nebrija, the first to conquer territory of people and the other to conquer the public mind through control of the printing press.

A second research strategy involves a comparative perspective. The work of Scribner and Cole (Scribner, 1979; Scribner and Cole, 1978) has provided a psychological base for this comparative research. Akin to this research, Goody (1977) has taken a more ethnographic approach.

We, too, have taken an ethnographic approach to the understanding of literacy in the West. We have selected as the focus of our work the socialization of children. In our work, we have paralleled the argument of Hymes (1966). Precedent to the question of the relation between literacy and thinking is the question of the functional role of literacy in the lives of individuals and the speech community.

A Literate-Oral Comparison

The Study Groups

We were interested in putting our own Western reality set into perspective by comparing it to another non-Western and also nonliterate realty set. Our field location was the community of Fort Chipewyan, Alberta, Canada, and our first two-way comparison was between the two reality sets we labeled *the bush concious-ness* and *the modern consciousness* (Berger, et al., 1973). The typifying example of the bush consciousness was the narrative performances of elder tradition-bearers. As the typifying example of the modern consciousness, we used the academic prose essay. In fact, the published report of the study became, somewhat para-doxically, a typification of that modern reality set (Scollon and Scollon, 1979).

The second comparison, also two-way, involved a young child who was in the process of being socialized into the modern literate tradition and the adult models of that same tradition. We also compared a young child who was in the process of being socialized into the bush consciousness with his elder models within that oral tradition. Those two children were compared to each other as well. Both of these studies have now been extended beyond the Fort Chipewyan speech community to include most of the Alaskan Athabaskan community (S. Scollon, 1982; Scollon and Scollon, 1981a).

In this work, we discovered an important interconnection between four elements of a community wide communication system. We found a mutually reinforcing circle of causation among discourse patterns, practices of socialization, assumptions made about interpersonal relationships, and universal strategies of display of "face" (Brown and Levinson, 1978). For the bush community, the primary assumption was one of nonintervention in interpersonal relationships. The reflection of this value in discourse is the traditional oral narrative. The abstract element of the story is contextualized in the current performance according to the needs and knowledge of the existing audience (Scollon and Scollon, 1981b). The discourse is structured by the relationships between storyteller and the audience, and the text is made to fit those relationships.

In the literate community, on the other hand, the author and audience are fictionalized into a set of conventional relationships that speak to one another through the medium of the decontextualized text. Text speaks to text. We found, then, that a child who typified this discourse pattern was socialized to signficant amounts of fictionalization of the self. The distance that in the bush tradition was assumed to exist between individuals was seen in the literate tradition to exist between the person of the author and fictionalized role of the author of text (Scollon and Scollon, 1981a; Ong, 1977b; Foucault, 1977).

An Interactive Approach

In the course of our work, our interest in comparing these two communicative traditions came increasingly to focus on interaction between the two traditions. These were two separate and, to a large extent, logically incompatible reality sets, and it was clear that wherever they came into contact there would be some level of conflict. At the lowest levels, this would result in simple misunderstanding; at higher levels, this misunderstanding would result in discrimination against members of the less powerful group (Erickson and Shultz, 1981).

It also was clear that in many cases we had observed, individuals were undergoing some personal negotiation of these two traditions. It was our belief that the conflict was no less severe in these cases than in the cases of interpersonal contact; it was simply less observable to people other than the individual seeking to make the negotiation.

More and Less Focused Interaction

In trying to develop a vocabulary that we could use to obtain a more interactive view of this conflict of reality sets, we began to think in terms of the degree of focusing of an interaction (Scollon and Scollon, 1980, 1981b). We argued that a particular interaction between people communicating with one another was more or less focused depending on three factors: timing, the medium, and the number of participants (and, of course, their roles). Generally speaking, the more participants there were, the more focused the interaction became. When some medium was interposed between the participants, the level of focus was higher than when the participants met face to face. Finally, the more hurried the interaction was, the more focused it became.

In this use of the term *focus*, we were attempting to quantify the amount of leeway each participant in an interaction has in determining the outcomes of the interaction. The more highly focused an interaction is, the less the sense of the situation can be negotiated among participants. With this terminology, we hoped to get beyond the simple literate-oral dichotomy. It allowed us to consider the medium as a variable of comparable importance to time or the participant structure.

We then sought to locate a variety of sites in which we could investigate simultaneously the conflict between reality sets and the role of the focusing constraints of time, medium, and participant structure.

Computers and Discourse

Having determined the premises and strategies of our study, we elected to observe communication between Alaskan natives and the community of the University of Alaska to investigate the interaction between individuals and modern bureaucratic institutions (S. Scollon, 1981; R. Scollon, 1981b, 1981c; Scollon and Scollon, 1982a). In some of our research, we looked at more focused face-to-face interactions such as those in classrooms and instructors' offices. We were interested, however, in seeing to what extent the characteristics that we had described for the modern consciousness and for literacy were attributable to the medium itself. To investigate this further, we became involved in research on telecommunications, particularly computer-mediated conferencing.

We guessed that computer-mediated conferencing might be an ideally focused type of interaction for mediating between individuals and bureaucratic institutions. We had in mind especially the asynchronous computer conference, in which participants use a central computer as a place to drop off messages. The conference extends over days or even weeks. Participants choose their own times and rates of participation and comment on subjects and messages of their own choice. This is a less focused medium than a face-to-face topic-oriented discussion in which participants must show considerable concern for topical cohesion and nonoverlapping participant exchange. On the other hand, computer conferencing is somewhat more focused than a casual conversation among friends in that it involves writing (although not necessarily nor usually print).

A second feature of the asynchronous computer conference is what Levin and others have called *multiple-thread discourse* (Black et al., 1981). Typically, messages include more than one topic, only some of which make reference to the immediately preceding topics. Because of different rates and times of participation, participants experience the discourse as a woven strand of many topical threads. This is very different from the topical cohesion typical for most other forms of discourse.

Reddy (1979) has suggested that our thinking about communication has been dominated by what he refers to as the *conduit metaphor*: That is, we tend to think of typical communication as starting with a message formulated by a speaker which then is transmitted as a well-formed package across a conduit to a hearer. Our interest in less focused forms for interaction led us to think that the conduit metaphor is most appropriate to highly focused forms of interaction but less appropriate to less focused interaction.

Thus, we began to look for a more appropriate communication metaphor. The Athabaskan metaphor of *berry-picking* (R. Scollon, 1980; S. Scollon, 1982; Scollon and Scollon, forthcoming) suggests that the role of the speaker is not so much to present a well-formed message as to present a set of choices; the role of the hearer is less that of a passive receiver of the message and more that of picking carefully through what is presented for a meaning that is of some use or importance to the hearer. We found the multiple-threaded discourse of the computer conference to be more consonant with this berry-picking metaphor for communication (Scollon and Scollon, 1981c, 1982b, forthcoming).

A New Type of Discourse

Our preliminary work with computer conferencing has led us to think that the current rapidly expanding use of computers in communication is bringing about change in the possibilities of discourse, possibilities not seen in the world at least since the introduction of widespread printing. If there is some basis for Illich's (1980) thesis that we have been engaged in a 500-year war on subsistence values, then literacy itself must have been intimately involved in this battle. The decontextualization that we see in early socialization to literacy may be the necessary prelude to successful integration into the bureaucratic and institutional world of the modern Western world. To the extent that this integration is a negative human experience, literacy may be thought of as one of its causes. It is, of course, even less clear whether computers will be a predominantly positive or negative development. To us, it is imperative that we begin extending our concern for literacy to this new form of discourse.

We are pursuing the question of the impact of computers in our world through four research programs. At the postsecondary level, we are engaged in university instruction using computer conferencing as the primary instructive medium. This allows us to research the learning of a new medium of discourse by adults who have been deeply socialized into traditional, even academic, forms of literacy. We have also been involved in faculty development, introducing colleagues to computer messaging, word processing, and other forms of computer use, especially the use of microcomputers (Scollon and Scollon, 1981c, 1982b.) To contrast with these studies of adult learning of computers and computer-mediated discourse, we have been working with the preschool on the campus of the University of Alaska, Fairbanks. Two microcomputers are currently being used by children as young as 3 years old in their regular preschool program. We are involved in training the preschool staff in the use of microcomputers with very young children. Finally, we have been studying the the the acquisition of computer knowledge by our own children. Rachel, who was 7 years old at the beginning of this study, is the same child we reported on as the "Literate Two-Year-Old" (Scollon and Scollon, 1981a). Tommy, who was 4 years old at the beginning of this study, is the child to whom we refer in the title of this chapter. In the following sections, we focus on the use of computers by children.

Educational Use of Computers

The predominant use of microcomputers for children is in drill and practice routines. The predominant metaphor appears to be that of the conduit. The presupposition is that the computer, or more specifically, the program or software, contains information that will be transmitted to the child as some form of learning or at least communication. The role of the computer appears to be a transparent, clear, open conduit between the ideas of the programmer and the child. Seymour Papert has referred to this situation as use of the computer to program the child (Papert, 1980). We believe that this use prevails largely because of the pervading influence of the conduit metaphor on the adults who organize this use of computers for children. It demonstrates the influence of traditional conceptions of literacy on computer-mediated discourse.

It is significant, then, that in our research children tend to avoid this sort of computer use. Children's widespread preference for games may well be an indication of their preference for more interactive uses of the computer.

Author and Audience

If the computer is a medium, then between what participants does it mediate? There are at least two cases to be considered. One is the interaction between the child using the computer and the designers of the hardware and software being used. The second is the interaction between two people, either two children or even a child and an adult, who are using a computer during their interaction. In both cases, there is no simple relationship between any one person as the author of a message and any other person as the receiver of that message. In fact, the notions of author and audience are of doubtful relevance in understanding computer-mediated discourse, even such a simple discourse as the playing of a computer game.

The role of the software writer or the hardware designer is not the role of someone communicating to someone else. Instead, it is a role in which a world—a *microworld*, if the pun can be forgiven—is created. Likewise, the role of the user is not a role of receiving any message but rather one of exercising the available options for creation of a discourse in the microworld presented by the designer.

In the literate model of communication, the creative role is thought to be filled by the writer, and in the oral model, by the speaker. In the discourse between the user of a computer and its designer, the creativity is shared. The designer set limits and suggests options and, within those limits and options, the user creates a discourse. We believe that it is this sharing in the creative role that is so attractive to young children and also so threatening to many adults who are operating on the basis of the sender-receiver conduit model of communication.

Microworlds of Discourse

In the spontaneous use of microcomputers by young children, the emphasis seems to be on the creation of worlds of discourse: Each world has its own rules and possibilities for action and interaction. A few examples are presented to give some sense of these microworlds.

One microworld is that of a word processor. The Writer's Assistant is the word processor program with which this chapter was composed. It is a modification of the Pascal editor developed at the University of California at San Diego for use in research on children's writing. The Writer's Assistant is easy to use and has been used in school environments by third graders for composition and editing of class newspapers. Our son Tommy has watched us write for some time using this word processor. Without any specific instruction beyond answers to his questions, Tommy now is able to create and save text files and print them out. The only thing he cannot do is read or write. Here is a sample file he created:

```
     #5
sgff#5
 #5
 #4
 #3
 #2
 #1


frr gsfvcdgcc


i

 dxs
```

Of course, as a message, this text is nonsense. It is analogous to the stories we observed Rachel "writing" at 2 years of age. The sequence of actions required to create and save this file is equivalent to writing characters on paper and putting the paper into a labeled folder in a file cabinet. The computer makes it much easier to generate legible nonsense than do paper and pencil. Instead of the fine motor coordination required to write with a pencil, the task requires handling disks and manipulating a keyboard. It also requires cognitive skills such as the ability to recognize if not completely read messages printed on the screen of the monitor and to know what keys to press in response.

Despite the nonsense quality of the previous example, Tommy's first file was created with the intent of communicating. It contained the message, "Hi, mom," which he had written on paper several times before. Our point is that although Tommy does not read or write any form of connected text, he already has an interesting level of competence in manipulating a discourse frame, the operating system of a fully professional word processor.

A second world in which Tommy operates at a framing level of discourse is music synthesis. The Alf music synthesizer is a screen-oriented synthesizer. It allows the user to enter music notation on a score displayed on a screen for later playback. It is a full editor analogous to a word processor. It allows simple insertions and deletions of music on a score as well as many other much more complex operations, such as calling up and inserting subroutines that have been stored elsewhere. It also allows the users to change the sound envelopes either for an entire piece of composed music or for sections at a time. With the synthesizer, as with the word processor, Tommy is able to enter notes on a score, edit them, and play them back through a stereo system. This was his introduction to conventions of musical notation. What he composes may be musical garbage at this time, but we believe that his interest in learning to operate this editing system shows an involvement with the computer at the level of operating systems of discourse frames rather than at the level of simple musical messages.

A third discourse system in which Tommy is very interested is Logo. Logo is a language and an operating system that allows (we might say, encourages) programming of very interesting graphics displays, among other things (Papert, 1980). As Papert has pointed out so often, it is a marvel to watch children as young as 5 years old discussing what amounts to the Pythagorean theorem in attempting to get the screen turtle to make its journey across the hypotenuse of a right triangle to arrive at exactly the diagonal corner. It is exciting to watch young children engaged in parallel discussions to try to get the turtle not only to make a square but to continue making it in an indefinitely recurring loop.

An interesting phenomenon that we have observed fairly commonly in very young children appears, on the surface, to be simple. It is the problem of getting a simple game up and running on a microcomputer. All our evidence tells us that a 4-year-old child is as likely to succeed at this task as any untutored adult. However, comparing our studies of adults and children we find this difference: The children in our studies are able to gain control of the general operating system, as distinct from the programs themselves or the languages in which the programs run, more quickly than the adults.

Are Computers Linear?

A common complaint from adults who use computers is that computers are too linear or too literal, that they are unforgiving of slight mistakes in typing or of slightly varied syntactic forms. We rarely have encountered this complaint from a child. While an adult is searching through his or her written notes about how to access a particular program, a child is returning to the overall operating system, calling up the catalog of programs, and rerunning the program. Failing that, the child turns off the system, turns it on again, and begins anew. Thus, the way young children and adults approach even such a simple task of running a program in BASIC is fundamentally different. The adult's approach is linear, literal: One typing mistake results in frustration. The child's approach is global and recycling: If something does not work, it is of small consequence; one begins again or does something else and comes back later.

We have argued recently that if computers are indeed highly literal, it generally is not at the level at which a user employs them (R. Scollon, 1981a). Such common uses as word processing allow and perhaps even foster a global approach to the task. In contrast, a computer program in its finished form definitely is highly literal. One line out of order may determine whether the program will run. Nevertheless, the writing of the program typically takes place in modules. An overall outline is sketched, and modules are completed as the programmer wishes. Then, the program is run many times, with returns to debug or edit it into its final shape. Only then does it take on its relentlessly literal form.

It is plausible that the development of linear logical forms of discourse may have reached their fulfillment in the programming of computers. Now that we have mechanized this possibility, human discourse may be freed from the necessity of such a relentless linear logic. Whatever the case (and at this point we can only speculate), it seems clear that the adults' complaint about the mercilessly literal logic of the computer is more a comment on their own approach to the machine than to anything inherent in the actual use of computers.

Conclusion: Effects of the Computer Age on Traditional Literacy

We now come to the question our title asks: Can Tommy in fact read? In computer jargon, *read* refers to a process by which the computer copies some information from one point in the system where it is permanently stored to another place in the computer where it is temporarily stored for some form of processing. With a microcomputer, the term generally means to copy some information that is magnetically stored on disk onto a chip in the computer where it can be used. In LOGO, for example, a procedure that will generate a star can be saved or written onto a disk and later recalled as part of another program.

Tommy's use of LOGO regularly requires him to read files from disk onto chips in the system for further use. In that sense, then, he can read. This is not just playing with words. It allows us to consider a problem that underlies the question of what it means to read or write, especially in reference to young children. We can say that Tommy knows what steps to take in a procedure to make a file accessible for use in LOGO. We are not sure that in some more explicit sense he knows what he is doing, but he can do what he needs to do to accomplish what he wants to accomplish, and this process is called *reading*. For more than a year, Tommy has been able to put in a disk, turn on the computer, type "CATALOG" to get the list of programs on the disk, type "RUN TRILOGY" to call up the game "Trilogy," and then play the game either alone or with some other competitor. Could Tommy spell *catalog*, *run*, or *trilogy*? We would have to answer that he could not: That is, if we asked, "Tommy, how do you spell *run*?" he could not (or at least would not) spell it. The same is true of the whole vocabulary of some fifty words (including *kaleidoscope*) that he could use in calling up programs on the computer. However, if we said, "Tommy, let's play Trilogy," he could easily sit down and type "RUN TRILOGY."

The question, of course, is what do we accept as evidence of knowledge? In some sense, Tommy knew how to spell many words. Many of them, such as *kaleidoscope*, are considered very unlikely ones for a 4-year-old to know. He had, however, no control over them as spelling words. His control over them was as procedures to be carried out on a keyboard to accomplish some other task such as playing a game. He had no need to spell them correctly the first time.

Our question regarding what evidence would indicate that Tommy knew something more important about spelling was answered one day when Tommy and his father were in a bookstore. There was a novel with the title *TRILOGY* standing in a long row of books. Tommy went up to his dad and said, "Daddy, what's that?" and his father replied, "Maybe you know." Tommy looked at the book, at his father, back at the book, and then whispered, "Trilogy!" He had made the incredible leap from a procedure to accomplish something in the world to a conceptualization of a relationship between a symbol and an idea. We believe that this leap has been made at some time by every child who has become a successful reader. Although we can make no causal tie between Tommy's use of the microcomputer and that leap, the use of the microcomputer has been the occasion for an encounter with literacy that goes far beyond the understanding of representational systems normally encountered by 4-year-olds.

Tommy regularly plays several games. One of these is the "Prisoner." It is a very challenging game for most players, child or adult, and depends heavily on learning a complex system of separate modules that begin to relate to one another only after a considerable amount of playing and thought. Another simpler game is "Little Brick Out." A dot (a "ball") bounces off a wall of bricks on the right of the screen, and the player keeps it bouncing back to the wall with a "paddle" that moves up and down the left side of the screen. As the ball bounces off the bricks, bricks are knocked out of the wall until finally they all are gone. Other players of "Prisoner" with a great deal of determination have learned the system well enough to escape from the prison. Some have managed to break into the actual program and have read it to see how the programmer designed the prison, thus finding a way out. What Tommy asked us was if we could rewrite the program so that "Little Brick Out" would be one of the options for escape from the game. We believe that this insight may be related to his understanding that the design of computer programs and computer discourse generally is at the level of the creation of microworlds rather than at the level of the creation of messages. This insight may reflect general concern for representational systems, not at the level of the message but at the superordinate level of the discourse.

Tommy's "trilogy" insight probably is made at some point by every successful reader. We wonder to what extent adults socialized to a literate environment are able to make the next level of insight into the creation of whole possibilities of discourse. Foucault (1976, 1977) has argued that our history has moved slowly from discourse to discourse. According to Foucault, it is the extremely rare thinker (Freud is an example) who has not given us just new messages in an existing discourse but who has actually created new ways of saying things. The use of microcomputers by young children may be fostering just that level of insight: It may be that the intrigue children experience with the computer does not lie in the possibility of saying things to the computer or in using the computer as a discourse medium, but in the possibility of creating a new kind of discourse altogether.

The printing press is now more than 500 years old in the West, but the scientific study of literacy itself is in its infancy. We have only historic records with which to reconstruct the social and cognitive consequences of the development of Western literacy. Small personal microcomputers are less than a decade old. We urge anyone with an interest in literacy to consider that the impact of microcomputers on society and thought may much greater than the impact of literacy has been. There is some tentative evidence that the possibilities of discourse that are growing up around microcomputers may constitute an integration (at last) with the more particularistic, vernacular discourse values of the period preceding print. We believe that the impacts may include the fostering of insights into the nature of representational systems that have previously been extremely rare. What other, perhaps darker, possibilities will be fostered is unknown.

PART III. LITERACY AND COGNITION

11. The Creative Achievement of Literacy

Frank Smith

The goal of the University of Victoria Symposium was to elucidate the ways in which children succeed or fail in becoming literate. I interpret literacy as the ability to make full sense and productive use of the opportunities of written language in the particular culture in which one lives. The manner in which illiterate children must detect and understand such potential sense and utility is my primary concern in this chapter, which includes some reflections on the nature of written language and on the ways in which children learn to make sense of their worlds in general.

I shall endeavor to look at literacy in relation to the learning brain, which I regard as having certain universal and inescapable characteristics, rather than in relation to learning or teaching situations, which may vary greatly within and between cultures. (An opposite perspective might be thought to be prevalent in education, one that assumes that universally effective instructional proceedings exist or can be found which provide all children with equal opportunities to learn, and that failures can be attributable to distinctive inadequacies of particular children.)

My two main points will be that children in the first few years of their lives know how to learn to read and write because written language presents them with problems similar to those they solve with spoken language, and that social interaction is required to make literacy learning possible but can also confound learning. Society cannot impose literacy on children, either through prescription or instruction. Rather, society must make literacy learning possible. Children require a particular kind of interaction to become literate. I shall characterize this interaction as an apprenticeship, or engagement with relevant demonstrations.

All children are born illiterate. This truism requires stating because illiteracy sometimes is perceived as a developmental defect or an inability to profit from instruction rather than the inevitable beginning from which every individual must move to make sense and use of written language. Illiteracy is a condition of not yet having acquired certain fundamental insights or understandings. Literacy is not achieved by learning the so-called basics or mechanics of reading and writing, such as the names of letters of the alphabet, phonic generalizations, spelling, and punctuation. Learning such mechanics would be pointless and difficult unless a child had already developed a foundation of insights into the nature and functions of written language. With such insights, though, a child will learn the mechanics far more easily, sometimes in the absence of formal instruction. These insights are largely independent of formal instruction, and children often gain and capitalize on them before they receive any formal instruction in reading and writing at school.

The insights to which I refer are concerned with language function and structures, with what written language does and how it does it in the particular cultures to which a child belongs. These are the issues being examined in this chapter. I endeavor to discover those crucial understandings that must be obvious, though not explicitly so, to every child who becomes literate. This is not an ethnographic study;

no particular written language environment is described or analyzed. Rather, I propose to look at the landscape of written language as a whole, to construct a general picture of the range of possibilities and problems presented to any young child striving to make sense of an unfamiliar world of literacy.

The Uses of Written Language

Differentiating Print in the Environment

Why should children try to make sense of written language? Why should they bother to differentiate print from the pattern of the wallpaper or the decorative borders of packages and books? Writing, after all, does not call attention to itself as does speech. Print exists whether or not people are looking at it, and it persists after the people who produced it have gone away. Indeed, it is rare to see anyone actually produce much of the more conspicuous written language in the environment—the *ambient print* of announcements, signs, and labels.

In the situations in which many children are most likely to see people write—food servers taking orders, teachers recording marks, and bureaucrats and other adults completing forms—writing must seem (and may be) a purely ritualistic and purposeless activity.

In much of the literature on literacy, a great deal is made of the need for children who are learning to read to relate to authors and to understand their purposes. However, the prime necessity must be for children to understand a *reader's* purpose, to see someone actually paying attention to print for a reason which must be self-evident.[1] It does not seem necessary for beginning readers to understand that writing is produced by people. How could they easily achieve such an insight? My interpretation of the research of Goodman (see Chap. 7) and others is that children discover a great deal about written language, whether in ambient print or in stories, without differentiating it from natural phenomena. Written language *exists*, and its primary relevance to the child (and often to the literate adult as well) is as something to be read, something to be used. It is in this respect that print is different from the patterns of the wallpaper, the colors of cars and clothing, and the configurations of the leaves on trees, none of which has any potential utility to the observer (or, at least, to most children). Thus, the first requirement for children who will become readers must be the recognition that written language exists, that there are aspects of the visual environment worth paying attention to in a particular way.

The Relationship of Spoken and Written Language

Halliday (1975) points out that infants do not learn spoken language as an abstract system which they then use for a variety of purposes. Language, whether spoken or written, produced or comprehended, always is related to intentions and purposes, and children learn about language as they strive to use it. (This includes that most overlooked and underrated use of language by children, as something to be attended to closely in order to decipher the feelings, intentions, and mysteries of people around them.)

Children are less likely to discover possibilites of written language from their own spontaneous experimentation with writing than they learn about spoken language from their babbling and early speech. They need to see what written language will do for readers or writers. They learn about language, spoken or written, in the process of doing other things for which language can be recruited, whether finding the exit or a preferred brand of candy in a department store or exploring the worlds of stories. Thus, children must be entirely dependent on literate others to lead them into literacy, to show them how written language can be used.

I have argued elsewhere (Smith, 1982, Chap. 4) that written language can be used for every purpose for which speech can be used (although some purposes are better served by speech and others by writing) and that speech can be used in support of every human intention. Thus, to catalog the possible uses of written language one would have to catalog every possible human intention, in terms of both understanding and producing effects. The actual range of language uses in any particular culture can be ascertained only by careful and extensive observation, by the researcher and by the child. The circumstances in which written language occurs in literate cultures are multitudinous and multifarious, and every circumstance is likely to have its own unique conventions. In other words, understanding the sense and uses of written language is not a general problem for a child but innumerable specific problems, each requiring largely unique solutions. A child has a great deal to learn.

The Manifestation of Written Language for Children

The ways in which written language becomes manifest to children varies with cultures. They vary not only in terms of differing uses and expectations, including the frequently highly artificial representations in schools, but also in terms of which manifestations have the greatest impact on illiterate or nearly illiterate children, the order (if any) in which children tend to pay attention to them, and the degree to which insights about particular manifestations of written language can be generalized to elucidate other manifestations.

Research to date has paid little attention to any particular order or structure behind the manner in which children become literate. (See, for example, Chaps. 2, 6, 8), although some of the broader details are beginning to be painted in.) By 3 years of age, many children in North American cultures have learned that print can be used to discover where certain fast foods are available and the contents of packages (Goodman, 1980); they can differentiate text from decoration even, perhaps, before they can identify particular written words. By age 3, they can understand that writing can be used for notes and reminders (Harste et al., 1981). Another more obvious use—one that often is assumed to be what reading essentially *is*—is for the enjoyment of stories, an insight that children can acquire even earlier (Scollon and Scollon, 1981a) if they have appropriate opportunities. In schools and other formal instructional situations, on the other hand, reading may be regarded as only those activities, often ritualistic, that are engaged in in the name of reading. Children, parents, and teachers come to believe that drills and exercises constitute important reading.

My overall conclusion is that children are capable of understanding any use of written language that is demonstrated to them, provided that they themselves understand and share the intention (behind the reading or the writing) of the particular manifestation of written language. What is critical is that which is demonstrated to the child, in terms of not only potential uses of written language, which give the child insights into function, but also the relationship of language and its uses, which provides the child with important insights about *form*.

The Form of Written Language

Olson (see Chap. 14) asserts that the two major problems confronting a child who is striving to become literate are the contextual and conventional nature of written language. In one sense, this assertion is indisputable; children will not become literate unless they understand how written language is contextualized and conventionalized. However, in another sense, these two aspects of written language are solutions rather than problems; they are the means by which children naturally explore any manifestation of language with which they become involved. I regard contextualizing and conventionalizing as psychological and linguistic universals, two aspects of language that children take for granted. Certainly, the two terms conveniently summarize important characteristics of print, and I shall therefore employ them in organizing my own exposition.

Contextualization

In many discussions of literacy, it is emphasized that written language is *decontextualized*. This is an overgeneralization. Not all written language is decontextualized in the sense in which the term is intended. In addition, decontextualization is not a unique characteristic of written language; spoken language frequently is decontextualized in the same way. Finally, it is not strictly correct to suggest that any language, written or spoken, could ever be entirely decontextualized.

A typical explanation of the decontextualization of written language—and of its alleged particular difficulty for children—is that, unlike much of the spoken language with which a child might be familiar, the written language of stories and newspaper and magazine articles is not related to the physical situation in which such texts are produced and read. There can be no appeal to external cues to meaning in the environment. In contrast, with spoken phrases such as "here are your boots," "why are you crying?" or "look at that dark cloud over there," the meaning might be apparent even if the listener did not understand or even hear the actual words. I have called such everyday spoken language *situation-dependent* (Smith, 1982), because the form of the language is determined by the situation or circumstances in which it is produced (including the intention of the producer). Words in situation-dependent utterances cannot be changed arbitrarily without damaging the meaning and confounding the intention. For example, one cannot say "pass the jam" if the salt is required. Situation-dependent speech clearly is important in the spoken language development of infants, because the physical setting provides the clues by which they learn to understand what is being talked about by people around them, and it provides feedback about whether their interpretation is correct. If a child thinks mother has just said "pass the jam" and father responds by putting the cat out, then a mistake has obviously been made.

The written language of storybooks does not, of course, function in this situation-dependent way. The language and meaning remain the same wherever the book is located and whenever it is examined, so that a child will not find clues to understanding or confirmation of hypotheses by looking around. This is the sense in which the language of written texts often is characterized as decontextualized: The texts are *situation-independent*; the physical setting does not determine the words or their meanings.

However, many manifestations of written language function in exactly the same situation-dependent way as the everyday spoken language to which I have referred. For example, the ambient print of signs and labels is determined by its physical setting and cannot be changed arbitrarily. The hamburger sign cannot be placed over the gas station, and the print on the detergent package cannot read "cereal." Thus, the physical setting of language can provide clues to meaning and feedback about whether hypotheses are correct. The evidence suggests that in Western cultures at least, it is through situation-dependent ambient print that many children find their way into literacy or have their first meaningful encounters with print (Goodman, 1980). This may be because there is so much ambient print in many environments (especially in television commercials), and because children are likely to be adept at using situation-based clues based on their experience in making sense of speech.

There are many forms of written language that remain independent of the physical situation in which they occur, but this is not an exclusive characteristic of writing. Many forms of spoken language also are situation-independent. These include the spoken language of oral story-telling, or reports, descriptions, explanations, and discussions, and sometimes the possibly critical fictionalization or externalization of self referred to by Scollon and Scollon (1981a). Such spoken language is as decontextualized as any text and may be as important for providing a child with essential experience in language detached from its physical setting as being read to. Although children from oral traditions frequently are regarded as underprivileged when compared with those from more literate backgrounds, familiarity with story-telling may be more advantageous to children approaching textual literacy than a wealth of ambient print, alphabet books, flash cards, and phonics drills.

Of course, functioning language, whether spoken or written, does not divide itself neatly into situation-dependent and situation-independent categories. Probably much of the written language that adults encounter has elements of both, as are the instructions on a package, the illustrations to stories and articles, and the majority of television commercials.

More importantly, however, no meaningful language is independent of context. Producers of extended discourse or text are no more free to be arbitrary in their choice of words than are the writers of product labels or street signs. Powerful constraints, and therefore clues, exist for situation-independent language, but they operate within the text or discourse itself. They are the constraints of sense, syntax, and other linguistic conventions such as lexical selection, cohesion, and discourse structure. These constraints function in exactly the same way as the environmental clues for situation-dependent speech and print: They permit the reader (or listener) to anticipate and monitor meaning and the learner to hypothesize and receive relevant feedback. The only time many children are likely to meet decontextualized language is during formal instruction.

All meaningful language is contextualized; it is sensitive to its environment (including the intentions of its author) and it is this context that permits comprehension and learning. What the learner has to discover for all forms and uses of language is the manner in which contextualization is achieved, which is always conventional. A child unfamiliar with what I call *context-dependent language* (paradoxically, often referred to as *decontextualized*), in which the constraints lie within the text rather than in the physical setting, will be unable to grasp the language to find out what makes it work, what makes it comprehensible and useful.

Conventionalization

Languages are complex systems of social contracts, implicit agreements that sounds or signs will be produced and interpreted in particular ways. The writer (or speaker) must say things in a manner in which the reader (or listener) will expect them to be said, and the reader (or listener) must anticipate the manner in which things will be said. In general, as part of the mutual trust to which Grice (1957) refers, we produce and interpret language the way we expect others in our culture and group to produce and interpret it. It is possible for language producers to be unconventional, but this always is assumed to be for a good reason, usually ignorance or because what is to be said cannot be expressed in conventional ways.

There are conventions for every aspect of language—for lexical choice and the application of appropriate syntactic rules in every dialect as well as for idiom (which overrides lexis and syntax), cohesion, paragraph structure, larger aspects of textual organization such as genre schemes, calligraphy, typography, neatness, layout, letter and line dimensions, spacing, indentation, capitalization, orthography, and punctuation. None of these are rules except in the sense that they involve relative internal consistency. Exceptions are always possible, provided they are reasonably conventional (for example, the spelling "tonite," or vertical lettering in advertisements). To use language, one must know the conventions. Literate people are familiar with and can use the appropriate written language conventions of their culture.

All language is conventional in that its forms must be respected, but it also is conventional in that its particular forms are arbitrary, a consequence of historic accident. The facts of language cannot be predicted or inherited genetically. Every aspect of language could be different, as is the case in different languages: *Oui* also means "yes," "yes" could mean "no," dogs could be called cats. Languages do not work because they are the sole or even the best way to achieve the ends to which they are put. We may become so chauvinistic about our own language that we have difficulty imagining an efficient alternative that does not employ capitalization, quotation marks, question marks, paragraphing, uniform spelling, or anything else that is among our conventions. However, it is the conventional nature of all languages, not their particular rules or reasons, that makes them work.

That language is so thoroughly conventional is not a problem for children; they expect it. All deliberate human behavior is conventional, or a reaction to the conventional, and children clearly are eager to discover what the appropriate conventions are. They are bewildered when others contravene convention and embarrassed to discover they have contravened it themselves. It is not difficult to conjecture why children have such an expectation: A world that was not conventional would be entirely random and unpredictable, even after relevant experience; in fact, there could be no relevant prior experience. The problem for children is always to discover what the relevant conventions are. After gaining the first insight that written language fulfills purposes, children then must progressively learn what those purposes are and how those purposes are conventionally accomplished. For every use of written language (as for every use of speech), there are clusters of conventions, and since there is a multitude of uses of language, the number of conventions with which a child must become familiar—the number of specific problems to be solved on the way to becoming literate—must approach the astronomical.

The Learning Child

How are so many children able to solve the numerous specific problems required to become literate? How do they group the manifold conventions by which written language becomes contextualized and thus meaningful and useful? These questions have been generally addressed in two earlier articles (Smith, 1981a, 1981b). The basic argument, which I shall not elaborate here, is that children are capable of accomplishing enormous amounts of learning about language (and many other matters, too) because they are learning all the time. Learning is not an occasional and specialized activity which must be extrinsically motivated, directed, and reinforced. Rather, children are vulnerable because learning is constantly taking place without the child's or anyone else's awareness. They can learn inappropriate as well as appropriate things about literacy. In addition, for children to learn about language, language must be demonstrated to them. They learn from demonstrations and what they learn is what is demonstrated (or, more precisely, their perception of what is demonstrated).

Demonstrations

A demonstration is an example of something being done, and of how and why it is done. Most formal school or schoollike instruction does not consist of meaningful, purposeful demonstrations (except in terms of the instructor's own intentions). However, an adult observing a traffic sign, drawing attention to a brand name on a package, or reading a book aloud is demonstrating the uses of traffic signs, package labeling, or books. Each demonstration shows an aspect of the *power* of written language. For a literate person, demonstrations of written language uses are as continual, unsuspected, and inevitable as the demonstrations of speech that adults provide for infants.

To reiterate Halliday's (1975) theme, children do not learn language first and then apply it to various uses. They learn language as they learn of its uses. A demonstration, in my view, is far more than an incentive for a child to learn. It is more than a model for the child to copy. Such abstract roles could not account for the enormous amount of language learning that is done inconspicuously, without overt direction, and so often error-free. Young children never speak approximate versions of their parents' or peers' dialect, and conventions and styles frequently emerge in their later speech and writing without preliminary indications of failure to achieve a desired model. Learning is not the consequence of demonstrations but a concomitant. The demonstration is when the learning occurs, and the demonstrator's act becomes the child's learning trial. In other words, language learning is both *incidental* and *vicarious*, two general aspects of learning that attracted much attention from experimental psychologists in the 1930s but that have been largely ignored by contemporary cognitive theorists.

I have discussed already the incidental aspect of literacy learning: Children learn about print by using it or by being involved in its use. In general, this might be called the *can I have another doughnut?* theory of language learning. Every child learns to say "can I have another doughnut?" not for the sake of learning to say it but to get the doughnut. What the child learns to say is incidental to the objective of getting the doughnut. Most children older than 3 years can identify the McDonald's sign, and it is not likely that this widespread ability is unrelated to hamburgers and french fries.

The vicarious aspect of language learning probably requires more elaboration. The general argument is that children do not have to do something themselves in order to learn. This is clearly the case with spoken language. Infants come to understand the speech of those around them without (or before) producing that speech themselves. After their initial, intensively experimental period of baby talk, they learn large numbers of new words, idioms, and grammatical constructions that tend to be produced correctly the first time (although the exceptions generally attract attention). Miller (1977) computed that infants are learning a new word every hour of their waking life, obviously without formal instruction, practice, or conspicuous trial and error. He reports this in a book felicitously titled *Spontaneous Apprentices*, a term which encapsulates the essence of children's language learning.

Children learn about spoken and written language by attaching themselves as apprentices to people who are using language as a tool to accomplish particular and self-evident ends. Children have to behave like language users, to share the *purpose* for which the language is being used, in order to learn *how* the language is used. A child learns that a sign signifies hamburgers when a person in his or her company uses the sign as an indication of the availability of hamburgers. If the sign is to be learned outside of an actual physical context, then it must be learned in an imaginary but equally relevant context, as part of a picture story or in play, for example.

There are several critical differences between demonstrations and formal instruction. Demonstrations provide opportunities for learners to engage in the purpose of the activity, to share an intention with the demonstrator, whether to construct a story, locate a hamburger, or discover what someone else is thinking or planning. Usually, there is little or no awareness on the part of either demonstrator or child that teaching or learning is taking place. Both concentrate on the purpose rather than on the process, and conventions are employed in context. Formal instruction, on the other hand, is self-conscious, particulate, and metalinguistic. It makes written language the object of reflection and analysis and fragments superficial aspects of behavior or of a product. It does not involve participation in a purposeful process. The amount of conscious awareness, if any, that a child requires to learn to read is an issue still open to debate. In my view, research has failed to show any necessity.

For written as well as spoken language learning to occur, it is essential for that which is demonstrated to be something that learners will want to do and will expect to be able to do. Therefore, children must perceive themselves as part of the particular language-using community, as "members of the club." Vicarious learning can take place only when learners fully assimilate into their own behavior that which is demonstrated, when they can *identify*—to use another venerable and recently overlooked psychological concept—with what the other person is doing. I call this process *engagement*, as immediate, direct, and invariable as the transmission of power and movement through the mechanical meshing of gears.

Thus, literacy is both individual and social—individual because the impetus must come from the child, but social because literate others must provide the demonstrations that engage the child as a literate member of society. Children do not become literate in a vacuum. On the other hand, children cannot anticipate society's uses for literacy (and perhaps would not become literate if they could). Literacy develops because the child sees what reading and writing can do, and because it is relevant to the child's own creative and constructive purposes.

The Creativity of Learning

The most focal element in learning about written language is imagination, the ability to relate possible contexts and conventional behavior. The creative nature of children's language learning has been illustrated in a number of aspects of early literacy—in invented spelling (Read, 1971), "mock writing" (Clay, 1975), and the construction of "first grammars" (McNeill, 1970). Many examples of the ways that children perceive context and seek conventions are provided in Chapters 6, 7, and 12. I subscribe to an even more general theory—that creativity is the essence of learning itself.

In Smith (1983), I argue that the currently popular metaphor for the brain as an information-processing device is inadequate and misleading. It would be far more appropriate and productive to regard the brain as a creative artist, except that it is entire worlds that are created. The actual world around us, if it exists in the mind at all (let alone as any kind of objective reality), exists only as one among a number of possible worlds that the brain continually creates. To guide all our behavior in and interactions with this "real" world, we compare our experience of it with constructed "recollections" of past experience and with constructed expectations and intentions for the future. All our fantasies of what we wish the world had been like in the past or might be like in the future are alternative worlds that the brain creates. Every hypothesis we entertain about the world or our place in it is a construction. Creative imagination is not a by-product of our interactions with the world but the basis of them.

This creativity is particularly noteworthy in many aspects of children's early years—in the role-playing of play activities, children's empathy for the feelings of others, involvement as observers of what is going on around them, and general interest in stories. Macnamara (1982) has recently noted that 3-year-old children can not only assess speakers' intentions (independently of language) but can also evaluate adult assessments of the child's own intentions. Such complex role-playing seems to support my view that children associate themselves completely with another person's purposes and behavior (to the extent that they share intentions) and that they learn at second hand what is available for the actual actor to learn firsthand. The demonstrator becomes the tool of the child's own creativity.

All of this leads me back to the original question of why children should bother to learn about the uses of written language in the first place. What, in general, motivates them to learn to read and write? I believe that the motivating force is not a largely mythical compulsion to communicate or a simple curiosity about what is going on around them, and it certainly is not a blind readiness to learn anything that happens to be part of their environment. Rather, I suspect that children happen to learn about written language, if appropriate demonstrations are available, because writing is a particularly efficacious means of accomplishing that which the child's brain is perpetually striving to do in any case—namely, to create worlds.

The sense that children make of all the ambient print in the environment—when they are able to make use of that print—is sense that is part of a world they are creating. This world is one in which children themselves are agents, if only in their imagination or vicariously, using written language in the process of achieving ends. Stories do not *represent* experiences for children; they *are* experiences as immediate and as compelling as actual events. The act of writing must be a particularly powerful device for children because of the power it gives them to construct, manipulate, and even erase entire worlds of experience and ideas which otherwise would never exist for them.

Conclusions

Literacy is more than utility and understanding for children. It is power, and power is not something that has to be explained to them; it is enough that it is demonstrated. All children are sensitive to the exercise of power by others and to its effects on themselves.

Earlier in this chapter, I observed that the enormous and continual learning capacity of children made them vulnerable. They are always likely to learn that which is demonstrated to them. Thus, if it is demonstrated that reading and writing are nonsensical, purposeless, or painful activities, that is what they will learn. Many so-called problem readers seem to have learned just that.

In cultures that are predominantly literate, there is another aspect of power to which illiterate children also are susceptible. As Anderson and Stokes (Chap. 2) point out, literacy can be a means of political control and manipulation. It can be used to categorize individuals and groups. Children can learn to reject literacy as alien to them (or to their social group) or as something that is used to underline or justify differences. The teaching of literacy in schools can never be devoid of cultural and political considerations, although these may escape well-intentioned teachers more often than the children who are the subjects of instruction.

Note

1. Conversely, I would argue that for children to learn to write—whether shopping lists or stories—it is more important for them to understand the author's perspective than to have a sense of audience.

12. The Underlying Logic of Literacy Development

Emilia Ferreiro

Developmental literacy cannot be fully understood by isolating some of its components from the others. Nonetheless, given the present state of our knowledge in this field, it seems very hard to analyze all the components at the same time and with equal depth. Therefore, in this chapter, I focus on only a single problem area (the one that I probably understand best at this moment)—that is, the psychogenesis of the production of written texts in the period that *precedes* the use of letters with conventional sound value (including invented spelling).

There are at least two very distinct ways of considering any written production of children—one that we may call *figurative* and one that we may call *constructive*. They are related to the kind of questions with which the researcher is concerned. The figurative aspects, which are traditionally considered the most relevant aspects, are those related to the quality of the graphic shapes. They appear when the researcher looks for answers to questions about the distribution of letters in the graphic space, the conventionality of the forms used, the orientation of the path followed (from left to right or otherwise), and so on. The constructive aspects (to which little attention has been paid until now) arise when we ask ourselves, about the same pieces of writings, other questions such as: What is the internal link between the graphemes that compose a given string? Are there systematic rules of production applied by children? What are the letters supposed to represent, from the point of view of the subject who produces them? The latter questions concern what is specific to a writing system, because they are related to the rules of composition that define the system itself.

To deepen our understanding of the processes of appropriation of the socially constituted writing system, we studied a group of thirty-three children over a 2-year period. The children were from two contrasting situations in terms of their access to written language. One group consisted of children from a slum in Mexico City. Most of their parents had no formal schooling. Their environment was characterized by a high degree of illiteracy, unstable employment, and low income. The environment provided few occasions for reading and writing, and few materials that could be used in reading and writing. There was a low incidence of participation in social acts in which written language is used and little opportunity for obtaining information from literate people. The second group consisted of middle-class children, and at least one of each of the children's parents had a university degree. There was a variety of reading and writing materials available in their homes, and their families made use of written language as part of their daily activities (for example, they read newspapers, wrote telephone messages, completed forms, and sent letters).

At the beginning of our study, there were twelve 3-year-olds, eleven 4-year-olds, and ten 5-year-olds. We interviewed each child at intervals of approximately 2 months. While the middle-class children were always interviewed individually at home, the lower-class children were interviewed individually as well as in small groups in a public park near their homes. All interviews were conducted according to the basic principles of Jean Piaget's method of critical exploration.

Of the aspects of literacy development explored in this research, only the evolution of the production of texts—that is, writing itself—will be discussed in this chapter.[1] We were trying to understand how children construct a piece of writing in various situations. We may distinguish four kinds of situations according to whether the pieces of writing are produced:

1. Without context (the writing of something suggested by an adult, for example)
2. In the context of other graphic activities (when we encourage the children "to put something with letters" in their drawings, for example)
3. In the context of pictures presented without texts (when we also encourage the children "to put something with letters" to magazine figures glued on a page, or to playing cards)
4. In the context of play with real objects (for instance, the organization of a market or a toy shop and preparation of the corresponding signs)

In this chapter, I will attempt to reconstruct the psychogenesis of writing through the comparison of the thirty-three case studies. The focus is on processes of construction and not the quality of the graphic shapes. I will not deal with copying, because a copy is a drawing of letters and not writing. The difference between copy and real writing is at least as great as the difference between deciphering and reading. I will not talk about the hand that takes up the pencil nor of the lines as a final product. Rather, I will talk about that which mediates between the hand and the result—that is, a subject who thinks, who assimilates in order to understand, and who should create in order to assimilate. Knowing subjects necessarily transform what they are learning; they construct their own knowledge to make the knowledge of others their own.

Drawing and Writing: Figurative and Spatial Relationships

One of the first problems that children face when trying to produce a piece of writing is to find the frontier that differentiates drawing from writing. It is the problem of finding the difference between the graphism-drawing, which is close to the shape of the object in its ways of organization, and the graphism of any form whatsoever, which is linked with the object only by an act of attribution (a "belonging relationship"). That such a graphism becomes capable of symbolizing is only a result of the relationship established by the subject and not due to any figurative similarity with the object. The transition from the search for a figurative relationship to the use of graphisms of whatever form is well illustrated by *Fermín* (LC):[2]

At the age of 4 years 4 months, all Fermín's writings were composed only of strokes and circular lines. However, in the market situation those graphisms were distributed according to the shapes of the objects: circular lines for round objects (such as apples) and straight lines for straight objects (such as green peas in their pods) (See Fig. 12-1A).

At 4 years 11 months, Fermín's graphemes still were not well differentiated, being mainly circles and angular strokes. Trying to put "something with letters that goes well

Fig. 12-1. (A) Graphic shapes that keep figural similarity with the objects (Fermín, 4 years 4 months old). (B) Graphic shapes without figural similarity with the objects (Fermín, 4 years 11 months old).

with the figures," he put a grapheme in the immediate proximity of each figure, but this time he is not looking for any figurative similarity. For each figure of two children, he used two small graphemes, each one being "of child" *(de niño)* (Fig. 12-1B).

A similar progression is observed in the case of the texts produced to accompany the children's drawings.

Nanis (LC), at age 4 years 1 month, tried to draw a doll. Then he was asked "to put something with letters." He made some circles inside the figure, but these circles were letters as well as the "noses" of the doll (Fig. 12-2).

The graphemes were placed inside the drawing for a precise reason: Nanis, as well as other children at the same developmental level, produces graphemes that are considered only as letters that do not yet "say" anything by themselves. A belonging

Fig. 12-2. *Graphic shapes inserted into the drawing ("letters" as well as "noses" of the doll) (Nanis, 4 years 1 month old).*

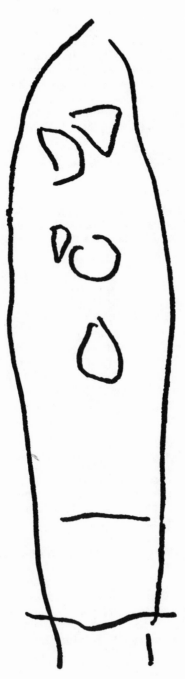

relationship starts to be established, but it is so weak that it would vanish if the incorporation of the graphemes inside the limits of the picture or drawing did not guarantee it. This is one of the many conflicting situations that play an essential role in this development, pushing children beyond their previous ideas. To be sure that letters really "say" what is intended, the children realize that they may need to put them inside the drawing, but in doing this, the letters (still poorly differentiated from the lines used to draw) may become a figurative part of the object.

To maintain the distinction between the drawing and the writing, the children feel obliged to move the letters outside the limits of the drawing. However, before they are actually placed outside, the writing sometimes outlines the figure. This sequence of inside-outside is well exemplified by *Silvia A.* (LC):

> At 4 years 4 months she drew four human figures, giving each one the proper name of a known person. She was asked "to put something with letters." As a result, she made some graphemes inside the figures, changing the color of pen used. We asked, "What did you put?" "The *i*, *i* (*la* i, i)" she answered (Fig. 12-3A).
>
> At 5 years 6 months (1 year later), she drew a clown. When she was asked to write, she made graphemes that outlined the hat. We asked, "What did you write?" "A, e, i." "Can't you write *clown*?" "I already did it," she answered, while pointing to the graphemes that surrounded the clown's hat (Fig. 12-3B).

This surrounding of the head, which a naive observer might confuse with the hat's decoration in Silvia's case, reappeared as a crown or as the antennae of a bee in Ana Teresa's case (MC, age 3 years 3 months) (Fig. 12-4). The importance of the spatial proximity as a determining factor for the attributed interpretation is very clear in this case. First, Ana Teresa drew the big doll (her sister) and wrote her name beside it, but when she drew herself (the small doll), the same letters were intended, by proximity, to say "Ana Teresa." She was not happy and rewrote both names above the head. When she wrote the name for the second drawing, we purposely asked her if it was a hat. She became upset and replied, "No!! They are letters." "What does it say?" we asked. "It is Ana Teresa *(Es Ana Teresa)*."

Variety and Quantity: The Conditions for Attribution of Meaning

At the beginning of the differentiation between drawing and writing, the graphemes are distributed freely on the page. This beginning might not necessarily be marked by an objective distinction within the graphemes themselves, but by the intention of the producer of them. There still is no linearity, and no attention is paid to the variety of characters or to their quantity. Once the activity of writing is initiated, the limits of the space are the limits of the activity. The progress consists, first, in organizing the graphemes one after the other in a linear arrangement and, second, in introducing some variety in the ordered graphemes (even if it is no more than alternating between circle and stroke, between circle and cross, and so on). The quantity of the graphemes seems to be out of control at the beginning, but at a given moment, and sometimes suddenly, a drastic reduction in quantity of graphemes takes place. This reduction may be so drastic that, for some of the children, to

Fig. 12-3. (A) Graphic shapes inserted into the drawing (Silvia A., 4 years 7 months old). (B) Graphic shapes that outline the drawing (Silvia A., 5 years 6 months old).

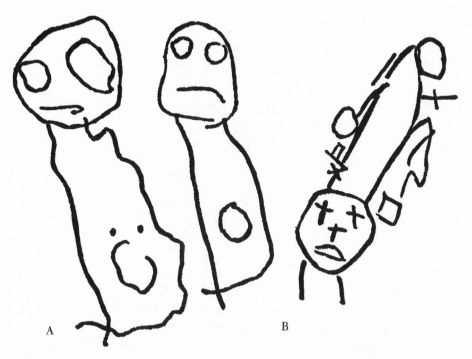

write something that goes well with a drawing, a picture, or an object means to make one and only one grapheme for each.[3]

This strict correspondence—a sign for each object in the picture—frequently appears simultaneously (and we will see that this is not merely a concidence) with the moment of passage from "letters-graphemes" to "letters–substitute objects." In other cases, it appears once the letters are not just letters anymore but "say something." It is impossible to understand the evolution of the construction of writings without bearing in mind this tremendous change.

Letters as Substitute Objects

Letters are not immediately considered as substitute objects—that is, as objects that represent something else. Once they are differentiated from drawing and ornamental marks, they are defined only negatively. The name assigned to this set defined as "that which is not drawing" may vary. It may be referred to as *letters, numbers, fives* (Jorge, LC, age 3 years 1 month), or *zeros* (Gabriel, MC, age 4 years 1 month). None of these names implies that letters are conceived as a set of elements that stand for something else.

Fig. 12-4. Graphic shapes are placed outside the drawing but their interpretation depends on spatial proximity to it (Ana Teresa, 3 years 3 months old).

The younger subjects of our LC sample allowed us to assert the reality of this level.[4] Some typical dialogues at this level follow:

Martín (3 years 5 months) was attending to a series of playing cards with pictures, some of which had a text.

Researcher	Martín
What is it? [Indicates picture.]	A doll.
What could be read here? [Points to text.]	Letters.
What does it say in the letters?	Letters.
In the letters does it say letters?	[He agrees.]
Look at this one. Does it have letters? [Shows picture without texts.]	[Negation gesture.]
What is it? [Indicates picture.]	A doll.
I am going to put letters on it. What may I put with the letters?	Letters.
Letters that say what?	Letters.

Jorge, at age 3 years 1 month, called all the texts *fives*, thus applying this name of a subset to the entire set as a generic term. At 3 years 4 months, the texts coupled with pictures were "*fives*" that said "*four*." Ten months later, the situation remained almost unchanged. At this time, we worked with texts belonging to different real objects.

Researcher	Jorge
[Pointing to a clock.] What is it?	A clock.
What did they put here? [Indicating numbers.]	The fives.
Why?	Because *(para que sí)*.
Does it say something there?	Yes.
What does it say?	Twelve.
[Shows text of a commercial bag.] What did they put here?	Twelve.
And here? [Shows another text.]	Fives.
Does it say anything?	[No response.]

Elami (the only MC subject who clearly was situated in this stage) used *numbers* as the only generic term from age 3 years 3 months to 3 years 5 months. At 3 years 8 months, she used the term *letters* instead of *numbers*. The texts were letters that said "*o, i, a*"; they sometimes were called simply "letters of *o* and of *a*."

All the children in the preceding examples shared the same basic assumption: Letters are particular objects of the external world and, like any other object, they have a name. The question "what does it say?" is not meaningful at that level because letters are not substitute objects that stand for something else. They are what they are. The letters cannot *say* anything or, at most, they can *say* what they really are. That is why the only answer to all such questions is "letters."

These children's answers appeared in the most diverse contexts and were preserved despite the changes of context. At this level, the pictures and the texts can share the same graphic space without entertaining any particular relationship between them. They are treated as two independent systems. How do children progress from this level to the systematic relationship that will characterize the next level, when they begin to suppose that the text represents the names of the objects shown in the pictures?

Victor (LC) will help us to understand the progression. Since he was 3 years 10 months old, Victor used the denomination *letters*. Until he was 4 years 2 months old all the texts, including his own, were "letters that said letters." Three months later, texts without pictures still were "letters that said letters," but when a picture was in the immediate proximity, there was a change:

Researcher	Victor
[Showing a picture of a guitar.] What is it?	A guitar *(una guitarra)*.
[indicating text.] What did they put here?	For the guitar *(para la guitarra)*.
What does it say?	Guitar *(guitarra)*.
[Showing a picture of a chair.] What is it?	A chair *(una silla)*.
[Indicating text.] What's this?	For the chair *(para la silla)*.
What does it say?	Chair *(siii-lla)*.

The sequence of events is very important: first, denomination of the picture, then a relation of ownership between text and picture, and finally attribution of meaning. It also is important to observe how the definite article disappears when Victor's reference changes from the picture to the text.

At age 5 years 1 month, Victor was given a picture. He called it a doll. We asked him to find, in a set of cards with different texts, one that would be suitable for the doll. Victor took the first one he found.

Researcher	Victor
What is it? [Pointing to letters in the card.]	Letters for the doll.
Read them!	[He takes a pencil and marks some circles beside the picture.]
What are you doing?	For the doll.
What are you doing for the doll?	Some letters.
What do they have to say?	Doll.

One month later, we presented to Victor a page with some pictures and gave him the general instruction, "Let's put something with letters." We attempted to learn whether Victor was able to anticipate before he began writing. He was going to write *gallina* (hen).

How many [letters] are you going to put there?	Three.
Three what?	Of hen *(de gallina)*.

His anticipation did not yet control the performance, and he ended up making six circles. He then made five circles for the picture of a fish.

What could be read there?	Fish.
Could fish be read here? [Indicating a picture.]	No. There is where the fish is. *(No. Ahí está el pescado*, [with strong emphasis on *está*].)

Victor is not the only child who showed us a progression of this type. At the oral level, the contrast between a name with the definite article to refer to the picture and a name without the article to refer to the text constitutes one of the most reliable cues to detect the beginning of the constitution of letters as substitute objects. Regardless of the length of the text, the letters are conceived as representing the name of the object. However, the transition from the letters that have a name but that do not stand for anything else to the letters as a representation of other names needs careful examination. Let us consider some examples:

Delfino (LC; age 3 years 11 months) looked to a book and said "this is of this one" or "for this one" ("*esto es de esto*" or "*para esto*") while he pointed to one text and one picture at a time. Sometimes, in the same situation, he said, "It is called boy," "It is called house," or "It is called tree." We asked, "But where is it called tree?" and Delfino pointed to the text close to the picture.

Enrique (LC; age 3 years 5 months) told us that the texts of a storybook were "of the bunnies" or "of the puppies" (according to the picture), but he also told us that the text was "his name" or "their name of these children" ("*su nombre*," or "*su nombre de estos niños*"), indicating, in each case, the text and the closer picture. In the same session, a bag of potato chips was called "food," and the texts of the bag was "its name" ("*su nombre*"). Five months later, the same child with another storybook said that the texts were "of the children," ("*de los niños*") "their name of these ones" ("*su nombre de éstos*"); "this is their name of these two" ("*éste es su nombre de estos dos*") (pointing to the picture of a man and a dog).

Thus, before the texts are truly substitute objects, they are the texts *of* someone or something or are *for* that something or someone, or they in some way indicate what the object or person *is called*, because his *name* is there. It would be wrong to think that the expression "his name" may in any way be considered as the representation of the sound pattern belonging to that object or person. We are close to that, but that is not exactly what these children are thinking. The *name* is only the set of letters, the text that is being related to a picture or an object. *Name* is what is written and not the interpretation of what is written. *Name*, at this transitional stage, refers to a category of what is written (which is differentiated from *letters* or its equivalent).

Elami, (MC; age 3 years 6 months) will illustrate how difficult it is to grasp the meaning of this transitional period. We were playing with Elami to look for cards with written texts that "may go all right" with different pictures, Elami put a long text of three segments below the figure of a man.

Researcher	Elami
What did you put?	A name *(un nombre)*.
What name did you put?	One that is here *(uno que aquí está)* [she points to it.] We could put this one to the puppy. [Places another long text.]
What did you put with the puppy?	A number *(un número)*.
Does it say something there?	Oh! This one fell. [She picks up a card that fell.] One arrow here. [She comments on some details of the card.]
Now we are going to play differently. I am going to place some of these [written cards] and you are going to look for a picture that could go all right with it. Let's see. For this card . . .	The lady. We are going to put the name here [matches picture with text.]
What name?	I already put this name *(yo ya le puse este nombre)* [pointing to the card that had just matched with the picture].

These marvelous moments, when the children throw out the interpretative schemes of the researcher are the most exciting in a study conducted with a Piagetian methodology. We enter into a kind of pseudo-dialogue between two systems (the child's and our own) that do not share the same presuppositions. Our question ("which name?") presupposes an interpretative answer. For the child, the same question implies only a pointing answer ("Which name? This one, the one I put. Or didn't you see it?").

The name, then, is the attributed writing, potentially but not necessarily and immediately interpreted. The interpretation will come shortly after. We have devoted much attention to documenting this transition between "letters that say letters" (letters as objects) and "letters that say something different from what they are" (letters as substitute objects) because these transitional periods are essential for the theoretical reconstruction of the psychogenesis of the writing system.

To build up the letters as a system related to but independent from the system of figurative graphemes, it first is necessary to state the conditions for the attribution of meaning. That the letters start to "say something" in the proximity of a picture does not mean that they still "say anything" outside this privileged condition. In addition, this first real interpretation of writing does not imply any conservation of the attributed meaning. If the letters that say *dog* are transferred to another picture (whatever that is), the same letters will say the name of the new object. The same letters, in the same order, could say different names depending of the relation that is established with the objects or pictures. Similarly, different letters could say the same name if they are attributed to the same object or picture. Out of the act of establishing a correspondence, the same letters will not say anything, or they simply will return to the category of "letters that say letters."

That the meaning of the texts is so dependent on the context is understandable: If the letters are substitute objects, they have meaning, and to know what their meaning is, they must be put in relationship with the elements of another system (the system of the objects of the world). Thus, the letters could be used *to represent an essential property of the objects that the drawing as such is not able to represent: the name.* Since the names constitute the prototype of that which can be written, let us proceed with the evolution of the writing itself, focusing on the writing of names. (As 3-year-old Santiago (MC) says philosophically, the letters of an object "say what it is" ["*dicen lo que es*"].)

The Problem of the Amount of Graphemes

Our data clearly indicate that the intepretation of the writings (the children's own writings and those of others) as the representation of names appears only when there is control over the quantity of signs that are written—a sign for each object or picture, or several signs for each object or picture, but with control over both the lower and the upper limit of this quantity.

As we have seen, the period characterized by written productions in which the quantity of elements depends exclusively on the available space is followed by a dramatic reduction in the amount of graphemes, which could lead to the extreme situation of a unique grapheme for each name. Of the fourteen subjects of our sample who passed through this stage, twelve progressed immediately to the requirement of "several signs so it can say." The two other children were close but did not arrive at this point by the end of our study.

We previously established the requirement of a minimum amount of graphemes as a condition for a text to be readable (Ferreiro and Teberosky, 1982). The longitudinal data we are presenting in this chapter confirms the psychogenetic importance of this requirement built up by the children. Below this minimum amount, a piece of writing is not readable—that is, it is not a representation of a name. The minimum amount of graphemes required by children to constitute a piece of writing is notably homogeneous: three, with a tolerance of one more or one less.

Once the lower limit has been defined, it becomes necessary to establish the rank of variations admitted and the reason for these variations. Two alternative solutions arise here: to look for an external criterion that allows changes in the maximum amount of graphemes, or to determine one time for all the minimum and the maximum, fixing the quantity of letters. This second solution is less sophisticated than the first, less stable, and more exposed to contradictions. The first solution does not always precede the second, although it has the tendency to do so. However it reappears many times, after failed attempts to find a general rule that allows control over the variations in the quantity of letters.

When *Fernando* (LC) was 4 years 11 months old, we offered him a poster with pictures glued on it that we chose expressly to stress the contrasts between singular and plural and big and small. For the first time, Fernando put only one letter for each picture, giving each one the interpretation of the corresponding name. With the picture of three cats, he put three letters, expressing the following justification: "Because they are three cats" (Fig. 12-5). He ignored the contrast of big and small between two butterflies but had it in mind when dealing with two corncobs. After having written three signs for three cobs, he put only one for a small cob but two for a big cob (Fig. 12-6A).

When he was 5 years 3 months old, Fernando ignored, in a similar situation, all the contrasts that he had previously considered. He always wrote three letters, regardless of whether there were several objects or only one in the picture and regardless of whether the object was big or small. Thus, for three apples he said he would write "apples with three" and he did so. For one apple, he announced he would write "also with three" (and he read "*man-za-na*"). For a picture of five children, he wrote niños (children) with three letters only, and for one child, he said he would put "also three" so that it would say "*niño*" (child) as well. The picture of two children also received three letters (Fig. 12-6B).

It is very important to note that, even if the quantity of letters remains unchanged, careful attention is paid to vary the composition of letters from one piece of writing to the next—that is, to differentiate one written word from another. Since this differentiation cannot be based on the quantity of letters, and since Fernando did not know many different letters, he could not change the letters to change the writings. The only solution was to make changes in the position of the letters in the lineal order (see Fig. 12-6B). Fernando intended only to differentiate one written word from another; it is clear that he was not using the same letters or the same order of letters for similar referents.

Let us now consider the other alternative of differentiation that children discover: to vary the quantity of letters over an already established minimum. The minimum number is not allowed to change, because it is one of the conditions that

Fig. 12-5. One letter for each object in the figure (Fernando, 4 years 11 months old).

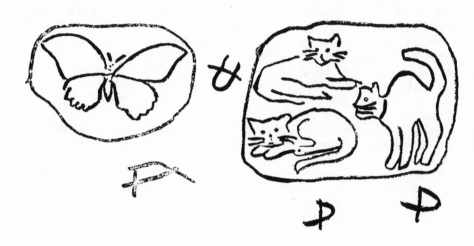

define the legibility of a text.[5] Using that minimum as a starting point, it is possible to look for criteria allowing quantitive variations. Thus, children may use more letters if the object whose name is going to be written is bigger, heavier, or older than other objects. For instance, *Antonio* (LC; age 4 years 11 months) proposed five letters for "elephant" because "he weighs about 1000 kilos!"

In the example of Fernando we saw that, by maintaining the same number of letters (minimum equals maximum), he produced different texts to allow for different attributions of meaning, changing the position of the elements. The opposite case also occurs: The exclusive centration in the variations of the quantity of letters leads the subject to keep the same sequence of letters, as happened with Paola (Fig. 12-7).

Paola (MC; age 4 years 11 months) prepared the cards for the market. For peas, she used three different letters (ϯOE). Then she verified how many peas there were in the set and added more of the same letters. She verified again and crossed out a letter, so that the number of letters and peas was equal (Fig. 12-7A). She put the same three letters for three peppers (Fig. 12-7B). For another set of six peas, she made two rows of three letters that she read as "*chi-charos*" (one part of the name over each row of letters) (Fig. 12-7C). She put exactly the same letters, in the same order, for six tomatoes. For five apples, she anticipated "five numbers so it could be five apples" ("*cinco números para que sean cinco manzanas*") (Fig. 12-7D). She followed the same procedure for four mangos, but when trying to read her writing, a conflict arose. "*Man-gos*" would require only two letters; she succeeded in stretching the word a bit to convert it to "*man-go-os*," but she felt obliged to cross out one of the letters (Fig. 12-7E). This happened also with the text for onions (*cebollas*). She began by making four letters, according to the number of objects; then she applied a syllabic reading ("*ce-bo-llas*") to her writing, and crossed out one letter (Fig. 12-7F).

Fig. 12-6. *(A) Transition between one letter for each object and variations in the quantity of letters according to quantifiable properties of the referred objects (Fernando, 4 years 11 months old). (B) Differentiations between the written names are obtained only by qualitative variations over a minimum amount of letters that is fixed one time for all (*Fernando, 5 years 3 months old).

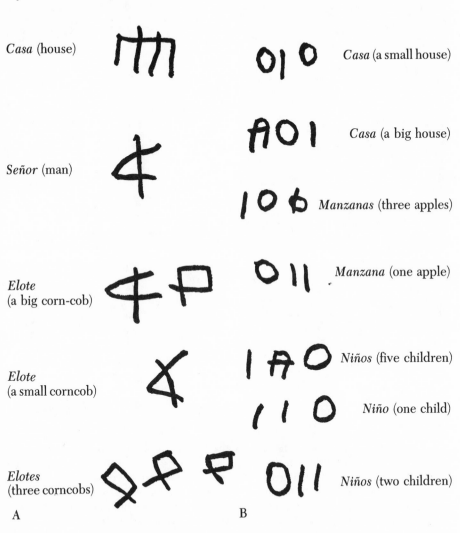

Casa (house)

Señor (man)

Elote (a big corn-cob)

Elote (a small corncob)

Elotes (three corncobs)

A

Casa (a small house)

Casa (a big house)

Manzanas (three apples)

Manzana (one apple)

Niños (five children)

Niño (one child)

Niños (two children)

B

Fig. 12-7. Differentiations between the written names are obtained only by quantitative variations, leaving aside qualitative ones. Quantity of letters depends heavily on the number of objects in each set, but starts to be controlled by a syllabic analysis of the word (Paola, 4 years 11 months old).

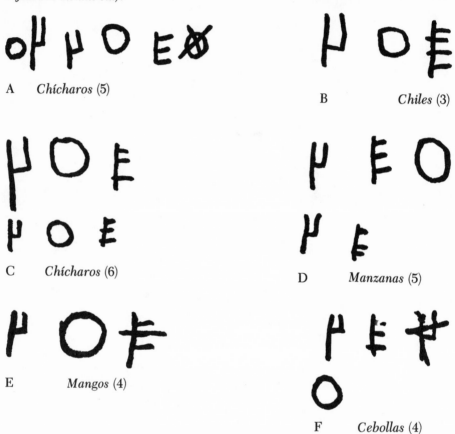

A   *Chícharos (5)*

B   *Chiles (3)*

C   *Chícharos (6)*

D   *Manzanas (5)*

E   *Mangos (4)*

F   *Cebollas (4)*

It is very difficult for the child to vary the quantity of letters, with a search for a criterion of control, while simultaneously taking care of the internal and external variety between the letters to avoid writing the same sequence twice. It is as hard here as in other domains of cognitive development, because to do this implies a great effort of coordination. One wonderful attempt at coordination is shown in the series of writings produced by *Abraham* (MC; age 4 years 7 months). The task was to prepare cards for a toy shop. The texts produced by Abraham (and the names they were intended to represent) are shown in Figure 12-8. With a stock of only five different graphemes, using a minimum of three and a maximum of five for each writing, and trying to maintain the internal variety but to avoid repeating the same letter more than twice, Abraham shows us how far children of this age can go when trying to be coherent with the internal principles they have constructed by themselves.

Fig. 12-8. Both qualitative and quantitative variations are kept under control. The number of letters is justified by a syllabic reading of the intended word (A–E and G) or by the number of objects in the given set (F and I). Only in one case (H) is there no justification of each one of the letters that compose a particular piece of writing (Abraham, 4 years 7 months old).

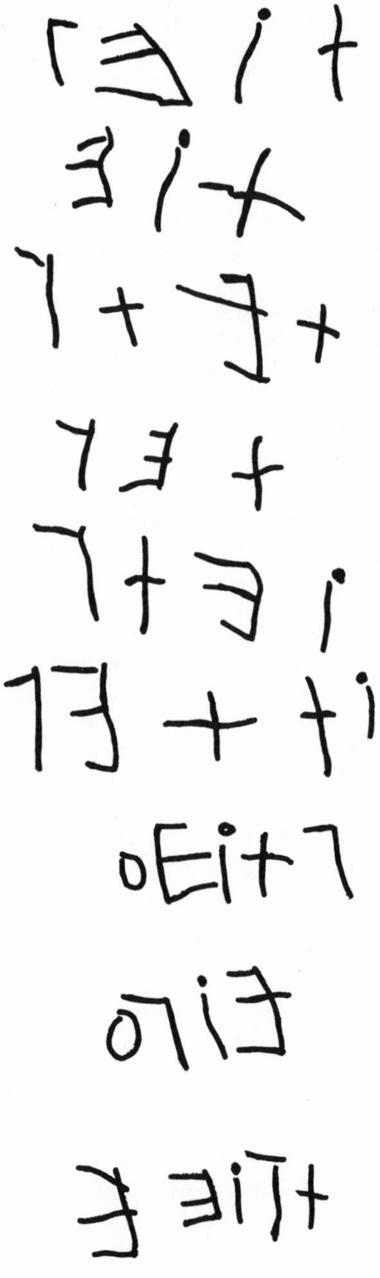

A — *mu-ni-e-ca* (doll)

B — *te-le-visión*

C — *ca-ba-lli-tos* (little horses)

D — *bar-qui-tos* (little boats)

E — *pa-ya-si-to* (little clown)

F — *autos* (cars)

G — pa-li-to-chi-no (chinese stick)

H — "llaves" (keys)

I — "cochinitos" (little pigs)

Although none of the letters receive a stable sound value, one of the main principles of alphabetic writing is applied in Abraham's writings: With a limited number of signs, different totalities are constituted by a combination of the elements. Paola and Abraham's examples also are relevant because they show how children can alternate the criteria they use to regulate the maximum quantity of letters. They may adjust the quantity of letters to the quantity of real or pictured objects, or they may adjust the quantity of letters to the quantity of syllables. This last procedure leads us to the next problem.

Beginning the Syllabic Period

Because a written name is a composition of parts (owing to the requirement of minimum quantity), children necessarily face the problem of the meaning of these parts, once the meaning of the totality has already been established. When children write five letters for a set of five objects, the meaning of each one of the letters is clear (as Paola said, "Five numbers so it could be five apples"). However, what is the meaning of each one of the letters when at least two or three are needed to have something readable and the referred object is a single one? It is at that moment that the parts become observable (in the epistemological sense of the term). The parts start being considered as elements of a totality when children try to understand the precise relationship between the parts and the totality. It is the beginning of the syllabic hypothesis, when children try to make a one-to-one correspondence between the ordered parts of the word (its syllables) and the ordered parts of the written word (its letters). (See Ferreiro [1979–1980] for more details about the syllabic period.)

At the beginning, the syllabic hypothesis serves only to justify a piece of writing already produced, without taking control over the process of construction. As the requirement of minimum quantity remains, the syllabic hypothesis will enter into conflict with words of only one or two syllables. Children try several compromise solutions to solve this problem. In Spanish, one of the most popular solutions is to use the diminutive form of the name to be written (which, in Spanish, makes the name longer). For instance, *Ana Teresa* (MC; age 4 years 8 months) read *bar-qui-tos* (small boats) rather than *bar-cos* (boat) and *pa-li-to* (small stick) rather than *palo* (stick) to obtain the minimum number of syllables required to justify the minimum number of letters required by her (three, in this case). (For more information about the relations between the parts and the totality, see Ferreiro [in press]).

Information and Assimilation

How does the specific information provided by the environment enter into this developmental path? In the preceding sections, we have been dealing with letters that have no consistent sound value. In each case, it is the subject who determines which letters fit in a given piece of writing that is being constructed. Once the piece of writing has been constructed, it is the meaning attributed to the totality that determines the value of each of the elements.[6] The quantity and variety of letters are the chief criteria. The syllabic hypothesis requires one letter—any letter—for each syllable, but it is not necessary to choose the same letter for the same syllable.

In both groups (MC and LC), the phonetic analysis of the word followed the syllabic analysis. In both groups, the vowels were the privileged letters (because they constitute syllables by themselves and because, in Spanish, they have a very consistent sound value). The consonants often acquired a syllabic value related to specific names (for instance, *J* became "ja" for Javier, *M* became "ma" for Mariana, and so on).

Lower-class and middle-class children face the same cognitive problems in attempting to compose their writing productions, but the two groups differ drastically in terms of the information available to them. Nonetheless, whenever information is provided by the environment, it must be assimilated (that is, processed) by the subject in order to be incorporated. It is not the information itself that creates knowledge. Many of the MC children show clear signs of not being able to assimilate the information given to them. The following is one striking example:

Santiago, one of the most precocious of the MC group, had a well-organized alphabet at the age of $2\frac{1}{2}$ years: *R* was *"la de Rubén"* (the [one] of Rubén); *A* was *"la de Ana"; L* was *"la de Luis"; I* was *"la de Irma"*; and so on.[7] At that time, one of the parents said to him that *L* was not only *"la de Luis"* but also *"la de Leonardo."* Santiago rejected this information by which he was bothered. However, at 2 years 8 months, he seemed to accept that a letter may belong to two different people, because he repeated the information that he had previously rejected. Regarding an *L*, he said, *"La de Luis pero también la de Leonardo"* (the one of Luis but also the one of Leonardo).

Then, at the age of 3 years, Santiago and his mother engaged in the following dialogue: Santiago drew a kind of *P*, saying, *"Es la de papá"* (it is the one of daddy). His mother replied that it also was the letter of Paula. Santiago was disturbed and looked for a compromise solution. Pointing to the round part of the letter, he said, *"La de papá,"* and pointing to the straight part of the same letter, he said *"La de Paula."* One month later, the same difficulty in accepting that a given letter may belong to two different names reappeared. He rejected the information that the letter for Ana could be the same as the one for Anne. He also rejected that Z could be *"La de Zorro,"* because he had previously indentified it as *"la de Nelson."* Only when he was 3 years 7 months old did he start to ask (first with resignation and then with genuine interest), *"De quién más es esta letra?"* (to whom else does this letter belong?).

Santiago took an entire year to accept that a given letter could belong to two different names. This exemplifies well how complex the interplay can be between the available information and the assimilation processes. Undoubtedly, the knowledge of letters as Santiago presents it was provided by his family and was assimilated quickly by this child. However, the family also provided him with the information that the letters belonged to more than a single name, and Santiago needed an entire year to accept that. Both facts need to be taken into account in our theoretical construction of literacy development.

Concluding Remarks

The construction of writing is not foreign to the construction of the more general logical schemes built up by the knowing subject. Trying to understand the writing system, children face problems of a logical nature. There are problems of one-to-one correspondence, of the relationship between a totality and its constituent parts, of serial order, of identity and conservation of a meaningful attribution, of classification, and of permutation and commutation. These problems arise in literacy development, just as they arise in many other domains, when children try to understand the world but the world resists the assimilation schemes of the growing subject. In literacy development, cognitive conflicts play a role similar to that played in the domains studied by Piaget (1977). It is important to remember that these conflicts are of two different types: (1) conflicts between the information provided by the environment and the assimilation schemes built up by the subject, and (2) conflicts due to lack of coordination between different assimilation schemes that lead to contradictory results.

When we consider these aspects, we can see that literacy development acquires epistemological relevance. Either we conceive literacy development as the acquisition of a set of marks, the functions of which become clear through social experiences while the structure remains opaque, *or* we admit that the structure of the system (more precisely, the reconstruction of it as a system) is a necessary part of the ownership process. Children pose deep questions to themselves. Their problems are not solved when they succeed in meaningfully identifying a letter or string of letters, because they try to understand not only the elements or the results but also, and above all, the very nature of the system.

Notes

The data reported in this chapter belong to a research project financially supported by a joint grant of the Ford and Spencer Foundations (Ford Foundation Project 78-203).

1. The aspects of literacy development with which this research dealt include: (1) the interpretation of texts (produced by children or by others); (2) the production of texts; (3) the evolution of the denominations (mainly the distinction between *letters* and *numbers* and between *to read* and *to write*); and (4) the evolution of distinctions among the objects that carry written texts (books, newspapers, calendars, and the like).

2. Hereafter we identify the two groups of children already referred to as LC (lower-class) or MC (middle-class). We are delaying with case studies and not with random samplings. We have not adopted any rigorous definition of *social class* in this chapter. Our major interest was the contrast between two opposite literacy environments.

3. To emphasize the similarities between the two study groups, let us point out that the percentage of subjects that at some point of their development pass through a period of one-to-one correspondence is very close in both groups: 42 percent (or 58 percent if we include the doubtful cases) in the MC group, and 48 percent (or 57 percent if we include the doubtful cases) in the LC group. To emphasize the differences, let us point out that the ages at which this procedure appears are drastically different in both groups: In the MC children, this way of organizing the relations between picture and text appears between the age of 3 years 1 month and 4 years 11 months, whereas in the LC children, it appears between the ages of 3 years 10 months and 6 years.

4. It is useful to point out that the interpretation of *reading* as if it were synonymous with *writing* also is typical of the level that we are considering. Children understand easily the action of writing as the production of marks on a surface, but if those marks are not substitute objects—that is, objects to be interpreted— then there is no reason to think that something could be done with them besides producing them. The following are typical answers to questions about reading at this level:

What do you need to read?	A pencil.
Go ahead and read!	[They write.]
Where do you read?	[They show a blank space.]

5. *Gabriel* (MC; age 4 years 7 months) stated it clearly. He wrote three letters, looked at the result, and said, "With all of this it can already say something" ("*con todo esto ya puede decir algo . . .*").

6. This applies particularly to the variety of syllabic writing in which letters with a sound value close to the conventional one are not used.

7. All these names belong to real people with whom Santiago is acquainted.

13. Speech and Writing and Modes of Learning

Margaret Donaldson

How Natural Are Reading and Writing?

A question central to the theme of this book is whether learning written language is the same kind of activity as learning spoken language. Are the two equally natural and able to be achieved in essentially similar ways?

Smith (Chap. 11) and Goodman (Chap. 7) are among those who stress the similarities. Smith (p. 143) says that children in the first 4 years of their lives "know how to learn to read and write because written language presents them with problems similar to those they solve with spoken language." Goodman, taking the view that learning to read and write is natural, gives numerous examples to illustrate the ways in which preschool children may pick up information about the nature and uses of written language in a society such as ours.

However, there is a fact that cannot be denied—namely, that all normal children learn to use and understand speech in the first few years of their lives without specific instruction but that very few learn to read and write with equal success within the same period of time. Bissex (Chap. 6) and Clark (Chap. 9) provide important evidence that some children teach themselves to read early and easily. However, the great majority do not, and even those who do have learned to speak sooner. Thus, there is a difference between the two achievements that we should not ignore.

It is fashionable nowadays to emphasize what children *can* do rather than what they cannot do. This trend has developed as a reaction against the practice of looking always for limitations to children's capacities, and it certainly is healthier than its predecessor. However, the pendulum is in danger of swinging too far. Some things are harder than others for children to learn. Some things take longer than others to learn and are achieved later or with less universal success. We do no good to children, or to science, by trying to deny it.

What, then, can be said about the nature of the differences that exist between learning spoken language and learning written language? Why should one be harder to achieve than the other?

To say that speech is natural but that writing is not is merely a way of dismissing the topic. However, if we reflect on the child's experience of the two linguistic modes, there are more illuminating comparisons to be made.

A notable difference is that speech issues in obvious ways from another person. It is seen to do so. The mouth opens, the lips move, the sounds are heard. And the speech, once heard, is instantly interpreted. Otherwise, it never will be interpreted for it has gone. Thus, the link between spoken language and its source is clear and immediate.

Written language also issues from a person, of course. It is coming, as this is being composed, from my moving hand. However, except in the unusual case in which the reader watches the moving hand and interprets the words as they reach the page, written language is separated from its author in space and time. When it finally reaches the reader for interpretation, it is impersonal. This is true even of *public* or *ambient print* (print that has an extralinguistic context, such as street signs or the writing on a cornflakes package). Indeed, in some ways ambient print is the most impersonal of all. Typically, the author of such print is unknown and of no concern.

When written words are read aloud, as in story-reading, then they once again issue from a human being. In this circumstance, though, what is received by the interpreters is of course the spoken version; and, certainly at first, children are apt not to understand clearly that the speech they are hearing is constrained by the marks on the page. (Soon, when a story is familiar, children may begin to be annoyed by any departures from the words they have come to expect, but what this implies about the extent of their understanding is far from clear.)

Listening and Understanding

Many consequences follow from this basic difference between interpreting speech and reading print. Of these, the most important probably is that the communicative function of speech is easier to apprehend than that of writing. Words spoken to young children commonly accompany actions to which the meaning of the words is likely to be relevant. What we say and what we do often supplement one another. For instance, a mother may hold a jug over the child's cup and ask, "Do you want more milk?" or she may point up into the sky and say, "Oh, look! There's an airplane!" Thus as Macnamara (1972) has argued, the personal context can provide clues to what the words mean, and these clues, which often are highly salient, probably contribute in crucial ways to the breaking of the code.

It is worth noting that if children are able to begin to figure out the meaning of language in this way, then there are at least two implications. First, children must be making the basic assumption that words and actions are in accord - that people do not do one thing and say another. Children must at least expect the two to be in harmony, or they would not be able to use one to make inferences about the meaning of the other. Second, children must have a good understanding of the meaning of the actions before they can use them in such a way.

This last postulate is well supported by recent research. In particular, Bruner (1975) and Trevarthen (in press) have shown that by the end of the first 18 months of life, children have achieved precisely the kinds of understanding that would seem to be needed. These include most importantly the understanding of what it is to be a person with goals to achieve, facing a world that affords opportunities and sets constraints. What 18-month-old children already know well is that some of these opportunities and constraints come from other people. They know that other people can help them to achieve their goals or can frustrate them. They know that other people have goals, too, which may relate in various ways to the children's own. They know that they must negotiate with other people to win them over and invoke their aid.

These kinds of understanding help to make language learning possible, but they do more. They make the usefulness of speech easy to discover. According to Hubley and Trevarthen (1979), a baby of around 10 months of age may already be more responsive, in cooperative play, to an instruction in the form of speech combined with gestures than to the performance of an action offered as a model for imitation. The baby already is eager to be *told* what to do so as to gain this special kind of help in learning to manipulate the inanimate world.

Yet as both Bruner and Trevarthen are well aware, to put this stress on cooperative problem-solving is to tell only half of the story. Children are not interested in other human beings merely as instruments or merely as specially interesting and manipulable objects in the way that John Watson (1972) has suggested. Children want to develop loving relationships. This means that in early exchanges between people, as in later ones, powerful emotions are at play. It is relevant to note that the human voice is expressive of emotion by its very quality, irrespective of the meaning of the words uttered. Marwick (personal communication) has found evidence for close and continuous relationships between changes in a mother's voice quality when speaking to her baby and changes in her mood or in her moment-to-moment intentions. Given that this is so (and Marwick's analyses confirm all our intuitions), we may reasonably expect that from a very early stage the voice will be for the child a focus of quite special attention.

The Role of Production

Thus far, I have concentrated entirely on the receptive process—the hearing and interpreting of speech. It is this that is the counterpart of reading although, curiously often, one finds reading compared with speaking rather than with comprehending. However, I believe it is not possible to make any effective comparison between the learning of spoken language and the learning of written language without recognizing the significance of production and the part that it plays in each of these enterprises. When children learn their mother tongue they do not merely listen; they also utter. In the personal encounters through which the learning proceeds, child and adult genuinely interact. The child is a true contributor even before speech itself appears. This active role becomes established in the course of what have come to be known as prespeech dialogues between mother and child.

The desire to communicate thoughts is strong in young human beings.[1] It can be powerful in ways that we do not yet understand well. Some years ago, I was working with a child, Laura, aged 2 years 9 months. I was interested in her knowledge of number, among other things, and, in the course of several sessions with her, I had searched in vain for any evidence that she could correctly use or comprehend number names other than *one*. Then it happened that she asked me to read her a story and I chose one about Desmond the Dinosaur who went to Loch Ness on a holiday. It comes as no surprise to the adult reader that when Desmond reaches the shore of the loch he meets the monster, but it came as a great surprise to Laura. A double-page illustration in the book shows Desmond on the shore looking at the monster in the water, and there is a marked similarity between the two creatures. When I told Laura that the animal in the water was a monster, her eyes grew wide. She pointed to Desmond, then to the monster, looked at me excitedly, and said, "Two monsters!" She had something to tell me—namely, that she realized that Desmond was also a monster—and her language was marshaled in the service of this communicative aim.

It has come to be recognized, in recent years, that St. Augustine was an astute developmental psychologist, and in the *Confessions* he has something to say about language learning that is relevant here. He is contrasting the learning of Greek, which was for him a second language, with the learning of Latin, his mother tongue:

> Time was also (as an infant) I knew no Latin; but this I knew (i.e., came to know) without fear or suffering . . . for my heart urged me to bring forth its own thoughts, which I could only do by learning words not of those who taught, but of those who talked with me; in whose ears also I gave birth to such thoughts as I conceived.

This passage, with its claim that the child cannot bring forth thoughts alone but that others must be there to talk and to listen makes a very modern emphasis on the social nature of cognitive development. At the same time, it recognizes that children want to learn language because they have things to say. Yet there now is reason to think that even this is not the whole story.

Children spend many years working toward a final state that may be called *knowing the language*. It would be a bold person who claimed to know any language fully and finally, but all normal adults eventually have a substantial shared or common knowledge of the mother tongue. Contrary to what Chomsky and his disciples originally believed, children do not achieve anything like completion of this process by age 3 or 4 years, however. They are still busy at it for long after that, as Karmiloff-Smith (1978) and Bowerman (1982a, 1982b) have recently made clear.

Now the question is: Why do children persevere? Why do they trouble to go on learning the language when they know enough to serve them for all practical communicative purposes? It seems that, to explain this tenacity, we probably have to agree with Karmiloff-Smith (1978) when she suggests that spoken language becomes for children "a problem-space in its own right." They want to understand and to be understood, but there is more to it than that. They want (consciously or otherwise) to discover the correct way to say things. In the process of finding out what is correct, it is a great help to be able to produce words and assess the response to them. To have to rely solely on the evidence of how other people use words would severely limit one's resources for discovery.

If we now take these arguments about the significance of production and look at written rather than spoken language, a sharp contrast appears. Eighteen-month-old children cannot produce writing. They lack the motor skill. Even at age 4 or thereabouts, a child has difficulty in handling a pencil well enough to write. It is, of course, possible by then to have the child say something and to have someone else write it down so that mediated production is achieved. Alternatively, as some reading schemes now do, it is possible to provide on cards a store of written words for the child to put together. The merit of such language experience methods is that they recognize how helpful it is for children to be language producers rather than merely language receivers; but it is difficult to see how such methods could be used in the first 3 or 4 years of life. Furthermore, they depend utterly on prior skill with speech.

Let us review the argument thus far. We have noted that speech is personal, immediate, expressive of human emotion, and obviously useful for purposes that young children can understand and entertain. It affords the opportunity for active participation in dialogue. This is satisfying to children in various ways and helps them to find out about the world and about the language. In short, children have some good reasons to want to learn and some good opportunities for doing so.

Writing, on the other hand, usually presents itself impersonally and is inscrutable as to function. Also, very young children, though they can produce speech, cannot produce writing. This greatly limits the potential value of writing for them, either as a tool that could serve ends beyond itself or as a means for testing hypotheses about the nature of the written language system.

Young Children's Ideas about Reading and Writing

Smith (Chap. 11) deals with these evident differences between spoken and written language by proposing that children can become interested in written language without knowing that it is produced by human beings, so that they initially treat it as a natural phenomenon. He also proposes that children need not directly use or produce writing to learn about it, since they can do this by identifying with the adults who use it, sharing in the adult purposes and becoming apprentices who learn by demonstration.

These are ingenious arguments, but I do not find them convincing. If children were given to thinking of written language as a natural phenomenon, they would be making a gross mistake as to its nature, a mistake that would be unlikely to help them appreciate its possible uses. Considered as a natural phenomenon, written language would be inert and uninteresting.

Moreover, some exploratory studies which I carried out a few years ago with children aged between 2 years 6 months and 3 years (Donaldson, unpublished) suggest that children first conceive of writing as something that people do. This may even lead them to deny the name *writing* to printed matter, and it is understandably apt to cause some confusion about the relationship between writing and reading. Thus, when I asked Laura if there was any writing on a cornflakes package, she answered "No." Then she seized a pencil and made a short vertical mark on the edge of the package. I asked her if her mark was writing and she said, "Yes."

Another child, Juliet, who often would ask me to write something for her (although admittedly it sometimes became evident that she really wanted me to draw) gave the following answers when I asked her about a book from which I had been reading her a story. The pictures were on the lefthand page and the text was on the right.

M. Donaldson: Which bit do you think I'm looking at when I'm reading?
Juliet: That bit [pointing to the picture].
M. Donaldson: Is that the bit you read?
Juliet: Yes.

This last observation is in line with the findings of Reid (1966). The children Reid studied were 5-year-olds who had been at school for 2 months, yet some of them still showed uncertainty about what reading entailed. One child declared that she was "past reading," having "finished it yesterday!" What she had finished was a pre-reading activity book containing no print at all.

Reid's research was replicated and extended by Downing (1970). Taking both of these studies together, we find that five of twenty-five children were not sure whether their own parents could read, and only three made any explicit reference to written symbols when trying to explain what their parents did when they read. These three spoke of looking at "the names," "the writing," and "the numbers," respectively. Another child said his parents read "by looking, " and two said simply "They sit down." When Downing showed his subjects a book and reopened the discussion of what adults do when reading, he obtained slightly better results, but much uncertainty still was evident.

The fact, of course, is that normal adult reading is a wholly covert activity. Thus, children are not typically, and in some unplanned manner, afforded the kind of demonstration that they receive when it comes to turning a key, or using a screwdriver, or even holding a pen and writing. They certainly do not get the kind of demonstration that is provided in spoken language by the sound of the human voice.

However, even if the covert character of most reading makes it difficult for a nonreader to apprehend the nature of the reading process, it still is possible that such an observer could arrive at some sense of the functions that reading serves. A nonreader might know what kind of information a reader gets, even without knowing how it is done. Almost everyone agrees that children are more likely to learn to read successfully if they see that reading can serve some useful purpose. Therefore, questions about the apprehension of function are important ones to ask.[2]

We should begin by noting that there are certain purposes for which writing is uniquely well suited, but which do not have much relevance to the lives of young children. Among such purposes are those for which writing presumably was developed in the first place, such as keeping exact records and obviating disputes over what has been agreed, as well as certain others not likely to have been foreseen by the original inventors, such as composing extended passages of prose and reflecting on their form and precise content. (See Olson [1977] for a valuable historical review.)

This last function of the written word has come to be of great cultural significance but, as Bruner (Chap. 15) observes, it cannot be what initially attracts children into reading. So then, what does? What uses of the written word in our society can preschool children be expected to understand? What uses will be both intelligible to them and intriguing enough to make them want to learn?

The Desire to Become Literate

One of the most easily apprehended uses probably is found in ambient print (street signs, shop names, and so on) where the extralinguistic setting lends to the written symbols something akin to the context that often is available to support speech. Children can fairly readily see the usefulness of distinguishing marks that help one to find things or to identify them quickly and surely. They also can grasp the communicative function of stop signs and the like.

A special instance of the distinguishing mark is the child's own name. This is in a category of its own, since its immediate usefulness may be less than evident, at least until schoolbooks or clothing have to be labeled; but it has a particular emotive power and often serves as a starting point, a way into the world of written language.

Another way in is provided by the sending and receiving of written messages. When someone well known to a child goes away and sends back letters or postcards, the child can readily be helped to understand that information has thus been conveyed, that the marks carry meaning. The urge to reply then can arise, with very good consequences. I have known this to have a powerfully motivating effect on a child who was not 4 years old. Yet another situation that can make sense even to a young child and that commonly arises in families of every social class is the one in which someone consults a written page for information about a television program. This is a prime example of a case in which the nature of the reading process may be totally obscure whereas the usefulness of its outcome may be completely evident.

So, do children learn to read in order to be able to deal with shop signs, postcards, and television programs? Perhaps some do, but Bruner (Chap. 15) suggests another less immediately practical purpose—the reading of stories, the entering into "possible worlds of human experience." I agree that, for some children, this motive becomes extremely powerful.

However, the topic of stories leads me back to my original theme. When they are very young, before they can aspire to read, children love to listen to stories. Yet, many who listen with evident pleasure never acquire a taste for reading fiction even after they have become competent readers. It would take me too far afield to discuss all the reasons for this, but there is a passage by R.L. Stevenson that is highly relevant: "To pass from hearing literature to reading it," Stevenson warns us, "is to take a great and dangerous step." And he goes on to speak of how those who once read aloud to us "sang to their own tune the books of childhood," whereas once we can read for ourselves, we have to "approach the silent, inexpressive type alone, like pioneers" (Stevenson, 1879). The point Stevenson makes is the one I have been making throughout this chapter—namely that our experiences of spoken and of written language are not the same.

Fifty years ago, Vygotsky (tr. 1962) said it also. We are mistaken, he assures us, if we suppose that written language is just speech on paper, able to be learned in the same way and used in the same way. He tells us that ". . . the psychological functions on which written speech is based have not even begun to develop in the proper sense when instruction in writing starts." And again: "Written speech is a separate linguistic function, differing from oral speech in both structure and mode of functioning." The first of these assertions can perhaps be challenged. The second seems to be unquestionably true.

Children might learn to read easily and spontaneously in the first few years of life if human foreheads were equipped with little windows in which visible symbols could be made to appear at will; if parents used these symbols frequently to express thoughts, feelings, and purposes that their children could comprehend; and if children could begin to produce approximations of the adult symbols at an early age. But even if all this were so, important kinds of further learning would still be entailed in the transition from dealing with these symbols in their immediate, transient, personal context to dealing with them when they appeared for scrutiny on the dispassionate page.

What Can Marks on Paper Represent?

The fantasy of windows in the forehead makes the assumption (a reasonable one in view of what we know about the sign languages of the deaf) that, if certain conditions were met, children would master a system based on visible symbols as readily as they master speech. However, if we now return to the realm of how things really are, there remains a further basic question to consider: Do children have difficulty with the very idea of written representation (other than drawing), as distinct from any difficulties they may encounter in learning a specific system? Is there a problem about apprehending the notion of meaningful marks on paper?

Ferreiro, together with colleagues in Geneva and in Mexico, has done important relevant work. She has been interested in the extent to which children in the preschool years construct their own notions on this subject, notions that may be substantially different from those of adults. For instance, using subjects who had not received formal school instruction in reading or writing, she has studied children's ability to relate parts of a written sentence to parts of the same sentence read aloud (Ferreiro, 1978). In this study, the experimenter wrote the sentence and then read it, running his or her finger along the text while reading. The children then were asked questions such as: "Do you think that I wrote ____ somewhere?" or "What do you think is written there?"

The results revealed much diversity in understanding, ranging from the realization that every uttered word, including the articles, is written separately to the notion that only the nouns are written or to a failure to establish any precise correspondence between spoken and written segments. Ferreiro (1978) concluded that at these earlier stages the text probably is not thought of as representing speech. Rather, it is seen as an independent representation of reality to which speech can be related. What is particularly interesting is the finding that, at first, it is only the static aspects of reality that are thought to be represented. There is no equivalent to the verb, no representation of movement or change. Yet, as we all know, certain oral representations of movement and change appear very early ("all gone," "up," and so on). Does this finding constitute evidence of a fundamental difference between the two modes, speaking and writing, in the functioning of the mind?

Recent work by Hughes and Jones (unpublished) complements Ferreiro's work in interesting ways, although it currently is restricted to the representation of number and numerical operations. The special significance of this research in relation to the present topic is that it involves challenging children to devise their own written representations. Thus, it is a study of production, but the child is not called on to grapple with the complexities of a conventional system.

Hughes and Jones conducted two studies with subjects of between 3 and 7 years of age. The first study used three tasks, in each of which the children were given a pen and some paper. In one task, the children were shown various sets of bricks and were asked, for each set, to "show how many bricks are on the table." In a second task, the experimenter either combined two piles of bricks into one or separated one pile into two, asking the children each time to show on paper what had happened. In a third task, the experimenter added or subtracted a small number of bricks to or from a large pile, saying: "Here's a big pile of bricks. I want you to show what I do to the pile. Can you show that I (took one brick away, put three more on, or the like)?" The number of bricks in the static sets ranged from zero to six, as did the number added or subtracted.

In their second study, Hughes and Jones (unpublished) used four identical, closed tins, each of which contained zero, one, two, or three bricks. The tins were shuffled around and the children were asked how many bricks were in each tin, which meant, of course, that they could only guess and often were wrong. They then were given the opportunity to mark each lid in such a way that they would know in the future what the tin contained, and their ability to use their own representations on a later occasion was observed.

From the results obtained, there is one finding that emerges as most relevant to the present argument. Although large numbers of preschool children could readily produce adequate representations of the static sets—even of zero, which was hardest—the representation of addition and subtraction proved to be extremely difficult. Not one child, even among the 7-year-olds, produced an adequate representation when they were asked to show two sets combined or one set divided. Most of them simply represented the state of the set or sets after the operation was complete. Some indicated the initial state or the number of bricks added or subtracted. A few got as far as drawing hands or arrows (Fig. 13-1), but there never was enough information provided about the direction of change to make possible an unambiguous interpretation.

When the request was merely to show how many had been added to or subtracted from a pile of indeterminate magnitude, there still was an almost total lack of success. The most common response was just to depict as a static set the number added or removed, with no indication of the fact that there had been change. Only eleven of ninety-six children made any attempt to distinguish addition from subtraction, and only four did so in a way that was intelligible without explanation, although some of the more obscure efforts proved to be highly ingenious. For example, one child drew the appropriate numbers of British soldiers marching from left to right to represent addition and of Japanese soldiers marching from right to left to represent subtraction! No child used the convention of crossing out to indicate bricks that had been taken away. Strangest of all, no child made use of the plus or minus signs $(+, -)$, although some had been receiving instruction in arithmetic for more than 2 years. This last fact gives rise to some disturbing speculations about how children conceive of the sums they do in school.

Aside from this, however, the most striking feature of these results is the support they lend to the view that there is a substantial difference in difficulty between using marks to represent events and using them to represent objects. Using marks to represent objects seemed to come quite readily, at least in this numerical context, to many 3-year-olds. Hughes and Jones (unpublished) report that 50 percent of the preschool children in their first study were able to produce adequate representations of one, two, or three bricks, and 19 percent could still succeed with set sizes of five and six. Further, it was not the case that the youngest children were the most likely to draw the bricks instead of using more abstract symbolism. In the first study, they made fewer drawings than did the older children and were more likely than older children to use simple tally marks. This may have been because the older children saw their task as one of providing information not just about how many things were on the table but also about what these things were; for, in the second study, in which it may have been clearer that the problem was to distinguish one number from another, the frequency of drawings among the school-aged children dropped to zero. It also fell substantially among the preschoolers.

This suggests that the children had at least a rudimentary sense of the difference between drawing and some other way of representing on paper. Gibson and Levin

Figure 13-1. Some children's attempts to represent addition and subtraction. (A) Leigh (6 years 11 months): Representation of five bricks subtracted from six bricks. (B) Rosanne (6 years 8 months): Representation of two bricks added to two bricks. (C) Denny (5 years 5 months): Representation of two bricks added to two bricks. (D) Niels (6 years 6 months): Representation of three bricks added to one brick.

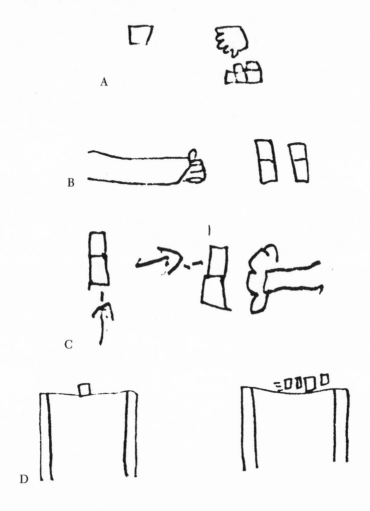

(1975) support this claim, quoting evidence obtained by Lavine (1972) to the effect that children from varied cultural backgrounds, including a remote Mexican village, could distinguish writing from pictures at the age of 3 years. Ferreiro (1978) also found that the distinction between drawing and writing was not absent among her youngest subjects, who were 4 years old, but she thought that the dividing line was apt to be vague. In a more recent report (Chap. 12), Ferreiro gives detailed, valuable evidence about the progression through which children move as they establish more firmly both the distinction between letters and pictures and the relationship that can exist between them when the letters finally become the bearers of meaning.

I believe Ferreiro's results are compatible with the view that, while young children are not limited to drawing as a means of representing reality, they are powerfully influenced by it. In this respect, too, learning written language is markedly different from learning spoken language. Children find it hard to break free from the constraints that drawing imposes and to conceive of wholly different possibilities - new ways of representing the world on paper that can deal with happenings as effectively as they deal with things. Eventually, though, they come to the moment of insight and realize that, instead of making marks to represent reality directly, they can make marks to stand for spoken language, a system capable of representing the dynamic and the static with equal ease.

Notes

1. Smith (Chap. 11) claims that the compulsion to communicate is largely mythical and is not what motivates children to become literate. I agree that it probably does not motivate them to become literate except in the case of wanting to send letters to some beloved person who has gone away; but I see no reason to call it mythical and none to doubt its significance for the process of learning to speak.

2. We should not forget the strength, in human beings, of the desire for sheer cognitive mastery. However, before this is aroused in any given instance, some sense of what it is that has to be mastered may well be necessary.

14. "See! Jumping!" Some Oral Language Antecedents of Literacy

David R. Olson

Literate Society, Literate Mind

It now is generally agreed that literacy is associated with both a distinctive form of social organization, a *literate society*, and with a distinctive form of thought and talk, a *literate mind*, although this view admits of many qualifications. The arguments for it are widely available (McLuhan, 1962; Goody, 1977; Eisenstein, 1979; Havelock, 1976; Olson, 1977), and so I shall not examine them in detail here. Rather, the question of concern is how do we explain the development of children's literate competencies? Do we look into the mental activities of children, an essentially piagetian undertaking, or do we look into the tutorial practices of parents, an essentially durkheimian, vygotskian, or brunerian undertaking? If we are tempted to do both, then precisely how are they threaded together? Psychologists tend to seek an explanation of children's literacy development in the learning activities of children. Thus, they expect changes to occur in the modes of thought and talk of children as they learn to read and write, a process that is not completed until early adulthood. In fact, this was our approach in our own research program at the Ontario Institute for Studies in Education (OISE). Some of the OISE work will be discussed later in this chapter. This approach attempts to account for what an individual child is doing and learning. The focus is on the abilities, knowledge, and intentions of individual children, on what is *learned*.

Sociologists and anthropologists, however, are quick to point out that literacy is not merely an individual achievement but a social one. Literacy is a part of the social order that is passed on from generation to generation through the process of socialization, particularly through literacy activities in the home and in school. Any knowledge or skill attributed to the child does not originate in the child; what the child does is simply a reflection of the transmission of this social order. From this perspective, the focus is on the role of literacy in the society and the ways in which familiarity with literacy is acquired by children—that is, on what the society, specifically parents and teachers, are doing rather than on what the individual learner is doing. In this view, the beginnings of literacy are seen primarily as cultural-historic rather than developmental. Thus, sociologic or anthropologic approach to literacy development emphasizes that which is perpetuated, transmitted, passed on, or *taught*, rather than what is *learned*.

The relation between individual development and social transmission is among the more challenging and pressing issues in psychology, but it takes a particularly interesting form in the discussion of the roots of language and literacy in which the relation between what is taught and what is learned is more conspicuous. Bruner (1982) has expressed the polarity well by describing as complementary the roles of the child's language acquisition device and the parents' language acquisition support system. A full account of language acquisition, he suggests, must include both the child's cognitive system for learning the language and the society's support systems for teaching that language. We may note, however, that these two systems are not fully commensurate: They involve different levels of description—the psychological and the social. One describes what is learned by the child, and the other, what is taught by the parent or teacher. Only if we assume, somewhat naively, an identity between what is learned and what is taught could we use the description of one to explain the other and so to specify the relation between the individual and the social. I suggest that the relation between what is taught and what is learned is very complex.

Nonetheless, there must be some relation between what is taught and what is learned, and it is that relation that I shall explore in regard to the antecedents of literacy. My suggestion is that the social assumptions about literacy influence what the child is taught in the course of learning his or her oral language. What the child learns from being taught these different things shall concern us later. Let us note first what it is that parents teach. Specifically, highly literate parents may teach their children a distinctive orientation to language in the very process of teaching them to talk. I propose that this orientation to language is expressed in part through a metalanguage. It is that metalanguage which differs from one part of the society to the next and which determines, at least in part, what parents teach and what children learn. In this chapter, I make and try to defend two main points. The first is that what varies from one subculture to the next is the knowledge and use of language about language, the *metalanguage*. Second, the locus at which the teaching of the adult and the learning of the child converge is the mastery and use of a common language. Let us examine these two points in regard to children's acquisition of literacy competence.

The Role of Metalanguage

As stated previously, literacy involves a distinctive mode of speech and thought. I must now specify what is distinctive about it. Psychologically, it is not very helpful to define literates as people who can read or sign their names or any of the other simple categorical criteria that are relevant to demographic concerns. Of greater significance is that, to a literate person, language is known as language. Literacy involves the knowledge that language exists as an artifact, has a structure, is composed of grammatical units including words and sentences, has a meaning somewhat independent of the meaning intended by the speaker, and, perhaps most importantly, that its structures may be referred to by means of a metalanguage. In short, it is the belief that language can be treated opaquely, as a structure in its own right. Derrida (1978, 12) puts it this way: "Inscription alone . . . has the power to arouse speech from its slumber as sign. By enregistering speech, inscription has as its essential objective . . . the emancipation of meaning." Elsewhere I have provided extensive if not conclusive arguments as to why that belief is tied to the existence of written artifacts. The central argument is that writing preserves surface structure, the words themselves, which can therefore be subjected to analysis, study, and interpretation, none of which are encouraged by oral language (Olson, 1977).

The literate assumption, then, is that language exists as an artifact independent of the intention it is used to express in any given situation. This assumption, which I have suggested is the key to the effects of literacy, need not be expressed or learned through reading and writing. It is this fact which makes the problem of the antecedents of literacy so puzzling. According to the preceding assumption, becoming literate is only indirectly related to learning to read and write. An awareness of language may be characterized either as a prerequisite—that is, a predisposition—to literacy or as a consequence of learning to read and write. These differing premises have formed the basis of numerous studies on what is referred to somewhat unfelicitously as *metalinguistic awareness*. Whether an awareness of language constitutes a predispositon to literacy or is a consequence of literacy depends, I suggest, upon the social practices and the forms of teaching, among which the child grows up.

What, then, are some of the parental assumptions about language and literacy that may influence a child's acquisition of the belief that language is an artifact, an automomous system. Goody (1982), in his study of the LoDagaa, a traditional African society, found that they do not treat language as a form of traditional knowledge that is taught but rather as a part of humankind's natural makeup. Unlike such activities as farming and cooking, which they believe were first taught to the LoDagaa by the gods and which they must in turn teach or pass on to the young,[1] talking, like motor development, is believed to involve simply an unfolding; therefore, it need not be taught. Conversely, if language is not considered a formal, autonomous structure, there is no need to teach it; indeed, it cannot be taught. Children can learn the language, but they cannot be taught the language as a language.

Among the LoDagaa, as in several other oral societies, there is a restricted metalanguage, which is further evidence that language is not considered an autonomous structure that may be analyzed, interpreted, and taught. Most conspicuously, the metalinguistic term *word* does not exist. There is a word for referring to speech, for what was said, but it can refer to any unit of speech ranging from a single sound to an entire poem and can apply equally to the expression or the intention lying behind it. We shall return to discuss the significance of such metalinguistic terms presently.

It is not only in oral societies that language is treated as transparent to the meanings and intentions that lie behind it. Heath (1982) points out that in a working-class black community in the Carolinas, in which most adults have some degree of literacy, a similar attitude toward the teaching and learning of language exists. Heath describes how children in this community learn to talk: They are not introduced to labels for everyday objects or for pictures or words in books, nor are they given a simplified input by adults. When asked about how she taught her son to talk, one adult said, "No use me telling him. . . . He just gotta learn." Again, the assumption is that language is not a piece of knowledge that must be taught systematically. It must be learned, but it need not be taught. To teach it is to treat language as an artifact, and to so treat it is, I suggest, central to a literate orientation to language.

Literate parents are those who, by my definition, tend to treat language as an object and who, therefore, have and use an elaborate metalanguage for referring to language. They believe that language is an object and that therefore it can be taught, somewhat systematically, to children.[2] Middle-class parents frequently introduce children to books as a means of teaching them to talk. Thus, written language is used as a means of teaching oral language. Bruner (1983) has described interactions between a mother and child around a picture book. The book provides a simple and stable environment suitable for teaching the names of objects. In these interactional formats, the adult points to a pictured object and solicits a name from the child. If the child fails to come up with it, the adult provides it. These naming games are considered paradigmatic of how some parents teach their children the language.

However, Heath's (1982) observations forestall the conclusion that these language teaching practices are universal. As we have seen in some societies and in some subcultures of our own society, the language is not taught at all; the children simply come to know it. The language teaching procedures that make up the naming game may reflect the literate middle-class assumption that language is an autonomous system or structure that must be taught to children if they are to learn to speak. This would explain the previously cited interactional formats and the simplified baby-talk register described by Snow and Ferguson (1977). Nonliterate parents or less literate parents may make no such assumption and, as a consequence, may engage in no such practices.

In an extensive study of the first words uttered by a group of infants of highly educated parents, Galligan (1982) made several observations that highlight these distinctive orientations to teaching infants to talk. Several authors have noted that some parents systematically teach their children the names for objects (nouns). Galligan observed that some parents treat the language learning task even more analytically and teach their children not only nouns but verbs in a somewhat systematic fashion. It is from a transcript of such a parent's lesson that the title of this chapter is taken. While pointing to a frog jumping into a pond, a mother said, "See! Jumping!"

What could motivate this parent to single out and attempt to teach the verb *jumping*? In the naming game, the objects usually are named by nouns; here, the action is lifted from context and explicitly taught. Presumably, it is part of the same explicit teaching program—first nouns, then verbs, then functors, and so on. The agenda is simply more striking when applied to a more abstract structure like a verb than when applied to a noun. A noun in isolation may at least seem like an eliptical demonstrative—"this is a cat," "this is a frog," and the like—and hence have a normal semantic context. To treat a verb in a way analogous to a noun requires a nominalization, a gerund treated like a noun: "This is a jumping." As a communicative sentence, it is decidedly odd. My conjecture is that the parent is not describing an event but rather teaching the verb *jump*. The resulting construction is a bit awkward, but it preserves the format of the teaching procedures that some highly literate parents use to teach nouns.

I suggest that such parents are teaching children to speak in a manner appropriated from the practice of teaching them to read.[3] In learning to read a word-based script, words are singled out into word lists and the like which then are taught to children in the form of a recognition vocabulary. The parent in this case is proceeding on an analogous basis, teaching the child not just how to use words but also the structure of language—language as an object composed of words, nouns, verbs, and so on. Thus, the parent teaches the word *jumping*.

There is other evidence that this technique is effective in acquainting children with language as an object composed of words and meanings. Children of highly literate parents have been noted to ask questions about language. One 3-year-old, for example, asked his mother, "What means 'old-fashioned'?" and later "What means 'by the way'?" Like their literate parents, such children come to recognize (or believe) that language has a structure, that it consists of words, that words have a meaning, and that these structures can be discussed by use of a metalanguage (Robinson et al., 1983; Gopnik, personal communication).

Teaching and Learning

In a sense, parents teach their children some nouns and verbs implicitly by using them in contexts that permit the comprehension of the utterance in which they occur. This is distinct from a parent's explicit teaching of the constituents, primarily single words, of language. Explicit teaching of words is a decontextualized form of tutoring. The parent has assumed that language is an object that has a particular structure, and he or she is systematically teaching the child that structure. The parent teaches the child words because he or she believes that language is made up of words; if the parent did not believe this literacy premise, he or she would be unable to teach the child.

This fundamental point may be seen more clearly by reflecting on the verb *teach* (Scheffler, 1960). Although the verb *teach* is used in a variety of ways, for our purposes we will consider *teach* in its role as an intentional verb. Intentional verbs mark actions done consciously and purposefully. If a child learns something from what a parent does but the parent did not intentionally attempt to influence the child, the parent cannot be said to have taught him or her. Hence, it can be said that a child learned to talk from his or her parents but that the child's parents did not teach him or her to talk.

In the intentional sense of *teach*, only those things that the adult recognizes as existing bodies of knowledge can be taught. One may teach farming, weaving, or cooking because these are believed to exist as specialized bodies of knowledge. However, as Goody (1982) pointed out, language is not considered such a body of knowledge in traditional societies, and so in such societies, language cannot be taught.

As we have seen, some parents attempt to teach their children to talk, and others apparently do not, but all children do learn to talk. The analytic techniques adopted by our highly literate parents seem to be no better than those adopted by less literate parents; both are successful. Therefore, the literate assumption that language is an object, subject to analysis, learning, and teaching, has nothing whatsoever to do with the acquisition of a native language. Why, then, do literate parents attempt to teach language? Although it has nothing to do with oral competence, teaching the language has everything to do with literacy. The literate parent is teaching the child an orientation to language which will not be relevant to learning to speak but which will be relevant to learning to read. The roots of literacy lie in how one learns to talk.

An explicit teaching procedure is not without risks, however. The child, in being exposed to the formal structure of language, may fail to grasp the meanings that language expresses, just as some children apparently fail to learn to read because they become confused about the functions of the visual shapes that they are learning to recognize (Smith, 1971).

Assuming a child succeeds in pairing forms with meanings and does learn to talk, it is important to know what else the child has learned through being taught language as an analyzable system. The literacy premise is a misleading representation of speech but an accurate representation of print. In learning to talk in this way, the child is taking the first step toward becoming literate.

At one level of description, we may say that literate parents transmit a literate orientation in the process of teaching their children to talk. Still, such a notion of transmittal cannot adequately account for what, precisely, the child has learned in learning to talk that explains his or her ease in learning to read and write. Although correct, it is clearly inadequate to say that highly literate parents have highly literate children, a relation that is evidenced by the high correlations between literacy skill and social class (Wells, in press). To explain this relation, we must turn from the social question "what specifically have the parents *taught?*" and turn to the psychological question: "what, specifically, has the child *learned?*" In other words, how is the literate orientation represented in the knowledge, beliefs, and skills of the children of literate parents?

My hypothesis is that the child is learning a set of concepts for referring to language per se, and this set of concepts is expressed largely (if not exclusively) through the terms of the metalanguage. It is in the metalanguage that the concepts critical to literacy are carried. As Reid (1966), Downing and Leong(1982), Wells (in press), Clay (1972b), and others have shown, children's knowledge of such things as words, letters, sounds, their names, and their correspondences correlates highly with their progress in learning to read: That is, children's knowledge of the metalinguistic nouns *sentence, word, letter, sound* is related to children's progress in learning to read and write. More importantly, these critical literacy concepts are part of the oral language competence of the children of more highly literate parents. Children who are taught to talk learn not only the language but also the metalanguage, and the metalanguage is relevant to learning to read a word-based script.

Nonetheless, only part of the metalanguage is represented in these structural nouns. Equally important are the set of metalinguistic verbs that have been discussed by such philosophers of language as Grice (1957), Searle (1979), and Vendler (1970). The central point of their theories is that there is a direct relation between speech acts and mental states and that these relations are made explicit in the set of speech act verbs and mental state verbs, which may be called *metalinguistic verbs* and *metacognitive verbs*, respectively. Specifically, to sincerely *assert* x, one must *believe* x; to sincerely *request* y, one must want or *desire* y; and to sincerely *promise* z, one must *intend* z. Of course, one may carry out these speech acts and entertain the corresponding mental states without knowing the metalinguistic verbs *say, ask, promise* or the metacognitive verbs *believe, desire,* or *intend,* but to carry the speech acts successfully, children would have to grasp the concepts expressed by these terms, and the terms would at least be useful in the clarification of these concepts. The words are important only because they represent concepts, and it is the concepts that are critical to learning the structure of written language.

In defense of this statement, we may note that a child need not know what the word *word* means to know what a word is (this is true for other nouns as well, such as *letter, sound, sentence,* and *language*), but it is the child's knowledge of the metalinguistic terms that correlates with learning to read. Presumably, this is because the words adequately represent the conceptual distinctions the child can make; the distinction is made clear by a linguistic expression.

In addition, we have some evidence from our own laboratory that children's knowledge of metalinguistic and metacognitive verbs is related to their progress in learning to read and write. First, children who become better readers use a greater variety of these terms in their free conversational speech. Examples are "I wonder what" "I think I know what." Second, a test designed to determine children's competence with such verbs as *mean, intend, think, know, pretend, wonder, decide, realize, remember, doubt,* and *deny* showed that knowledge of these verbs was indeed related to the child's acquisition of literacy skills (Torrance and Olson, in press). Third, in a more careful analysis of one particular pair of these metalinguistic and metacognitive verbs, namely *say* and *mean,* we have found that children's competence is closely associated with the acquisition of literacy. For example, preliterate children are unlikely to say, "He said x, but he meant y." Moreover, those children who do make this distinction come from more highly literate homes in which a parent has explicitly marked the distinction with a metalinguistic verb.

Finally, there is a logical reason why knowledge of the metalanguage is related to the development of literacy. As previously stated, in some traditional societies there is no conception of language as an autonomous system or structure of knowledge that can be intentionally taught to children. The metalanguage, including a name for language, permits reference to language, and it creates entities—language, sentence, words, and the like—which, when recognized as such, may be intentionally taught to children.

Thus, to understand talk about language and to think about language or to be taught about language, the child must have access to the concepts represented in the metalanguage. Children from more literate homes learn an explicit set of concepts, represented in the metalanguage, for referring to and thinking about language and its structure, the very structure they will use in learning to read and write. Other children presumably will learn this same set of concepts and the metalanguage for representing them in the course of learning to read.

Frank Smith (personal communication) has argued that it is possible for children to learn to read and write without a metalanguage just as they learn to talk and understand without one. Whereas children can learn without a metalanguage, they cannot be *taught* without one. Teaching, in the intentional sense, requires the metalanguage, and reading and writing, more than talking, seem to depend on explicitly being taught. To this extent, learning to talk and learning to read and write are dissimilar. I do not believe a child could learn to read without knowing he or she knew how to read and still be a fluent reader. Certainly, a child could not do so and still be literate in the sense that this chapter describes.

Fowler (1981) recently has reexamined the famous Terman studies of genius (1918) with a view to determining the role that parents played in such precocity. He found two patterns—parents who explicitly taught their children and acknowledged their roles and parents who disavowed that role but who nonetheless spent "numberless hours weekly over periods of months and years in responsive labelling, question answering, and reading to the child" (Fowler, 1981, 353). Fowler concludes that the patterns were equally effective in developing precocity whether the teaching was direct or indirect. For our purposes, it would be interesting to know if the indirect forms relied as heavily on the metalanguage for coordinating reference as does the explicit, direct form of teaching. My conjecture is that the metalanguage is used and acquired in both cases.

Conclusion

My conclusion about the role of the metalanguage in literacy is not significantly different from the traditional assumption that the antecedents of literacy lie in the knowledge of the language and that children from more literate homes have a larger vocabulary than those from less literate ones, both because their parents have larger vocabularies and because they are exposed to the larger vocabularies of books. It alters that view only in claiming that the important and relevant part of their vocabulary is that pertaining to the structure and meaning of language—that is, to the metalanguage—and to the mental states implicated by the metalanguage. Although the metalanguage is designed to cope with problems of referring in written texts, it is applied to oral language by literate parents and taught to their children as part of ordinary speech.

The link, then, between the structures of society and the structures of the individual are to be found in their sharing of a common language which, in this case, is the metalanguage for referring to language. It is in this common language that we may find an identity between what is taught and what is learned.

Notes

1. Edwina Taborsky (mimeo.) recently has suggested that literacy encourages not only the differentiation of language from speech, but also the differentiation of the knower from the known.
2. This is not to imply that there is only one possible set of assumptions about language and literacy that are accepted by literate parents or that there is one view of reading that these parents accept. Heath's (1982) and Schieffelin's work (Chap. 1) indicate some alternative views.
3. After this chapter was written, I discovered that Ivan Illich had made the same observation:

   I observed that these two people, generous people beyond any question . . . *did not speak to their children.* Rather, at every moment they acted as if *in loco magistri,* not the teacher in place of the parent but the parent deputed by the teacher. They taught their three young children English either by speaking to them as if they were in the classroom, or by saying things to me so simply and so clearly (although it was not at all what we wanted to discuss) that the children also could understand them. There, I understood how commodity intensity, dependence on products, could be rooted right in the family, how vernacular language could be destroyed. (Illich, 1981.)

15. Language, Mind, and Reading

Jerome Bruner

In this chapter, I will consider the nature of the newer forms in which language has manifested itself, the kinds of problems these forms create, and ways in which these problems can be obviated. I mean, of course, written language principally, but I wish to include also all uses of language that occur outside the immediate context of ongoing action. This will necessarily include the use of language whose referent and topic is language itself, because I believe this use is an intermediate form between spoken language and written language.

I want to begin with a commonplace, one raised by several other authors in this book. Although written language has many special and unique features of its own, it is still only *one* of the uses of the language. It cannot be understood independently of the other uses to which language is put. Written language is not merely a page-put version of spoken language. The same can be said of virtually any register in which one creates a set of conventions—lover talk, therapy talk, pedagogic talk, or whatever. To be understood, reading and writing, like all these forms of spoken language, have to be placed in the context in which people use them.

To begin with, language in any form represents an external, conventionalized system of communication that exists prior to the individual's entry into the society. As such, it contains a great many devices, forms, and presuppositions that characterize it as a *tool* of communication. Tools inevitably shape and bias the acts of those who use them. One of the ways in which a culture "forms" its members is by giving them a set of tools or prosthetic devices by which they enter into interaction with the natural and the social world. The tool system of language is, however, strikingly different from other tool systems. Such systems reflect sociotechnological requirements to which the individual must conform in order to enter the cultural system for exchanging goods and services.

But with language, there is something else that enters. Language as a tool creates realities; it is constitutive. It has an illocutionary or performative function that brings social realities into being. A promise, a threat, or a supportive utterance creates events that are sufficiently real to have even physical consequences, like jails for those who promise and do not fulfill. We do not acquire language for its own sake but for the sake of doing something with and to somebody else. How you acquire a language is affected by the uses to which you put it in the process. As speech-act theorists have insisted, acquiring a language also gives form to the intentions to which communication is put. When you ask somebody why she said that, she will answer you in terms of what she said it *for*, her "speaker's meaning" rather than the "timeless meaning" of her utterance.

What I have said thus far rests on the capacity of language to be intercalated with life as it is lived, with actions, intentions, and events that are ongoing. This, of course, is the well-proclaimed context sensitivity of language. But there is no *natural* way in which the context sensitivity of language can be understood. The context dependence of any utterance is governed by conventions: syntactic, semantic, lexical, prosodic, and even cultural. (Cultural conventions include many so-called pragmatic conventions, as in speech acts in which declarative utterances may be correctly interpreted as requests by virtue of seemingly extralinguistic conventions.) In fact, such conventions are *not* extralinguistic: They relate to the conduct of discourse and are supersentential. This is not to say that you do not use syntax, semantics, or lexis (as these are commonly understood) to achieve your supersentential intentions. Rather, you use them in ways not wholly related to the well-formedness of a sentence or the semantic restrictions on words and phrases within a sentence. I agree with Olson (Chap. 14) that the use of a written language rests on its *contextualization* and on its *conventionalization*. "What constitutes the context?" and "What are the conventions?" are critical questions governing the use of any language, but context and convention are somewhat different in written language and in spoken language.

Let me go back to a distinction that C.S. Peirce (1932) made between three levels of language functioning: indexical, intralinguistic, and metapragmatic. The *indexical* level involves a use of language that depends entirely on deixis. It is virtually a pointing or ostensive use of words, as in a label for an object. The indexical symbol points directly at the extralinguistic world. The *intralinguistic* level entails the beginning of the translation of symbols into other sets of symbols, as in the well-known description of the relation between proper names and descriptors—for example, *Saul Kripke is the Princeton philosopher who writes about proper names and descriptors*. The *metapragmatic* level involves talk about text: It is, in effect, *explication du texte*. At its simplest level, it is talk no more complicated than quoting, citing, or paraphrasing what another person has said. At a higher level, it is more like the kind of activity that goes on in analytic philosophy—delving into an utterance to extract its underlying proposition. The development of metapragmatic competence has not been studied much though there are interesting beginnings in the work of Silverstein (1983) and Hickmann (1983).

I think it will be obvious that the dividing line between intralinguistic and metapragmatic functioning is necessarily fuzzy, principally owing to the existence of the device of topicalization. There is virtually no limit linguistically on what can be topicalized, up to and including John Stuart Mill's topicalization of the "idea of everything." Insofar as one creates overarching topics about which comments can then be constructed, one slips gradually into metapragmatic functioning. I do not mean to make anything special of this technical point, any more than I want to make something of the subtleties of anaphora whereby one operates intralinguistically to relate a topic (text) to its antecedents (context). I mention it only to store up a point about problems in reading and writing—problems having to do with text coherence—to which I want presently to return.

Very few human beings have trouble learning spoken language. But the work of Basil Bernstein (1970) and others on restricted and expanded codes certainly suggests that there may be large differences in the extent to which people can achieve freedom from the here and now in their spoken language. Indeed, Joan Tough (1970) has reported that children from economically poor backgrounds are delayed and even disoriented in mastering pronominal anaphora. It seems that nobody has any difficulty achieving indexical competence or, indeed, advancing far into intralinguistic usage (for which there is enormous support in infant-mother interaction, as illustrated by Bruner [1983]). All of this would certainly suggest that children at the time they are required to learn to read are unequal in their habitual competence with the spoken language, at least in respect to their ability to operate at the textual level of metapragmatics. Later in this chapter, we will explore whether this inequality may have something to do with their approach to the task of reading. But there are some other matters that need discussion first.

Let us begin by getting rid of some old wives' tales. The prime myth is that reading instruction should consist exclusively of teaching phonics, vocabulary, and grammar. I have no doubt that intending readers must master some elements of grapheme-phoneme or even grapheme-morpheme correspondence. But the claim that there is something very special and difficult about learning such correspondences seems, on the basis of the testimony of nobody less than Frank Smith, to be grossly exaggerated. There is little evidence that children learn their working vocabularies from reading exercises. As for grammar, there seems to be widespread agreement that instruction in formal grammar in the context of written language is of little help in mastering reading. On the basis of the evidence offered by other contributors to the University of Victoria Symposium the hoary triad of phonics, lexis, and syntax cannot be at the heart of the problem of reading (or writing, for that matter).

A more interesting hypothesis is that reading requires that language be under-stood outside of its immediate context. It is not clear in written text what the context is in which language is being used; it is not clear what is the .riter's intent; it is not clear what "belief system knowledge" one is supposed to operate on (that is, what the "microcosm" of the writer is). To dig these matters out of the text requires a metapragmatic approach to language or, in Jakobson's (1965) terms, a metalinguistic approach whose objective is to relate what is said to some sort of code. And given the nature of text, there is no support from the here and now of action and intent to guide the reader extralinguistically.

As Bissex (Chap. 6) points out, written language is *taught*. The teaching, she rightly points out, is based on the pedagogic conception that children know nothing and that anything they learn must get there through feedback from outside. We teach letters, words, and grammar all as if they were something new. In fact, there is very little feedback from outside. The way in which reading is taught, however, prevents our equipping the children to be their *own* teachers to the degree we know them to be able to. In certain crucial respects, we even discourage them from testing their own hypotheses about text as a guide to learning. Bissex deftly demonstrates that children generate hypotheses about written language just as they do about spoken language. Ought we not be discussing these hypotheses with the children to help them better use or repair their guesses, guesses not only about phonics, lexis, and grammar, but also about text and its alternative meanings? I agree with Bissex that we prevent children from using their natural astuteness as problem-solvers through the very way we teach them.

Return for a moment to the different uses to which language is put and consider the written language. In Chapter 13, Margaret Donaldson comments: ". . . Speech is personal, immediate, expressive of human emotion, and obviously useful for purposes that young children can understand and entertain. It affords the opportunity for active participation in dialogue. This is satisfying to children in various ways and helps them to find out about the world and about the language." In contrast, "writing . . . usually presents itself impersonally and is inscrutable as to function." The "purposes [that language originally served] do not have much relevance to the lives of young children." These purposes are, she states, for "keeping exact records and obviating disputes about what has been agreed" and "for communicating over distances in time and also in space."

I agree with everything that Margaret Donaldson says. What puzzles me is why *anybody* (save cranky lawyers and argumentative intellectuals) would be motivated to learn to read or to write—save by sheer compulsion—if that is all that there is to the story. But Donaldson adds another point. The written word allows the composing of text that permits us to reflect on form and content in a way that more transitory spoken language cannot do. Is that enough to lure children?

I think there may be more here than meets the eye. "Reflecting on the form and precise content" is a rather highbrow idea of what children do with "extended passages of prose." I have no doubt whatsoever that it is what intelligent readers are enabled to do eventually and that this is why reading is such a boon to metapragmatic functioning and reflection in general. But there is something that precedes it. I want to make the claim that what initially attracts children to reading and into mastering all the mechanics of it is the opportunity that text provides for penetrating possible worlds, worlds beyond the mundanities of here and now.

I want to argue this point from the background of research on children's play and the auxiliary knowledge that children's language use (during acquisition) is most daring and most advanced when it is used in a playful setting. If Vygotsky (1978) is right about the props or toys with which children conduct their early play—the stick between the legs serving as a horse and such—then consider for a moment the kind of prop that written text provides. It is a way into worlds unheard of and undreamed, the worlds of Maurice Sendak and Dr. Seuss, of Snow White and E. B. White, even of the comics and the television advertisements. It may be banal to say that children love stories, fantasies, and secret worlds: It is nonetheless true. It may also be banal to say that there is a very severe limit on the number of occasions on which adults will serve as oral storytellers to children, either singly or in groups. Children can and do make up and act out their own stories or dramas, but there seems to be a considerable shortfall between what they can do for themselves and what others will do for them. And so enter the book, the comics, and, of course, television.

Writing down stories was not among the very earliest uses of writing, but the record, such as it is, suggests that it was not long in appearing in an indirect form—most usually in mystical, religious scripts rather than stories for their own sake. If we may make a wild guess from recorded history (and that is all we have to go on), the first written stories were sacred-in-the-saying, ritual accounts of creation and struggle such as the Koran or the Upanishads, inscribed to protect the sacred word from degradation. Probably, the first form of literary or textual analysis was the comparison of variorum texts. As long as the society interacted primarily face to face and as long as there were tellers of tales in the sense that Lord (1960) has described them, there was no need for writing down story and drama. Besides, there was no audience to read them. Literature for its own sake does not become a genre until relatively late in human history. The novel in its recognizably modern form (concerned with reconstrual of the ordinary in dramatized form) has yet to celebrate its second centennial. It comes into being only as the "mythologically instructed community" (Campbell, 1956) begins to fall apart. Indeed, the genres of "creative" literature are probably responses to increased social complexity and differentiation within society. In any case, what brings them into being is not nearly as important for our purposes as the impact that they have on reading. Let me turn to that in connection with learning how to read.

I want to consider stories, or accounts of adventure, fantasy, mystery—what Borges (1982) refers to as "guided dreaming." When comprehended, stories have personalness, emotion, and nearly all of the rich things that Margaret Donaldson properly ascribes to spoken language. What they lack, and must necessarily lack, is embedding in dialogue, which is one of the most critical vehicles in the pedagogy of spoken language. But what must not be overlooked is that children already know enough about stories as texts or scenarios to treat them as subject to interpretation, and the interpretations that children bring to what I am calling stories can easily be made to have some of the properties of dialogue—dialogue once removed. That is, the structure of story text or scenario easily conforms to the speech acts, the stances (a term I shall return to in a moment), and the discourse structures of dialogic exchanges. Even more striking, perhaps, is the fact that dramatic scenario is of a form that lends itself to an appreciation of alternative texts. Stories can come out in surprising ways that violate expectancy or, indeed, that conform to expectancy with a funny twist or variorum reading. I recall the account of a Head Start class whose teacher read them *Little Red Riding Hood*. When the story reached the climax at which the wolf, disguised as Grandmother, responds to Red Riding Hood's remark about her big teeth by proclaiming, "All the better to eat you, ho ho!" one of the children snarled, "That mother-fucking son-of-a-bitch." This is not very highbrow metapragmatics, but the teacher was clever enough to ask the children how the story *should* have gone at that point. "She shoulda killed the wolf!" was the response. The teacher asked, "And then what?" And then there *was* a good discussion—not great, but good for 4-year-olds. It was not quite about text, but at least it was about different ways in which a scenario (or was it life?) should have turned out. The children, arguably, were enroute from being intralinguistic to being metapragmatic; once they became involved in making up stories on their own and agreeing on what their teacher should write down as a record of the story, they were much closer.

Stories and the dramatic form have the capacity to recapture intention in the voice of the text, particularly by the use of *stance markers*. Stance markers (Feldman, 1974) are pragmatic devices by which the attitude of the speaker-writer toward the topic or referent are expressed, and they are carried by such simple lexical markers as *even* and *only*, as in the following sentences:

Jack loved Jill.
Even Jack loved Jill.
Jack loved even Jill.
Jack loved only Jill.
Only Jack loved Jill.

They are terms of great simplicity that carry great pragmatic weight, are freighted with easily understood presuppositions, and are the stuff of dramatic discourse. They are, moreover, excellent targets for discussion. I do not mean to make a big and exclusive case for their use but mention them only in reference to the form of text that might be most easily penetrable by children by virtue of their already established knowledge of the nature of dramatic scenario.

I have two further points to make about this established knowledge of scenarios, one theoretical and one practical. The theoretical point has to do with the nature of dramatic action as a *natural kind*. I take the view that the simplest form of representation (though some may not wish to use that word for it) is representation by procedure—knowing *how* rather than knowing *that*. Knowing how is constituted in skills, in generative habits, and in procedures. I have always found myself in sympathy with theories of mind and of language that argue for the primacy of action and the schemata that constrain and guide action. Tolman's (1932) theory of learning was based on one such premise: the concept of means-ends readiness and the substitutability of means for the achievement of invariant ends. Fillmore's (1968) conception of case grammar is another example: Grammatical cases, in his terms, originate as arguments of action that place the verb in a determinative position, with cases comprising an *agent* of action, a *recipient*, an *object, instrument, direction, locus*, and so forth. And, of course, it is Piaget (1937) particularly who has argued that operatory schemas develop from the internalization of actions that have been rendered reversible.

There are probably two epistemically primitive action patterns: *cause-effect* and *intention-outcome*. We developmental psychologists have, in the main, concentrated on the first of these and neglected the second, though the latter is probably earlier and more pervasive, as indicated by the primacy of animistic interpretations over causal ones in the young child. There are other ways of referring to these two natural kinds of action attribution: interpersonal versus physical, narration versus explanation, or even deontic versus epistemic. By whatever name and through whatever conceptual cut, the two represent complementary modes of knowing the world. Each mode, fully developed, achieves an elaborated form in adult thought: cause and effect in science and mathematics, and intention and outcome in drama and poetry. Each uses language in a unique way to create possible worlds, and each is subject to different forms of representation. There is enough evidence now available on cognitive development to indicate that the two start early in life (See Leslie [1979] on the early appearance of Michotte-like causal perceptions in the infant, and Stern [1982] on the "first relationship"), although, as already mentioned, the primacy of animistic thinking suggests that the appreciation of intention-outcome precedes and remains always more accessible than the comprehension of cause-effect.

Having said that much, let me only comment on the bearing this has on reading and writing. If we wish to be assured that the child is able, in approaching reading, to deal with context and stance in what he is attempting to read, then we would be well advised to use the story medium in as personalized and as "possible-word" a dramatic sense as we can without terrifying the child or pandering to his daydreams. And if we err in the texts we provide, let it be in the direction of melodrama or the horror flicks. Let this first approach to text be accompanied by the full exercise of reflection on whether the form in which the text was encountered is the best or the most exciting or even the most lifelike. I would even be tempted to introduce children to writing (at least in part) by having them rewrite what they have read to make it better conform to the standards they wish to apply to it. Let them kill the Big Bad Wolf in act 1 and see where they can take it from there. (In case any of this should seem pedagogically unreal to any of you, I would suggest you look at Vivien Paley's remarkable volume, *Wally's Stories* [1981].)

This brings me to the practical issue—the materials used in introducing children to reading (and writing). After the First World War (egged on, I fear, by "reading experts" enamored of the mechanics of reading), it was thought that readability of text was best assured by simplification. This is not a bad idea, provided one has the proper simplicity metric. Unfortunately, the metric was based on the three ancient maxims of phonics, lexis, and grammar. Somehow text and context got lost in the details. For example, in the early 1920s, first readers contained, on the average, 645 different words, while those published in the early 1960s were reduced to fewer than 100 words. And what words! They were the ones that had the highest frequencies in *The Teacher's Word Book* and they are implacably banal. By the time you have thrown in such nouns as *boy, girl, dog, cat, house* and *shoe* and such verbs as *run, walk, come, take, call,* and *give,* you have used up 10 percent of the quota, without even getting to the tacks and twine of articles, demonstratives, copulas, and quantifiers. It is conceivable that you can write a fable, a folktale, or drama on such rations, but it is not easy. Anyway, few tried. What they *did* write was not only not dramatic (it was supposed to depict the familiar, although it is difficult to imagine why a child would prefer a recital of the familiar in a vocabulary of 100 words rather than one that tempted him beyond the familiar couched in fancier verbal dress); it was also too impoverished in content to provide a context in terms of which the child could understand what was put before him. It was far from dialogue, without stance markers, and altogether inconceivable as a domain of knowledge. What, indeed, is "Run Jane run. Catch the ball." about?

Finally, the enormous virtue of the dramatic form is that it keeps firm hold on the constitutive function of language—the warnings, threats, promises, and spells that create social and personal reality. Everything we know about early language points to the early development and elaboration of performatives, the instruments of constitutiveness. Their inclusion in written text is crucial.

My own conclusions are best expressed in some lines borrowed from a recent annual report of the Center for the Study of Reading at Bolt, Baranek, and Newman, Inc. (1980), in Cambridge.

> Our position is that language is always *situated*. It is produced by an author or speaker with various communicative, educational, or entertainment purposes, with the expectation that it will be interpreted by a listener or reader who tries to understand that set of purposes. In short, authentic text is as much an instance of the social action of communicating as is face-to-face conversation. . . . Children approach the task of learning to read with varying degress of knowledge about the pragmatics and functions of text. Children who have been exposed to different types and uses of text at home may come with a fair appreciation of what reading is all about. Others may find text, and especially basal readers, to be alien territory. We suspect that, for many young readers, the communicative functions of text are not perceived. Rather, for them the reading of text amounts to a

decoding game. This should not be surprising inasmuch as a major goal for the author of a basal reader is precisely that of developing students' decoding skills. On the other hand, language-as-a-decoding-exercise will not only be foreign with respect to many children's communication experiences but, further, is orthogonal to the communication experience for which it is meant to prepare them.

The Bolt, Baranek, and Newman group is trying to find ways of importing into text a workable and recognizable transformation of skills established in the spoken language. I, too, believe that this is the direction in which we must go, whether by interactive computer procedures or any other invention.

The brunt of my proposal is that we already have an invention that we are not using to its fullest extent. It is the dramatic story, the personal narrative full of stance and scenario. It is only one of the ways to proceed, but I favor it not only because the evidence indicates that it works, but also because it prepares readers to enter the world of possibility in a fashion that is not open to them in more impersonal domains. It makes reading an adjunct to and a tool for a form of understanding that human beings never fail to find compelling. Indeed, it is a world of possibility that can be entered through literature not only as a written medium but as an enacted one through television, which could, in fact, be used as an ancillary to the teaching of reading. When the curtain goes down, there is the text to brood over.

I have not attempted to give an overview of the whole field. If I had attempted to, it would include some conclusions such a these:

1. Written language is a problem space in which hypotheses and the capacity for self-correction are present in abundance. It should be treated as such rather than as some sort of mysterious assembly line of bits and pieces to be put together. The problem of reading seems more and more to be a function not of the difficulty of reading per se but of the difficulties created by the way in which we *teach* reading. Education is the problem, not the solution.

2. Misstatement of the problem has magnified the difficulty of reading by suggesting that you need to oversimplify what you are about to teach to make it teachable by the foolish method you have used. Consequently, we use readability scores and simplify text so that it cannot possibly have a context. Stance markers and affect are taken out, information is leached out, and component skills are emphasized without there being any emphasis whatsoever on use.

3. The constitutive function of the language used is destroyed. Plays keep it. Games in which language must be used as part of the ritual reality are rarely, if ever, used.

At the end of this long and dreary process, we produce children with so-called reading difficulties. No wonder many children then regard the process of reading not as a collaborative effort but as an adversary process, with their teachers opposing them by asking impossible questions. The "errors" of reading are treated as stupidities rather than as interesting hypotheses. The activity of reading is trivialized.

My suggestion is that we begin by making reading an instrument for entering possible worlds of human experience—as drama, story, or tale—in order to bring it as close as possible to the forms in which children already know spoken language best. And just as the human condition is the favorite topic of human reflection, so the text depicting that condition can become the basis of that reflection.

Commentaries

i. The Discussion: What Was Said

Hillel Goelman

Fourteen independent virtuosos with no common score, no prior rehearsal, and a strong sense of their own perfect pitch are unlikely to produce anything but improvisational music. It should not be surprising then, that many themes and ideas arose at the University of Victoria Symposium that remained divergent and incomplete, at some times dominant and other times muted, occasionally concordant but more often counterpointed, as individual participants responded more to the prevailing mood and rhythms than to the actual notes that others were playing. It is impossible to capture in writing the true richness and quality of improvisational music or lively verbal discourse (a weakness of literacy?), and certainly not the excitement that it can engender in performers and audience alike. What follows is one observer's attempt to present the harmonious along with the discordant and to trace some of the nuances that 4 days of intense interaction generated.

This discussion respects the order in which the papers were presented at the symposium, which does not mirror the order of chapters as they appear in this book. Each session was chaired—conducted would certainly not be an appropriate extension of my metaphor—by a different participant, and presenters were allowed approximately 15 minutes to talk about their respective papers. The discussion usually veered off quickly in directions beyond the control of the presenting participant or chairperson. Therefore, this chapter does not summarize the content of the papers or even the discussion directed to that content; rather, it describes the ways in which symposium participants responded to one another and to the issues that most involved them.

First Day (Anderson, Jacob, Scollon)

Two major themes were sounded in the opening sessions which remained unresolved throughout the 4 days of the symposium. Both concerned fundamental definitions, the first of literacy and the other of culture. The question of exactly what constitutes literacy arose in the reactions to all three of the papers presented on this first day. Many of the participants supported the notion that literacy involved more than the ability to read books. Anderson's research showed children involved with written language in a variety of ways, from consulting television guides to observing adults compose shopping lists. Ron Scollon wanted to broaden literacy beyond what he termed 'Western essayist traditions,' arguing that a broader definition would allow for musical notation, computer literacy, and non-Western literacies as well. The narrow definition of literacy as the ability to read books seemed to be rejected in favor of a broader reference to literacy as a "pattern of discourse."

Much discussion was provoked by Jacob's observations of "pretend literacy" and "preliteracy" activities among preschool children in Puerto Rico. Her use of these terms raised questions regarding the difference between such activities and "true" literacy activities, as well as the question of necessary and sufficient precursors to literacy. Her attention to nonlinguistic abilities including shape discrimination and number awareness in relation to literacy prompted some comparisons with traditional reading readiness activities and initiated debate concerning whether training in such perceptual and nonreading tasks is related to, facilitates, or influences children's acquisition of literacy.

Many of the speakers agreed that play, children's creative and imitative involvement with literacy activities, is an important developmental stage in becoming literate. Schieffelin reported data that supported Jacob's finding of sex differences in the types of play literacy activities in which the children were involved. Schieffelin cited the example of boys who were observed to be more involved in public aspects of literacy, such as score-keeping, whereas girls tended more to private aspects such as keeping diaries. Jacob acknowledged some drawbacks to the method of observation she used and said that in follow-up studies the play would be observed for longer periods of time to capture the contextual aspects of the play.

The debate about culture followed a pattern similar to the debate on definitions of literacy in that it was far easier to reach agreement on what culture probably was not rather than on what is was, especially as it might relate to literacy. There was agreement that culture was neither a neat categorization of people nor a meaningful description or explanation of behaviors. Anderson made the point that culture has been used as a shorthand explanation, usually pejorative, for people who are illiterate or not able to become literate. Anderson's failure to detect differences between Black Americans, Mexican-Americans, and white Americans, Jacob's findings of literacy activities in rural Puerto Rico, and Scollon's cross-cultural observations of white North American and Alaskan Athabaskan natives were all accepted as evidence of the lack of descriptive or explanatory power for the term *culture* as it is used in relation to literacy. One working definition that was not opposed and that bore similarity to the working definition of literacy as a "pattern of discourse" saw culture as "an organized pattern of behavior shared by a group of people." Anderson said he hoped for a moratorium on the use of the term 'culture' but that he could live with this operational definition.

Both Anderson and Jacob argued strongly that the literacy events they observed in families and in play were embedded within the child's environment. Both of these participants reported that the children themselves initiated many of the literacy activities. This claim was considered problematic by a number of the other participants. The question arose as to what constitutes the initiation of such an activity. Could a perceived initiation be a response to or a continuation of an earlier activity? Anderson suggested that since all these activities are so firmly embedded in social contexts, the precise initiation and termination of activities may not be accurately observable or useful.

The discussion on this first day focused largely on issues of culture vis-à-vis literacy and literacy vis-à-vis culture. Some comments by Bruner toward the end of the session put the day's deliberations in perspective and set the scene for the discussions of the coming day. Bruner noted that Anderson's paper showed how children's contacts with literacy, literate adults, and literacy activities occur within a wide range of social domains within the family, serving to connect the family with institutions and the outside world. Something was being transmitted to those children as they were cognizing their world within a social environment. What was it specifically, Bruner wondered, that was being transmitted? Although Jacob's paper discussed the importance of play and raised the question of precursors to literacy, we still do not know enough about possible necessary and sufficient conditions, activities, or other components that make literacy possible. Bruner observed that both Anderson and Jacob demonstrated how young children engaged in what he termed *run-ups* to literacy, in their interaction with their environment and through their early attempts to understand and gain power over the rules of discourse.

In pointing out the evidence on the importance of the social environment and the individual's interaction with that environment, Bruner posed what he called a number of puzzles. First, could those social activities that would relate to specific skills or uses of skills by individuals be identified? If literacy is a tool, an instrument of technology (a point which would surface and be debated many times) that an individual learns to master, how does that mastery interact with the social uses to which the tool is put? In gaining mastery and power over the tool, how do children gain entrance to the domain and participate in the rule-making of that domain?

These questions regarding the interface between the social conditions that facilitate literacy and the individual skills, abilities, or needs that allow individuals to master literacy remained major issues throughout the entire symposium.

Second Morning (Heath, Bissex, Bruner, Schieffelin)

The second day of discussions continued to focus on the social-personal interface puzzle that Bruner proposed at the end of the previous day. Questions raised in the presentations and discussion of the papers dealt with literate and nonliterate people's encounters with literacy from the perspectives of individual mastery and competence and the social contexts of the interactions. Shirley Brice Heath's paper, presented by Suzanne Scollon, attempted to document the way one young woman and her children in a particular sociocultural environment encountered literacy within their family. The research is part of a continuing inquiry into differences in literacy encounters among middle-class and Black lower-class families. The family in this study belonged to the latter group. The evidence seemed to suggest that adult-child language interactions were different in the two settings and that patterns used in Black lower-class families might be more creative and poetic but do not facilitate learning to become literate in a "schooled" sense.

Many participants again had reservations about the use of social class as a convenient or meaningful categorization of people or families in society. Some felt that such generalizations were prone to overgeneralization and stereotyping. Individuals in North America today may belong to different and overlapping groups. Other reactions focused on research citing greater differences within groups than between them.

Bissex's presentation on how some individual children became literate in the absence of formal instruction expanded on themes presented by Anderson and Jacob on the first day. She struck responsive chords with her observations that young children encounter literacy within meaningful social contexts and learn (as distinct from being taught) to view literacy as a way of making sense of the world. Many participants supported the view that formal instruction in literacy tends to be linear and devoid of much of the real-life social and meaningful contexts in which literacy has been observed to develop. It was argued that, from a child's viewpoint, real-life contexts are more powerful and meaningful than those which formal instruction tends to offer.

This argument subsequently introduced a number of questions into the discussion. Is literacy "teacher-proof?" What is the relationship between formal instruction and literacy? At this time in the discussion, the predominant view was that children encounter literacy in a social environment and without formal instruction, which is not necessary and therefore, perhaps, has no role at all in developing literacy.

During his presentation, Bruner attempted to refocus attention on the balance between the social and psychological perspectives. While arguing that social conditions give context and meaning to literacy and its uses in society, he was concerned with the connection between those formative social functions and what the individual brain is doing with or through literacy. Bruner proposed that the brain was performing a "metapragmatic" function in moving from speaking to writing, from oral to written language. Language in general, and written language in particular, allows people to go beyond their current reality and to create possible worlds in which other realities and events can occur. Written language, Bruner argued, gives children the power to transcend immediacy, although he agreed with those who commented that possible worlds could also be created through oral discourse and in dramatic presentations. He argued that any means of constructing scenarios would be acceptable but that the technology of literacy facilitates the use of written language. Olson agreed that the artifactual nature of literacy and the permanence of print tends to distinguish oral from written language and therefore tends to particularize and distinguish the products appropriate to the two modes of language.

The focus of discussion then shifted back to the socioanthropologic perspective, and Schieffelin's paper introduced some consideration of the phrase *literacy before schooling*. Since the terms *literacy* and *culture* had been broadly defined on day 1, Schieffelin offered broadened interpretations of the word *before*. Her research was concerned with three disparate groups—an entire society, a segment of suburban preschool children, and some new immigrants—before and as they were becoming literate.

In all three of these situations, the social context and environment were considered to be of primary importance in the development of literacy. In the suburban setting, story-telling and the ongoing use of literacy in the nursery school and at home were major orientations in the child's encounters with literacy. The inner-city Chinese children had a different set of social realities. They were becoming literate before their parents and then assumed literacy-related responsibilities in dealing with the outside world. The social environment, therefore, organized the acquisition and use of literacy and also altered traditional family patterns. Similar considerations and dynamics were found with a previously nonliterate tribe in New Guinea. According to Schieffelin, literacy arrived "packaged" and did not constitute a new form of cognitive or individual activity without further effects. Rather, the effects were socially profound and had a strong impact on the Kaluli way of life. The packaging of literacy included economic reorganization in the form of the institutionalization of a more capitalistic economy and had religious ramifications in that Bible-reading became an important literacy activity.

Schieffelin's paper and the subsequent discussion refocused attention on whether literacy is a neutral force, a benign tool to be used for any purpose, or whether it is a pattern of discourse that is value-laden, with widespread effects and ramifications on people in different cultures and on forms of societal and family organization. These issues, she said, were still being studied.

Second Afternoon (Ferreiro, Olson, Smith)*

Up to this point the discussion had dealt primarily with the social, familial, cultural, and environmental aspects of literacy. With the presentations of Ferreiro, Olson, and Smith, the central concern shifted to literacy as an individual cognitive and psychological phenomenon and dealt with questions regarding what it is the brain is doing with or through literacy. These papers drew attention to how the individual understands and engages in literacy (Ferreiro, Olson) as well as why the individual does so (Smith).

Ferreiro described her research on young children's explanations and descriptions of what they were doing when they were making marks on a page. She provided evidence for a developmental sequence, with children first seeing the marks as representations of real objects and only later as representations for letters that stand for sounds. She demonstrated that the children's explanations always were creative and reasoned and showed intentionality and an internal sense of logic and consistency.

Despite her focus on the psychological aspects of literacy, Ferreiro acknowledged the importance of social context by conducting her study with two different groups— middle-class children with considerable access and exposure to literacy and lower-class children with less access and exposure to literacy. Although she found the same developmental sequences in both groups of preschool children, she later said that after the initial run-ups to literacy had been accomplished, lower-class children, in subsequent years, were deprived of formal instruction in literacy as a result of social factors.

A number of questions were raised regarding the children and some of the cultural perspectives of Ferreiro's study. Asked whether the children were exceptional in any way, Ferreiro said they were typical of the groups from which they were selected. She said that children in both groups had experience with writing in one form or another. Whereas the middle-class children had pens, pencils, and crayons, the lower-class children had experience of writing with chalk, sticks, and brick. A number of the participants speculated on whether children growing up with a pictographic system of writing, such as Japanese, would go through the same stages of development as children learning a syllabic and phonetic writing system.

Olson's paper also dealt with representational functions of the brain but in a different sense from that of Ferreiro. Olson's major point was that in becoming literate, an individual comes to conceptualize and represent language as an object. That is, the individual learns a metalanguage which can be used to describe and define aspects of language itself. Some of Ferreiro's examples of children who were beginning to use the terms *letter* and *word* could be taken as evidence of such metalinguistic awareness. Olson argued that parents predisposing children toward literacy provided them with a literate metalinguistic orientation to language, and that this orientation is part of the structure of literate competence and is necessary in becoming literate.

This line of argument stimulated much discussion. There was resistance to assigning so much importance to the representational function of the brain in isolation from social context. There was also doubt about whether metalinguistic awareness is a necessary or sufficient condition for becoming literate, which in turn revived the issue of whether a list of precursors could be generated. Counter-evidence was cited in support of alternative views; some children with metalinguistic awareness did not become literate and children without this awareness did. Discussion also focused on how parents might provide this awareness. Did they teach their children language, metalanguage, or an orientation toward language?

Thus far, the symposium participants had heard support for the positions that either social context or representational functions of the brain were the most important factors to consider in the child's becoming literate. Smith took issue with the importance assigned to social context by claiming that while environment may make literacy possible, it also can limit possibilities for becoming literate. Psychological factors must also be considered but, Smith argued, they must extend beyond the issue of representational functions. A major consideration must be what the brain does, or indeed, what the brain needs to do. The brain needs to create, and this creative process is facilitated through language. Written language in particular can construct any reality or possible world that is desired. The writing down of language allows for exceptional control over the creator's creations.

The discussion of Smith's paper raised questions regarding the facilitation of the creative function of the brain and the relationships between the creative function, literacy, and the concept of authorship. Participants wondered whether it was appropriate for schools to provide opportunities for the creative and imaginative functions of literacy. The possible means and consequences of such facilitation were questioned by a number of speakers, all of whom supported the importance of the creative aspect of literacy but who expressed some uncertainty as to how it might be aided in young children. Olson said the technology of writing and print and the permanence of the creative product had led to the notions of ownership and authorship of ideas, which were, therefore, a consequence of literacy. Others disputed this, claiming that the notion of authorship and stories, ballads, and poems existed prior to literacy, and that specific products of the oral tradition could be attributed to specific people just as the products of written language are attributable.

At the conclusion of the second day of discussion, some of the earlier dominant themes receded and newer ones emerged. There was less attention to the definitional questions of literacy and culture and more attention paid to the questions that Bruner had posed at the end of the first day. Specifically, participants were concerned with how the interface between the individual's cognitive factors and the social, cultural, and environmental ones could be studied. This issue generated a number of related questions: What individual and social factors are involved in children's "running up" to literacy? How is literacy learned? Can it be taught? What does the brain do, need to do, or develop to do to perform the representational or creative functions associated with literacy? Just as improvisational musicians break between sets to tune their instruments, the participants recessed for dinner at what seemed to be just the right time, and formal deliberation gave way to informal talk and reflection on the increasing complexity of the discussion.

The discussion of Smith's paper raised questions regarding the facilitation of the creative function of the brain and the relationships between the creative function, literacy, and the concept of authorship. Participants wondered whether it was appropriate for schools to provide opportunities for the creative and imaginative functions of literacy. The possible means and consequences of such facilitation were questioned by a number of speakers, all of whom supported the importance of the creative aspect of literacy but who expressed some uncertainty as to how it might be aided in young children. Olson said the technology of writing and print and the permanence of the creative product had led to the notions of ownership and authorship of ideas, which were, therefore, a consequence of literacy. Others disputed this, claiming that the notion of authorship and stories, ballads, and poems existed prior to literacy, and that specific products of the oral tradition could be attributed to specific people just as the products of written language are attributable.

At the conclusion of the second day of discussion, some of the earlier dominant themes receded and newer ones emerged. There was less attention to the definitional questions of literacy and culture and more attention paid to the questions that Bruner had posed at the end of the first day. Specifically, participants were concerned with how the interface between the individual's cognitive factors and the social, cultural, and environmental ones could be studied. This issue generated a number of related questions: What individual and social factors are involved in children's "running up" to literacy? How is literacy learned? Can it be taught? What does the brain do, need to do, or develop to do to perform the representational or creative functions associated with literacy? Just as improvisational musicians break between sets to tune their instruments, the participants recessed for dinner at what seemed to be just the right time, and formal deliberation gave way to informal talk and reflection on the increasing complexity of the discussion.

Third Morning (Leichter)

Opening the third day of discussions, Leichter's presentation drew attention to the family as the dominant social context in which literacy is first encountered by young children, shifting the focus back to issues introduced by Anderson on the first day of the symposium. Leichter's specific concerns were precisely where literacy is found in the context of family life, and, methodologically, how literacy in the family is to be studied. Whereas Anderson had attempted to define nine *domains* within which literacy events were found, Leichter proposed three *climates* that provide contexts for literacy within the family. These were the physical climate (the actual presence of print materials and written language), the interpersonal climate (in which the stream of family activity literacy is found), and the emotional climate (the hopes, fears, and expectations that family members may have regarding literacy and the process of becoming literate.)

A major focus of the subsequent discussion was a new element Leichter had introduced—namely, the presence and importance of affective aspects of becoming literate. Until this point the discussion had dealt largely with cultural and social aspects of literacy (organized patterns of behavior) or the cognitive aspects (the creative and representational functions of the brain). Now attention was directed to the emotional aspects of children's encounters and interactions with literacy. Included was the tension that could be observed surrounding school-related or schoollike literacy activities. Smith noted that this view seems to oppose one of the previously mentioned assumptions about literacy, that it tends to reduce tensions. The discussion proceeded from talk about tension and schools to the question of power and then, for the first time in 2 days, back to some of the definitional issues raised on the first day of the symposium.

Bruner suggested that what was particularly tension-producing was the notion of obligatory literacy, such as that presupposed by what schools do and how success in school is defined. A number of participants spoke of the broad context of the family's relationship to school in general. In particular, families showed evidence of fear of failure to meet school criteria for success in literacy, a fear manifested in the performance of school-like or school-related tasks at home.

Smith suggested that power underlay these fears and tensions concerning literacy and school-defined success in literacy. Reading and writing represented power, but there could also be different biases toward literacy in society, including a specific dominant bias toward literacy for social power. He questioned whether the bias should not be simply toward literacy as a tool, an instrument of technology that could be used for a variety of purposes.

However, Ron Scollon doubted whether literacy is always the benign tool that Smith described. He suggested that literacy might be a value-laden phenomenon, possibly laden with negative values. Citing the work of George Steiner, R. Scollon argued that this negative side of literacy might be seen in the example of Germany, conceivably the most literate nation in modern times. Bruner refuted this argument, saying that culture has nothing to do with literacy but much to do with the way literacy is put to use, and the uses are numerous.

Olson pointed out that these two different lines of argument—the one that literacy is a unique phenomenon, unlike anything else, and the other that literacy is not at all unique but is a manifestation of social and environmental contexts, uses, and forms—made it necessary to go back and clarify (that is, define) literacy by looking first at what literacy does. He proposed that literacy creates a newer and broader social community, a reading public from whom authors are distanced. This situation in turn creates a need for conventionalized meanings for printed work and hence for the creation of dictionaries, giving everyone equal access to those conventionalized meanings.

A lively discussion ensued in which the role, impact, and importance of dictionaries in literacy and definitions of literacy were of major concern. Some speakers felt that relating literacy to dictionaries was far too restrictive and did not allow for the social as well as the affective aspects of literacy brought out in the discussion of Leichter's paper. Paralleling the earlier exchange on whether literacy is a benign or value-laden phenomenon, some speakers argued that the creation and use of dictionaries have served to control people.

Reflective discussion about the discussion itself followed, and it reappeared at various times until the symposium was ended. Speakers addressed themselves to the fact that dichotomies were being proposed with little talk of middle grounds or resolution. Dichotomous issues such as culture versus the individual, formal learning versus informal learning, and play or pretend literacy versus real literacy were seen as mitigating against general agreement or consensus. The discussion slowed at this point and momentarily came to a complete stop. Smith eventually commented, "Well, that reduced us to silence," to which Suzanne Scollon replied, "Reduced?" This brief fragment of conversation seemed to epitomize some of the differences in perspective that the symposium participants had brought with them. It also made clear that there were differing expectations for the symposium itself. The implicit quest for certainty and consensus with which the symposium had begun was no longer so apparent.

Third Afternoon (Clark, Goodman, Teale)

Clark's presentation brought some earlier themes back into focus with the help of additional findings from her research. Regarding the question of initiation of literacy activities which had arisen in the discussion of Anderson's and Jacob's papers, Clark preferred the concept of ongoing interaction since the precise beginning and termination of a literacy event is difficult to ascertain. It would be better she said, to assume that such events are part of an ongoing pattern of interaction within the home. Her view is consistent with remarks made in regard to Leichter's paper.

Clark also argued that young children show evidence of their awareness of the power and function of literacy. She reported on a young girl who claimed that "I can cut my egg because I can write my name." Her self-perception as a participant in literacy enhanced her self-image as a competent and, in her environment, powerful person. Another child's awareness of functions of literacy was apparent when she made up a shopping list in her play. Reminded to list sweets, her response was, "Oh, we won't forget sweets."

The discussion of Clark's paper highlighted the different aspects of literacy children could be seen to acquire. Bissex made a suggestion with which many of the participants subsequently agreed. She said that the underlying assumption in the previous discussions seemed to be to find those universals or common conditions under which literacy occurs, but perhaps it would be better to look instead for the *different* conditions under which literacy can occur. The presentations had all demonstrated, in different ways and to various degrees, that children in different cultures demonstrate the ability to begin to become literate. Several speakers alluded to the different aspects of literacy that had been researched and discussed at the symposium, expressing some doubt about whether all these aspects would contribute toward some larger group consensus or understanding of whatever universals might exist for an individual to become literate.

Goodman's presentation expressed concern about some of the concepts and categories in psychological research that might tend to impede an understanding of literacy. In particular, she argued that the notion of metalinguistic awareness as a necessary component in becoming literate was not supported in her research. In questioning others' attempts to make statements of universal relevance on metalinguistic awareness, Goodman followed the line of argument introduced by Bissex—that people can and do become literate in a variety of different ways. Referring back to Ferreiro's presentation, Goodman presented examples which she claimed demonstrated children's creative and individual approach to working out the uses and characteristics of written language.

The final paper presentation, by Teale, based on his research into storybook-reading, introduced new perspectives on the possible importance of narrative in becoming literate. Although many speakers had mentioned that children who have been read to in preschool years appear to develop facility in reading and writing, there was general agreement that not enough was known about why being read to was so important. Many participants concurred with Teale's point that too little is known about the diverse ways in which stories are read to children and the effects that different story-telling or reading styles may have on children's becoming literate. Nonetheless, Teale raised a number of possibilities regarding the particular relevance or power that exposure to narrative patterns of discourse might have in the acquisition of literacy. It is possible, he said, that narrative is a "primary act of mind," that all individuals are continually "writing their own autobiography" and, in some ways, are living a narrative which can be reflected in written form. Narratives can give structure to personal stories and can exist in the realm of the unconscious, in archetype, or as myth. Teale emphasized that he considered narrative a very important but not a determining factor in literacy development.

Clark said that in her research on young fluent readers she observed great diversity in the quantity and quality of story-reading experiences of young children. Bruner cited a program in London in which schoolchildren compose, edit, and publish their own narratives, acquiring a sense that narrative is "made, not born." Smith wondered what connection there might be between what the reader was doing and what the child was doing during story-telling episodes. He argued that story-reading episodes work because the child has a brain that wants to create and the story gives children experiences to recreate and reconstruct.

Participants also commented on the relationship between social and cognitive aspects of story-telling. Teale said that children have to be personally, actively involved in the story-telling episodes but that the episodes must be seen in their social contexts as well. The interpersonal relationship between reader and listener, and gestural, intonational, and positional factors all must be considered more closely, together with the way story-reading fits into other family activities. Other factors requiring research include children's reactions to being read to for the first time as opposed to subsequent times and children's reactions to new stories versus known stories.

This third day of discussion concluded with a demonstration by Ron Scollon of some of the microcomputer word-processing programs being used by preschool children in Alaska. Cited among the positive features of microcomputers was the production of neat, clean, consistent orthography, so that what a child produced would look identical (in terms of orthography) to the production of an adult. Bruner commented that by viewing a text before it was printed, the child could repair any possible mistakes so that the final product would look error-free. It was a way in which children could match their intended statements with those they actually produced.

Goodman agreed that microcomputers could be exciting additions to classrooms and might enhance literacy learning in a variety of ways, but she questioned whether it was necessarily good that children could eliminate errors easily. Why, she asked, are errors assumed to be bad, wrong, or something to be avoided? She argued that children can learn from their errors and that seeing them even in finished products can be beneficial.

The computer was discussed as an instrument of technology which, like literacy, is a tool. The use to which the tool is put and the mastery with which individuals will use the tool remain open to question. Scollon said that the new technology does not necessarily eliminate errors but may produce new kinds of errors, so that error-free might be an inaccurate representation of this tool. Computers could have profound effects on society in general and literacy in particular. In fact, future symposia may take place in which participants interact via a series of remote terminals rather then by conversing orally while seated together in a single room.

Fourth Day

On the final day of the symposium, Smith presented the participants with a list of statements regarding literacy. He asked whether, after 3 days of deliberation, a group of researchers all concerned with literacy could reach general consensus on any of these issues. The list of statements is reproduced here:

1. There is no single definition of literacy.
2. There is no single most important function of literacy.
3. Literacy creates cultural, psychological, and social tensions.
4. All children can learn to read and write.
5. Formal instruction is not necessary for literacy to happen.
6. Literacy creates biases.
7. Not all societies (and individuals) regard literacy as an unmixed blessing.
8. Literacy is a means of discrimination.
9. There is no central core of literacy ability which generalizes to all of its uses.
10. Literacy is learned in social contexts.
11. Literacy is acquired through collaborative experience rather than through explanation and precepts.
12. Literacy is learned in supportive environments.

The discussion of the list was conducted on two levels. On one level, the focus was on the content of the list, specifically on issues pertaining to the social-individual continuum, literacy as a tool, and the role of formal instruction and schools. On the second level, the focus was on the problems and issues involved attempting to generate a list of general, inarguable statements about literacy.

Olson thought the symposium had tried to deal with three separate issues. First, there was the question of the social contexts of literacy. Second was the psychological question of the structure of language use, comprehension, and production and how the individual comes to master that system regardless of the social context. The third question was the interface between the social and psychological aspects of literacy. When questioned about ways that the social and psychological aspects could be separated from each other, Olson replied that the creation of specific alphabets and syllabaries would reflect the representational aspects of human cognition. Anderson believed that the symposium had tended to emphasize social aspects of literacy but claimed that this was a reaction to research traditions in the study of literacy which had long favored the psychological perspective to the near exclusion of the social perspective.

The statement that literacy is a tension-producing phenomenon produced a number of comments concerning the social context and the uses to which literacy is put. Suzanne Scollon said that in some social contexts (for example, in North America), obligatory literacy is tension-producing because of its close relationship to compulsory education, school-oriented definitions of literary achievement, and unnecessary attention to and emphasis on formal instruction. Alternatively, Emilia Ferreiro argued that in Third World countries such as Mexico, the withholding of literacy from people produced tensions and that hopes for raising the literacy level are linked to the creation of accessible public schooling for more people. "School," she said, "is a great opportunity to become acquainted with print." Schieffelin reiterated that whether or not literacy is tension-producing, it never is simply a neutral phenomenon and always comes "packaged" with values and societal implications.

The role of formal instruction in the achievement of literacy in North America also was questioned. Many participants agreed that formal instruction may not be necessary for becoming literate, but there was debate over the term *formal*. Some participants argued that valuable, meaningful, noncoercive literacy learning can take place in schools through informal education. Some linked the listed item on the importance of collaboration in literacy as an example of the kinds of informal instruction that schools might make available.

Discussion of the attempt to draw up a list of generalizations centered around whether it was a possible or desirable task. If it were desirable but not possible, what needed to be done to contribute to such a list? Some participants objected to the creation of the list because, they argued, not enough was known yet about the many different ways and conditions in which people become literate. The good news, it was suggested, was that the symposium had aired many important, accurate, specific details about the different ways literacy is learned; the bad news was that much more detail is needed.

Leichter and Ferreiro each contributed a methodological suggestion. Leichter thought that rather than focusing exclusively on either detail or generalizations, it would be better to develop what sociologists call *theories of the middle range*. Such theories do attempt to abstract from discrete details but not to the "blurry level of generalizations." Ferreiro argued that a two-pronged effort must be made. On the one hand, more detail and specific information is needed. These details, however, must fit into what she termed a *theoretical network*. As a collection of pieces of information, the value of the detail is limited. As contributions to a theoretical structure, details take on greater meaning and contribute to a better understanding of the phenomenon of becoming literate.

Although the discussion had been opened periodically to the audience during the previous 3 days, audience participation had been limited mainly to informal conversation with speakers during the breaks. On the final day, Smith, who was chairperson for the session, explicitly invited audience participation and gave priority to the audiences's questions and comments. The resulting discussion dealt primarily with what the symposium participants could pass on to teachers and teacher-educators, if indeed the participants had any of the kinds of information that practitioners want and need.

Several speakers from the audience were eager to know if the participants could agree on a view of the child as an active learner. They referred to research findings presented at the symposium that supported this view and urged that if some sort of explicit, agreed-on statement to this effect could be produced, it would be of great benefit for those working directly with children. The participants were not able to produce such an unequivocal statement. Schieffelin commented that this view of the child as an active learner is not universal across cultures or, in a historic sense, across time in our own culture. Such an unqualified statement, Schieffelin believed, might not be helpful when working with some children from a culture in which this view is not accepted within a larger culture framework.

Speakers from the audience disagreed with one another about whether it was appropriate to pose these kinds of questions to the participants. One speaker claimed that the participants presented descriptive data that could illuminate a problem but was not a legitimate basis for "ought" statements—that is, statements that could provide prescription or direction for practitioners. A second speaker wanted participants to agree at least on their descriptive data—for example, to agree that all the data show that children are active learners. If such an assertion could be made based on the various disciplines and research studies, he felt that practitioners could construct their own "ought" statements regarding practice.

Although uniform agreement on the question of children as active learners was not accomplished, the term *active learner* was given greater definition and clarification by both audience and symposium participants. A speaker from the audience said that a misperception of the active learning concept is the one that views learning as a solo effort, whereas in her perception active learning must be conducted in collaboration with teachers and other children. Another speaker argued, from her experience of working with adults, that at the community college level as well as at the preschool level, the notion of active learning is important. Teachers at both levels, she argued, must engage their learners in more active ways. As she put it, most teachers at all levels "do all the doing" themselves.

As the concluding session drew to a close, Smith said that there was still much to be talked about, but that an afternoon of sailing awaited the participants. He asked, "Which is more important, sailing or talking?" Perhaps it was appropriate that for these symposium participants who had wrestled so hard with various dichotomies, the group consensus was, as Smith summed up, "Right, they're both more important."

Notes

* Margaret Donaldson was scheduled to speak at this session. Due to illness, she could not attend the symposium. Her paper was distributed to the participants at this time.

The Symposium: What It Meant

Antoinette A. Oberg

Many words were generated in a variety of media by the University of Victoria Symposium. There was the written language of papers, prepared in advance, shared at the symposium, and reviewed, revised, and later edited into the form in which they appear as chapters in this book. There were notes, letters, telegrams, timetables, programs, memoranda, and an overhead projector. There was talk over the telephone, face-to-face talk, and talk for the tape recorder. Every aspect of spoken language interaction, from whispers to speeches, occurred. There was even a word-processing computer. What did it all mean?

Meaning comes not only from what is written and said but also from the way events unfold and who participates in them. This was a literate event and the participants were all highly literate, with diverse and complex backgrounds. Literacy was pervasive, not simply as the topic of the symposium but in the way the symposium was organized, in the way participants talked to and challenged each other, and in the very manner in which they thought. What follows in this chapter is an interpretation of what happened at the symposium and of what came out of it.

Beginnings

Plans for the University of Victoria Symposium arose out of its historic context and the interests of its originator. Historically, the symposium occurred at a time when language researchers for the most part were redirecting their inquiries from formal aspects of language in isolated instances to its functional use in social and cultural contexts. In the process, language research was becoming an interdisciplinary endeavor. Thus, it was fitting that a psychologist, Frank Smith, should bring together a group of sociologists, anthropologists, and linguists as well as psychologists and educators to discuss the topic of literacy. The primary concern was education, and the hope was that insights from each of the disciplines could be distilled and blended to make clear the essential ingredients and conditions of children's learning to become literate.

The stage was carefully set to encourage productive interactions. When participants came together early in the damp and windy October of 1982, they were seated—in alphabetical order, of course—around a horseshoe-shaped arrangement of tables, facing one another and an academic audience of approximately forty people who were seated mostly at the open end of the horseshoe. The setting was sufficiently small and informal for exchanges to be conducted in conversational tones. The organization was deliberately nondirective, but the expectations were clear: The hope was that a statement of general principles about literacy would evolve.

The Interactions

A technician pushed the "record" button and the talking began. There were a few opening remarks and then the initial papers were presented by their authors. The discussion was polite, formal, moderated at first by the chairperson-organizer who also took the role of a discussant. Few of the participants knew any of the others outside their own discipline, and so there was genuine interest. Participants talked but they also listened. The short presentations were followed by long discussions in which participants explained the data according to individual rules of interpretation. There were wide-ranging comments, short interchanges, and questions that soon hinted at challenge and disagreement. The diversity among participants' positions began to become evident as they struggled to understand one another's interpretive frameworks. Questions were directed not at the literal content of what was said but at the presumptions made in saying it. Comments were made about the conceptual categories used to describe what was found in a particular study, the impact of the methodology employed on the nature of the findings, and the use of the term *culture* as an explanation. The histories and conceptual frameworks of the participants did not mesh, and what was a neutral term for one was a critical concept for another. The moderator gave up his role, and timekeeping tasks rotated among the participants. By the middle of the first afternoon, the symposium began to be carried along by its own momentum.

Through 4 days the conversations continued both in the formal sessions and between them, over meals, and on into the evenings. Discussion ranged over countless topics, some of which were considered more than once but few of which were resolved. In the end, the participants could not agree on a list of principles about literacy.

Still, the engagement had been enthusiastic and honest; most would even say it had been enriching and fruitful. Important statements were made about literacy (these will be described later in this chapter), but they were not the hoped-for seminal generalizations anticipated at the beginning of the symposium. This was despite the careful selection of participants who were at the edge of their own disciplines and crossing over into others, who were willing and able to share and develop insights about literacy. It was despite the care taken to allow participants the freedom and support to structure and direct the discussion in ways they found most profitable. Why had the generalizations failed to materialize?

Backgrounds of the Participants

The fact that the participants represented four different academic disciplines—psychology, sociology, linguistics, and anthropolgy—in pure or applied form (those in the applied field called themselves *educationists*) meant that at least four distinct communities of discourse were in operation, each with its own characteristic conceptual frameworks, modes of inquiry, presumptions, specialized language, history, and interests. Each paper was prepared from the discipline orientation of its author, and without a specific and well-formed topic to address, each took its shape more from the source discipline than from the issue at hand. Despite these differences, there were some significant common interests among group members which were sufficiently strong to have motivated them (in combination with other motivations that can only be guessed at) to attend the symposium. All participants were concerned with education in the sense of understanding the optimum growth of language in children, all had a professional history of reasearch in language learning, and all seemed to share a feeling that the traditional approach to language learning in schools was not consistent with current understandings about becoming literate.

Commonalities motivated and enabled the members of the group to engage in lively discussions for 4 days of formal and informal meetings, but differences prevented the hoped-for cumulation of ideas. There was an obvious and shared tendency among all present to reason from observed evidence and to base conclusions on the data at hand. The evidence gathered by individuals in their separate researches was remarkably uncontradictory, but the way participants reasoned from their evidence was notably different. At least two major paradigms were in use. In one (a paradigm usually associated with experimental psychology), the method of inquiry was to begin with a well-formulated set of theoretical contructs usually phrased in the form of an hypothesis and then to gather data to test the usefulness of the construct or the validity of the hypothesis. The other method (a paradigm most often associated with anthropology) was to begin with the data with as little prior focusing as possible, to gather descriptions as accurately as possible, and then to examine those data for meaningful patterns which could be cast in theoretical terms to enhance understanding of them. Participants who worked in the second paradigm were careful to take nothing for granted and to avoid imposing one set of cultural values on another situation. They were content with a collection of specific cases, each with its own internal logic. Thus, their sensibilities were easily offended by the evaluative and theoretical biases of the hypothesis-testing researchers.

It is ironic that the meeting of the multiple paradigms which was intended to uncover new awarenesses in fact clouded some of the issues addressed. It also is ironic (at least some of the participants would argue) that it is only by virtue of our being literate that we have been able to develop the complexity of thought embodied in these paradigms.

Conflict of paradigms was acknowledged implicitly but never addressed openly by the group. The conflict surfaced most explicitly in recurring discussions about whether and what generalizations could be made about literacy. With some participants arguing that each situation must be interpreted in its own terms, it became impossible for the group to reach consensus on any significant general statements.

Thus, each participant remained rooted in his or her own personal disciplinary background. Each presented a carefully constructed and internally consistent case, as each participant had written and spoken about it many times before. Such case-making is part of what it means to be literate and scholarly in an academic world. The participants sometimes acknowledged competing assumptions, but they could not resolve them. They listened to one another, but no one stepped far enough outside a personal frame of reference to penetrate another's. There was remarkably little talking at cross-purposes, but there was little sense of direction. The discussions were intelligible but unpredictable, more of a series of reconnaissances than an organized inquiry.

Broadness of the Topic

The topic of the symposium was intentionally stated broadly to permit approaches from many different points of view. The context was narrowed—children before school—but the definitions were not. As a result, an early and continued preoccupation of the group was with the definition of *literacy* and its related terms. There was an evident wide variation among the working definitions that participants had brought to the symposium. Some participants defined literacy according to what someone needs to know to be literate, and others defined it in terms of what someone who is literate can do. However, for some reason that remains unclear, participants were unwilling to exclude any particular definition. They opted instead to define literacy by the equally vague phrase *patterns of discourse*. Adoption of this global definition prevented exploration of the differences between written language and spoken language, even though insights about spoken language were offered as bases for important hypotheses about written language and how it is learned.

The adherence to a broad definition of literacy combined with the natural tendency for all participants to use rather than to reexamine their own frameworks meant that there was no way to focus the topic. As a consequence, there was very little use of technical terminology. The discussion was constrained only by the conventions of literate academic discourse patterns.

Presence of an Audience, Present and Future

Despite the absence of a topic focus, participants seemed compelled to contribute, if not by the format of a symposium in which every participant is expected to play a part, then possibly by the ever-present tape recorder which promised that the proceedings would include not only the written papers but also an account of the dialogue. However, it was not always easy for participants to decide where to enter and what to say in the undirected and unpredictable flow of comments. Consequently, initiatory behavior sometimes tended to take the form of making points or taking stances. Assertions often had to be supported by the degree of confidence with which they were presented. Yet, although there was a potential for conflict, contests over ideas never blossomed into full-fledged power plays, perhaps because of the participants' respect for one another or perhaps because of the tempering effect of the audience and the taperecorder.

The audience might have been happier had such contests taken place. The inability of participants to achieve consensus, the disjointed nature of the discussions, and the reluctance of the participants to push an issue to its limit were all disappointing to an audience looking for new understandings rather than familiar arguments. However, members of the audience expressed their disappointment only in hushed voices, and the participants apparently did not hear them.

During the concluding session, on specifically being invited to do so, members of the audience proclaimed their biases for eduactional action rather than scientific or political theories about literacy. Their concern was with what schools, especially teachers, might do to enhance literacy. They responded enthusiastically to the portrayal of the child as an active learner in the various studies presented. Brushing aside the anthropologists' caution that value attributed to this notion is culture-specific, the audience pressed participants for ways to support and foster active learning, and participants responded but always with caveats attached to their proposals. This pressure to consider the practical implications of literacy learning studies might have shaped a good deal of the discussion had it been allowed to surface earlier in the symposium.

The Nature of an Academic Event

An academic symposium defines a certain context for participant interaction. It produces certain rules to govern the interchange. Such rules are that people talk one at a time, control emotions, keep the talk going, make supportive as well as critical comments, respect the others' ideas, ask questions primarily to clarify and sometimes to challenge, use formal rather than personal language, address the whole group and avoid private conversations, yield the floor, pay attention to the speaker, remain focused on the topic, and try periodically to summarize. The participants were not forced or even requested to adhere to these conventions, but they did. Their respect for the conventions did not constrain the direction of the discussion but clearly prevented it from becoming a more probing analysis into personal meanings and perspectives.

Although, from the beginning, it was intended that the symposium be preceded and followed by writing, the symposium itself was exclusively oral, and this undoubtedly is part of the reason that it wandered over many different subtopics. Papers were written and perused in advance, but the symposium did not use them as its starting point and did not delve into their presuppositions and claims. A book was to be compiled, but there was no plan, no table of contents, to give the discussion a focus. That the oral interchange did not center on written arguments and rarely cited written work limited its power and sophistication. Relatively few notes were made by individual participants; there was no cataloging, diagramming, or written compilation of ideas or points. The control that can be gained over complex ideas by writing them down was absent. Occasional attempts to put more structure into the proceedings (usually by the psychologists) were inevitably resisted (usually by the anthropologists).

Undoubtedly, the oral nature of the symposium also accounted for many of the positive feelings among participants which persisted throughout the symposium. They engaged each other in friendly terms, and all left the symposium feeling the efforts had been worthwhile. In an oral event, the engagement is immediate and personal, and involvement is high. These features are intensified when the participating group is small, as it was in Victoria, and when participants are committed to the topic at hand, as was each of the participants in the University of Victoria Symposium.

When the symposium ended, it was clear that the ambitious nature of the symposium and the diversity of the participants accounted for the absence of generalizations and that literacy itself resisted any simple, single explanation. By way of summary, the concerns displayed at the symposium can be discussed under three broad headings: what it means to be literate, becoming literate, and the results of being literate. The underlying concerns are with definition, education, and power, respectively.

What It Means to Be Literate

Being literate means many things, and it means different things to different people. For the anthropologist, this statement is unobjectionable: It acknowledges a primary tenet that all meanings arise from the cultural context of the individual. Thus, it is possible to be more specific about what literacy means only in a particular case. For the psychologist, the opening statement is uninformative and indicates a lack of consensus on the cognitive knowledge and skills that constitute literacy. The only definitional statement that survived the onslaught of multiple perspectives was that literacy is a pattern of discourse that operates in a social context according to certain culture-specific conventions. However, even this statement does not represent a functional consensus, for underlying it is a range of interpretations of what it means to be literate. Participants' definitions of literacy ranged from being able to function appropriately with written and spoken language in everyday social arrangements to being able to analyze and discuss characteristics of language by means of a metalanguage.

Although there was no consensus on an operational definition of literacy, the idea of literacy or patterns of discourse was sufficiently well understood to permit 4 days of intelligible, dynamic discussion on the topic. Indeed, aspects of the function of literacy seemed to be more easily agreed on than elements of structure. It was agreed that literacy is embedded in social interaction and that skills of social interaction are necessary for an individual to learn to become literate and to demonstrate literacy once learned. The social context in turn shapes both the language and actions of individuals through a variety of culture-specific conventions.

Learning to Become Literate

It is tempting to label this section of the chapter, or at least to include in it, "implications for schools." Schooling was a concern common to all symposium participants, and becoming literate certainly is central to schooling. However, schooling is a normative enterprise, predicated on statements about what ought to be and why, and it is not possible to derive such prescriptive statements from the scientific studies and descriptive statements of academics at a symposium. Moreover, in studying preschool literacy, researchers were uncertain about such crucial issues as whether *metalanguage*—language used to talk about language—is necessary to literacy, or exactly which resources and experiences in the preschool environment fall into the category of *leading to literacy*. To suggest what should be done in schools with regard to literacy, positions must be taken not only on the contentious issues of what it means to be literate and how literacy develops but also on the roles and responsibilities involved in teaching, and these must all be preceded by statements about what ought to be learned. If the earlier summary statements about what it means to be literate are accepted, and the statements about learning to become literate that follow are correct, then the implications for schooling are self-evident. The sorts of instructional practices implied would be characterized by the purposeful use of language, greater emphasis on frameworks than on content, and concern for asking rather than answering questions. Curricular implications are more complex and far-reaching. They would begin with a curriculum that permits individual teacher variations in accord with the characteristics of a particular group of learners.

Despite the lack of consensus on a specific definition of literacy, a number of noteworthy theses about the process of becoming literate were proposed. One thesis characterized the process as self-motivated hypothesis generation and hypothesis-testing in a literate context in pursuit of individual ends. As observed in children, the process is one in which learners, trying to make sense of their environment, experiment with various forms and uses of language, eventually, and apparently independently, moving closer to conventional forms and uses. Whether metacognitive functioning is part of or necessary to this process remains unclear. Comparisons between the process of becoming literate as it pertains to written language and to spoken language remain problematic.

However, it seems clear that certain features of the cultural context within which a child becomes literate have some relationship to the degree and quality of literacy attained. Values and beliefs, roles, functions, and purposes shape the physical environment, emotional climate, interpersonal interaction, and language patterns from which and through which children learn to become literate. These contextual features do not always vary according to cultural group, social class, or ethnic background. The most reliable unit of literacy transmission probably is the family. Hence, a child's literacy or lack of literacy cannot necessarily be linked to cultural group, social class, or ethnic background.

In the family context, most literacy learning occurs incidentally and in relation to purposeful acts. In the process of being socialized into family life, the child has the opportunity to observe, participate in, and identify with language used to accomplish the real-life purposes of daily living. In many cases, formal instruction is absent, yet the child learns to become literate. Sometimes, as in immigrant families, the socialization roles are temporarily reversed when youngsters learn the language of the new country before their parents do and then help to socialize the parents into the new culture.

Learning to become literate in school is usually (but not necessarily) different from learning to become literate in the family. In school, children are *taught* language. Instruction is formal and intentional. The teacher mediates between the children and the environment and, in so doing, preempts the children's opportunity to hypothesize. Print is used not to engage in purposeful acts but as the focus of what is to be learned. To understand the instruction, one must understand the metalanguage. Thus, language becomes detached from the real-world situation that gives it meaning. Literacy learning in school lacks the purposefulness and the contextualization characteristic of literacy learning in the family. Children are obliged to master a decontextualized form of language to succeed in school. Some children succeed and others do not. Severe tensions may arise for those who do not, especially when the family values success at school. These children are labeled school failures, not only by the school but often also by the society at large.

For children who fail, schools could be said to have impeded literacy. On the other hand, as the only instrument for the conscious development of literacy in the Third World, schools may be considered essential for literacy. It is important to note that these contrasting views of the functions of schools and literacy are due to differences in social conditions and not to differences in the nature of learning or of literacy.

The Power of Being Literate

People who are not literate may lack aspects of the power that literacy makes possible. In the view of symposium participants, literacy is the power to gain knowledge, to communicate ideas, to reformulate or advance knowledge, to create possible worlds, and to achieve understanding and insight. It also is the power to go beyond circumstances or to detach oneself from them, to fantasize, to free oneself from the limitations of time and space. Literacy gives individuals the power to direct or decide situations or to use instruments by virtue of some special knowledge. Finally, literacy permits individuals or groups to exert political, economic, or social control over others. Any of these aspects of power that literacy makes possible can be used for good or for evil.

When some people in a society are literate and others are not, tensions may result. At a low level, these tensions can occur in the form of misunderstanding; at a more serious level, they appear as discrimination. Schools play a significant role in the achievement of or failure to achieve literacy, and consequently, they are seen as instruments for distributing power in society.

Conclusion

What did all the words achieve? Did they lack an ultimate meaning because the symposium ended without an agreed-on definition of literacy or a description of how preschool children often achieve it, let alone a set of guidelines for how literacy might be taught? It could be argued that these negative demonstrations constitute the symposium's most important outcome, a clear sign that neither language nor culture can be neatly pigeonholed or taken for granted.

A list of the positive outcomes of the University of Victoria Symposium might include the following:

1. Many diverse disciplines have relevant observations to make about literacy.
2. None of these disciplines can expect to have the last word or claim to possess the ultimate truth about literacy.
3. Many important insights and much data relevant to literacy exists—possibly more than any one individual or even one discipline can be expected to know or to take account of—but there also is a great deal to be learned.
4. Literacy is complex and multifaceted, and so it should not be surprising that individuals fail to agree on its nature or on how it should be taught.

Perhaps the most significant points of broad agreement in this symposium concern children's self-motivated quest to make sense of their own environments and their remarkable capacity to do so without formal instruction. The implications of this statement for education must always be derived with reference to culture-specific values and presumptions.

No representative of all anthropologists, all psychologists, all sociologists, or all teachers could distill the essence of everything discussed in the symposium and all the written language associated with it. The main lesson must be that children, literacy, and culture are too complex to be dealt with in terms of a few concepts, slogans, objectives, techniques, or materials. Teachers and theorists alike should reflect on the symposium's implications and uncertainties in light of their own experience and responsibilities, and then they should continue the inquiry.

References

Almy, M.C. *Children's experiences prior to first grade and success in beginning reading*. New York: Teachers College Bureau of Publications, 1949.

Anderson, A. *Literacy resources: How preschoolers interact with written communication*. Quarterly report to the National Institute of Education, July 1980.

Anderson, A.B., Teale, W.B., and Estrada, E. Low-income children's preschool literacy experiences: Some naturalistic observations. *The Quarterly Newsletter of the Laboratory of Comparative Human Cognition* 2 (1980):59–65.

Anderson, R.C. The notion of schemata and the educational enterprise. In R.C. Anderson, R.J. Spriro, and W.E. Montague (Eds.), *Schooling and the acquisition of knowledge*. Hillsdale, N.J.: Lawrence Erlbaum Associates, 1977.

Applebee, A.N. *Tradition and reform in the teaching of English: A history*. Urbana, Ill.: National Council of Teachers of English, 1974.

Applebee, A.N. *The child's concept of story: Ages two to seventeen*. Chicago: University of Chicago Press, 1978.

Baghban, M.J.M. Language development and initial encounters with written language: A case study in preschool reading and writing. Ph.D. dissertation, Indiana University, 1979.

Barker, R.G., and Wright, H.F. *The midwest and its children: The psychological ecology of an American town*. Hamden, CT.: Archon Books, 1971. Originally published 1955.

Berger, P., Berger, B., and Kellner, H. *The homeless mind: Modernization and consciousness*. New York: Random House, 1973.

Bernstein. B. *Language and poverty*. Chicago: Markum, 1970.

Bissex, G.L. *Gnys at Wrk: A child learns to write and read*. Cambridge: Harvard University Press, 1980.

Blachowicz, C.L.Z. Semantic constructivity in children's comprehension. *Reading Research Quarterly* 13 (1977–1978):188–199.

Black, S.D., Levin, J.A., Mehan, H., and Quinn, C.N. Real and non-real time: Cross-media analysis of instructional interaction. Laboratory of Comparative Human Cognition, University of California, San Diego, 1981.

Bolt, Baranek, and Newman, Inc. *Annual Report of the Center for the Study of Reading*. Cambridge, MA., 1980.

Borges, J. Convocation speech at New York Institute for the Humanities, October 1982.

Bourdieu, P. Systems of education and systems of thought. *International Social Science Journal* 19 (1967):338–358.

Bourdieu, P. Cultural reproduction and social reproduction. In R. Brown (Ed.), *Knowledge, education, and cultural change: Papers in the sociology of education*. London: Tavistock, 1973.

Bowerman, M. Starting to talk worse: Clues to language acquisition from children's late speech errors. In S. Strauss (Ed.), *U-Shaped behavioural growth*. New York: Academic Press, 1982a.

Bowerman, M. Reorganizational processes in language development. In L. Gleitman and E. Wanner (Eds.), *The state of the art in language acquisition*. New York: Academic Press, 1982b.

Branscombe, A. Giving away my classroom: Teacher as researcher. In D. Goswami and L. Odell (Eds.), *Teacher as researcher*. Sharon, CT.: Boynton-Cook Publishers. In press.

Briggs, C., and Elkind, D. Characteristics of early readers. *Perceptual and Motor Skills* 44 (1977):1231−1237.

Brim, O.G., Jr. *Education for child rearing*. New York: Russell Sage, 1959.

Brocher, T.H. Toward new methods in parent education. In M.D. Fantini and R. Cardenas (Eds.), *Parenting in a multicultural society*. New York: Longman, 1980.

Brown, P., and Levinson, S. Universals in language usage: Politeness phenomena. In Esther Goody (Ed.), *Questions and politeness: Strategies and social interaction*. New York: Cambridge University Press, 1978.

Bruner, J.S. *The process of education*. New York: Vintage Books, 1960.

Bruner, J.S. The ontogenesis of speech acts. *Journal of Child Language* 2 (1975):1−19.

Bruner, J.S. *Child's talk*. New York: Norton, 1983.

Bruner, J.S. *Acquiring the uses of language*. New York: Norton. In press.

Bruner, J., Jolly, A., and Sylva, K. (Eds.). *Play—its role in development and evolution*. New York: Basic Books, 1976.

Burroughs, M. The stimulation of verbal behavior in culturally disadvantaged three-year-olds. Ph.D. dissertation, Michigan State University, 1972.

Calkins, L. Children learn the writer's craft. *Language Arts* 57 (1980):107−213.

Campbell, J. *The hero with a thousand faces*. New York: Meridien Books, 1956.

Cebuliak, D.W. Patterns of avid readers. Master's thesis, University of Alberta, 1977.

Chomsky, C. Stages in language development and reading exposure. *Harvard Educational Review* 42 (1972):1−33.

Clark, M.M. *Young fluent readers*. London: Heinemann Educational Books, 1976.

Clay, M.M. *Reading: The patterning of complex behaviour*. London: Heinemann Educational Books, 1972a.

Clay, M.M. *The early detection of reading difficulties: A diagnostic survey*. London: Heinemann Educational Books, 1972b.

Clay, M.M. *What did I write?* Auckland: Heinemann Educational Books, 1975.

Clay, M.M. *The early detection of reading difficulties* (2nd ed.). Auckland: Heinemann Educational Books, 1979a.

Clay, M.M. *Reading: The patterning of complex behavior* (2nd ed.). Auckland: Heinemann Educational Books, 1979b.

Clay, M.M. Early writing and reading: Reciprocal gains. In M.M. Clark and T. Glynn (Eds.), *Reading and writing for the child with difficulties* (*Educational Review* Occasional Publications no. 8). Birmingham, England: University of Birmingham, 1980, pp. 27−43.

Cochran-Smith, M. What is given is no more than a way of taking: Children learning to make sense of texts. Paper presented at the World Congress of Sociology X, Mexico City, August 1982.

Cochran-Smith, M. *The making of a reader*. Norwood, N.J.: Ablex, 1983.

Creesy, D. *Literacy and the social order: Reading and writing in Tudor and Stuart England*. Cambridge: Cambridge University Press, 1980.

Cremin, L.A. *Public education*. New York: Basic Books, 1976.

Cremin, L.A. *Traditions of American education*. New York: Basic Books, 1977.

Cremin, L.A., and Cremin, A. *American education: The colonial experience 1607−1783*. New York: Harper & Row, 1970, p. 131.

Cullinan, B.E. (Ed.). *Black dialects and reading*. Urbana, IL.: National Council of Teachers of English, 1974.

Derrida, J. *Of grammatology*. Trans. G. Spivak. Baltimore, MD.: Johns Hopkins University Press, 1976.

Doake, D.   Book experience and emergent reading in preschool children. Ph.D. dissertation, University of Alberta, 1981.

Donaldson, M., and Reid, J.   Language skills and reading: A developmental perspective. In A. Hendry (Ed.), *Teaching reading: The key issues*. London: Heinemann Educational Books, 1982.

Downing, J.   Children's concepts of language in learning to read. *Educational Research* 12 (1970):106–112.

Downing, J.   Children's developing concepts of spoken and written language. *Journal of Reading Behavior* 4 (1971–1972):1–19.

Downing, J., and Thackray, D.   *Reading readiness* (2nd ed.). London: Hodder and Stoughton, 1975.

Downing, J., and Leong, C.K.   *Psychology of reading*. Toronto: Macmillan, 1982.

Durkin, D.   *Children who read early*. New York: Teachers College Press, 1966.

Durkin, D.   A six year study of children who learned to read in school at the age of four. *Reading Research Quarterly* 10 (1974–1975):9–61.

Dybdahl, C.   Learning about language. In Y. Goodman, M. Haussler, and D. Strickland (Eds.), *Oral and written language development research: Impact on the schools*. Urbana, IL.: National Council of Teachers of English, 1979–1980, pp. 21–30.

Eisenstein, E. *The printing press as an agent of change*. Cambridge: Cambridge University Press, 1979.

Erickson, F.   Taught cognitive learning in its immediate environments: A neglected topic in the anthropology of education. *Anthropology and Education Quarterly* 13 (1982):149–180.

Erickson, F., and Shultz, J.J.   *The counselor as gatekeeper*. New York: Academic Press, 1981.

Fantini, M.D.   The parent as educator: A home-school model of socialization. In M.D. Fantini and R. Cardenas (Eds.), *Parenting in a multicultural society*. New York: Longman, 1980.

Feld, S.   *Sound and sentiment*. Philadelphia: University of Pennsylvania Press, 1982.

Feldman, C.F.   Pragmatic aspects of language. In M. LaGaly et al. (Eds.), *Proceedings of the Chicago Linguistics Society*, vol. 10. 1974.

Ferreiro, E.   What is written in a written sentence? A developmental answer. *Journal of Education* 160 (1978):25–39.

Ferreiro, E.   The relationship between oral and written language: The children's viewpoints. In Y. Goodman, M. Haussler, and D. Strickland (Eds.), *Oral and written language development research: Impact on the schools*. Urbana, IL.: National Council of Teachers of English, 1979–1980.

Ferreiro, E.   Literacy development: A psychogenetic perspective. In D. Olson (Ed.), *Literacy, language and learning*. Cambridge: Cambridge University Press. In press.

Ferreiro, E., and Teberosky, A.   *Los sistemas de escritura en el desarrollo del niño*. Mexico: Siglo Veintiuno, 1979.

Ferreiro, E., and Teberosky, A.   *Literacy before schooling*. Exeter, N.H.: Heinemann Educational Books, 1982.

Fillmore, C.   The case for case reopened. In P. Cole and J.M. Seadock (Eds.), *Syntax and semantics*, vol. 3. New York: Academic Press, 1968.

Fodor, M.   The effect of systematic reading of stories on the language development of culturally deprived children. Ph.D. dissertation, Cornell University, 1966.

Fortes, M.   Social and psychological aspects of education in taleland. In J. Middleton (Ed.), *From child to adult*. New York: Natural History Press, 1970.

Foucault, M.   *The order of things*. New York: Random House, 1973.

Foucault, M.   *The archeology of knowledge*. New York: Harper & Row, 1976.

Foucault, M. *Language, counter-memory, practice.* Ithaca: Cornell University Press, 1977.

Foucault, M. *Power/knowledge: Selected interviews and other writings 1972–1977.* Ed. Colin Gordon. New York: Pantheon Books, 1980.

Fowler, W. Case studies of cognitive precocity: The role of exogenous and endogenous stimulation in early mental development. *Journal of Applied Developmental Psychology* 2 (1981):319–367.

Galligan, R.F. Individual differences in learning to speak: A study of the use of whole phrases, jargon and intonation. Ph.D. dissertation, University of Toronto, 1982.

Gardner, K. Early reading skills. In *Reading skills: Theory and practice.* London: Ward Lock Educational, 1970.

Garvey, C. *Play.* Cambridge: Harvard University Press, 1977.

Geertz, C. Deep play: Notes on the Balinese cockfight. *Daedelus* 101, no. 1 (1972):1–38.

Gibson, E.J., and Levin, H. *The psychology of reading.* Cambridge: MIT Press, 1975.

Glaser, B.G., and Strauss, A.L. *The discovery of grounded theory: Strategies for qualitative research.* Chicago: Aldine Publishing Co., 1967.

Gleason, J., and Weintraub, S. Input language and the acquisition of communicative competence. In K. Nelson (Ed.), *Children's language*, vol. 1. New York: Gardner Press, 1978.

Goodman, Y. The roots of literacy. In Malcolm P. Douglass (Ed.), *Claremont reading conference forty-fourth yearbook.* Claremont, Calif.: Claremont Graduate School, 1980.

Goodman, Y. El desarrollo de la escritura en niños muy pequeños. In C. Ferreiro and M. Palacio (Eds.), *Nuevas perspectivas sobre los piocesos de lectura y escritura.* Mexico: Siglo Veintiuno, 1982.

Goodman, Y.M., and Altwerger, B. Print awareness in pre-school children: A study of the development of literacy in preschool children. Occasional Paper no. 4. Program in language and literacy, College of Education, University of Arizona, September 1981.

Goody, J. *The domestication of the savage mind.* New York: Cambridge University Press, 1977.

Goody, J. Alternative paths to knowledge in oral and literate cultures. In D. Tannen (Ed.), *Spoken and written language.* Norwood, N.J.: Ablex, 1982.

Goswami, D. (Ed.). *Teacher as researcher.* Sharon, CT.: Boynton-Cook Publishers. In press.

Graff, H. *The literacy myth: Literacy and social structure in the nineteenth-century city.* New York: Academic Press, 1979.

Graff, H. *The legacies of literacy: Continuities and contradictions in Western society and culture.* New York: Academic Press, 1983.

Grice, H.P. Meaning. *Philosophical Review* 3 (1957):377–388.

Halliday, M.A.K. *Learning how to mean: Explorations in the development of language.* New York: Elsevier North-Holland, 1975.

Harding, D.W. The role of the onlooker. *Scrutiny* 6 (1937):247–258.

Hardy, B. *Tellers and listeners: The narrative imagination.* London: Athlone, 1975.

Hardy, B. An approach through narrative. In M. Silka (Ed.), *Towards a poetics of fiction.* Bloomington: Indiana University Press, 1977.

Harkness, F., and Miller L. A description of the interaction among mother, child and books in a bedtime reading situation. Paper presented at the seventh annual Boston Conference on Language Development, Boston, October 1982.

Harman, D., and Brim, O.G., Jr. *Learning to be parents: Principles, programs and methods.* Beverly Hills: Sage Publications, 1980.

Harste, J., Burke, C., and Woodward, V. *Children, their language and world: Initial encounters with print.* National Institute of Education Final Report. Bloomington: Indiana University Press, 1981.

Harste, J., et al.   Children's language and world: Initial encounters with print. In J. Langer and M. Smith-Burke (Eds.), *Bridging the gap: Reader meets author*. Newark, DE.: IRA. In press.

Harty, K.F.   A comparative analysis of children who enter kindergarten reading and children of the same age who require additional readiness for reading. Ph.D. dissertation, University of Wisconsin, 1975.

Haussler, Myna.   A young child interacting with language in a print-oriented society. Master's thesis, University of Arizona, 1977.

Haussler, Myna.   A psycholinguistic description of beginning reading development in selected kindergarten and first grade children. Ph.D. dissertation, University of Arizona, 1982.

Heath, S.B.   The functions and uses of literacy. *Journal of Communication* 30(1980a):1.

Heath, S.B.   What no bedtime story means: Narrative skills at home and school. Paper prepared for the Terman Conference, Stanford University, November 1980b.

Heath, S.B.   Toward an ethnohistory of writing in American education. In E. Whiteman (Ed.), *Variation in writing: Functional and linguistic cultural differences*. Hillsdale, N.J.: Lawrence Erlbaum Associates, 1981.

Heath, S.B.   What no bedtime story means: Narrative skills at home and school. *Language in Society* 11 (1982a):49−76.

Heath, S.B.   Protean shapes in literacy events: Ever-shifting oral and literate traditions. In D. Tannen (Ed.), *Spoken and written language*. Norwood, N.J.: Ablex, 1982b.

Heath, S.B.   Ways with words: Ethnography of communication, communities, and classrooms. Cambridge: Cambridge University Press, 1983.

Heath, S.B.   Taking language apart and building institutional talk: Critical factors in literacy development. In S. de Castell, K. Egan, and A. Luke (Eds.), *Literacy: What is to be done?* In press.

Henderson, Edmund H., and Beers, James W.   *Developmental and cognitive aspects of learning to spell: A reflection of word knowledge*. Newark, Del.: IRA, 1980.

Hess, R.   Experts and amateurs: Some unintended consequences of parent education. In M. Fantini and R. Cardenas (Eds.), *Parenting in a multicultural society*. London: Longman, 1980.

Hickmann, M.   The implication of discourse skills in Vygotsky's developmental theory. In J. Wertsch (Ed.), *Culture, communication and cognition: Vygotskian perspectives*. New York: Academic Press, 1983.

Hiebert, E.H.   Developmental patterns and interrelationships of preschool children's print awareness. *Reading Research Quarterly* 16 (1981):236−260.

Hildreth, G.   Developmental sequences in name writing. *Child Development* 7 (1936): 291−303.

Hoffman, S.J.   Preschool reading related behaviors: A parent diary. Paper presented at the third Ethnography in Education forum, Philadelphia, March 1982.

Holdaway, D.   *The foundations of literacy*. Sydney: Ashton Scholastic, 1979.

Howard, R.   A note on S/Z. In R. Barthes (Ed.), *Introduction to S/Z*. New York: Hill and Wang, 1974.

Hubley, P., and Travarthen, C.   Sharing a task in infancy. In I. Uzgiris (Ed.), *Social interaction during infancy: New directions for child development*, vol 4. San Francisco: Jossey-Bass, 1979.

Huey, E.B.   *The psychology and pedagogy of reading*. New York: Macmillan, 1908.

Hughes, M., and Jones, M.   Children's spontaneous written representations of number and arithmetical operations. Department of Psychology, University of Edinburgh, 1982.

Hutt, C.   Exploration and play in children. In J. Bruner, A. Jolly, and K. Sylva (Eds.), *Play—its role in development and evolution*. New York: Basic Books, 1976.

Hymes, D.   Two types of linguistic relativity. In William Bright (Ed.), *Sociolinguistics*. The Hague: Mouton, 1966.

Hymes, D.   Models of the interaction of language and social life. In J.J. Gumperz and D. Hymes (Eds.), *Directions in sociolinguistics*. New York: Holt, Rinehart and Winston, 1972.

Illich, I.   *Shadow work*. Boston: Boyard, 1981.

Iredell, H.   Eleanor learns to read. *Education* (1898):233−238.

Irwin, O.   Infant speech: Effect of systematic reading of stories. *Journal of Speech and Hearing Research* 3 (1960):187−190.

Jacob, E.   The influence of culture and environment on cognition: A case study in a Puerto Rican town. Ph.D. dissertation, University of Pennsylvania, 1977.

Jakobson, R.   *Child language, aphasia and phonological universals*. The Hague: Mouton, 1965.

Karmiloff-Smith, A.   The interplay between syntax, semantics and phonology in language processes. In R.N. Campbell and P.T. Smith (Eds.), *Recent advances in the psychology of language*. New York: Plenum Press, 1978.

Kellogg, R.   *Analyzing children's art*. Palo Alto: Mayfield, 1969.

Krippner, S.   The boy who read at eighteen months. *Exceptional Child* 30 (1963):105−109.

Kroeber, A.   *Anthropology*. New York: Harcourt-Brace, 1948.

Lamme, L.L.   Just one more book, PLEASE? The story of an early reader. University of Florida, n.d.

Lavine, L.O.   The development of perception of writing in pre-reading children: A cross-cultural study. Ph.D. dissertation. Cornell University, 1972.

Leichter, H.J.   (Ed.).   Some perspectives on the family as educator. In H.J. Leichter, (Ed.), *The Family as Educator*. New York: Teachers College Press, 1974.

Leichter, H.J.   The concept of educative style. *Teachers College Record* 75 (1978):239−50.

Leichter, H.J.   Families and communities as educators: Some concepts of relationships, In H.J. Leichter (Ed.), *Families and communities as educators*. New York: Teachers College Press, 1979.

Leslie, A.   The representation of perceived causal connection in infancy. Ph.D. dissertation, Oxford University, 1979.

Lockridge, K.   *Literacy in colonial New England*. New York: Norton, 1974.

Lord, A.B.   *The singer of tales*. Cambridge: Harvard University Press, 1960.

McDermott, R.P., Gostodonoff, K., and Aron, J.   Criteria of ethnographically adequate descriptions of concerted activities and their context. *Semiotica* 24 (1978):245−275.

Macnamara, J.   Cognitive basis of language learning in infants. *Psychological Review* 79 (1972):1−13.

Macnamara, J.   *Names for things: A study of human learning*. Cambridge: MIT Press, 1982.

McNeill, D.   *The acquisition of language: The study of developmental linguistics*. New York: Harper & Row, 1970.

Mandler, J.M.   A code in the node: The use of a story schema in retrieval. *Discourse Processes* 1 (1978):14−35.

Mandler, J.M., and Johnson, N.S.   Remembrance of things parsed: Story structure and recall. *Cognitive Psychology* 9 (1977):111−151.

Mason, J.M.   *Prereading: A developmental perspective*. Technical Report no. 198. Urbana, Ill.: University of Illinois, Center for the Study of Reading, 1981.

Mason, J.M.   Acquisition of knowledge about reading: The preschool period. Paper presented at American Educational Research Association convention, New York, March 1982.

Mead, M.   *Blackberry winter: My earlier years*. New York: Morrow, 1972.

Mehan, H.   *Learning lessons*. Cambridge: Harvard University Press, 1979.

Miller, G.A.   *Spontaneous apprentices: Children and language.* New York: Seabury, 1977.

Miller, P.   Early socialization for schooling in a working-class community. Paper presented at the University of Pennsylvania Ethnography in Education Research Forum, 1981.

Miller, P., Nemoianu, A., and DeJong, J.   Early socialization for schooling in a working-class community. In B.B. Schieffelin (Ed.), *The acquisition of literacy: Ethnographic perspectives.* Norwood, N.J.: Ablex. In press.

Miller, S.   Ends, means and galumphing: Some leitmotifs of play. *American Anthropologist* 75 (1973):87–98.

Moon, C., and Wells, C.G.   The influence of the home on learning to read. *Journal of Research in Reading* 2 (1979):53–62.

Ninio, A.   Picture-book reading in mother-infant dyads belonging to two sub-groups in Israel. *Child Development* 51 (1980):587–590.

Ninio, A., and Bruner, J.S.   The achievement and antecedents of labelling. *Journal of Child Language* 5 (1978):5–15.

Nunberg, G.   Reading, writing and thinking. *New York Times Book Review* December 1981.

Ochs, E., and Schieffelin, B.B.   Language acquisition and socialization: Three developmental stories and their implications. In R. Shweder and R. Levins (Eds.), *Culture and its acquisition.* Chicago: University of Chicago Press. In press.

Olson, D.R.   From utterance to text: The bias of language in speech and writing. *Harvard Educational Review* 47 (1977):257–281.

Ong, W.   *The presence of the word.* New Haven: Yale University Press, 1967.

Ong, W.   *Interfaces of the word.* Ithaca: Cornell University Press, 1977a.

Ong, W.   The writer's audience is always a fiction. In W. Ong (Ed.), *Interfaces of the word.* Ithaca: Cornell University Press, 1977b.

Paley, V.   *Wally's stories.* Cambridge: Harvard University Press, 1981.

Papert, S.   *Mindstorms.* New York: Basic Books, 1980.

Payton, S.   Readiness for reading as an aspect of language growth. Master's thesis, University of Birmingham, England, 1982.

Peirce, C.S.   *Collected papers.* Cambridge: Harvard University Press, 1932 et seq.

Piaget, J.   *The construction of reality in the child.* London: Routledge and Kegan Paul, 1937.

Piaget, J.   *Play, dreams, and imitation.* New York: Norton, 1962.

Piaget, J.   *The development of thought: Equilibration of cognitive structures.* New York: Viking Press, 1977.

Platt, P.   Grapho-linquistics: Children's drawings in relation to reading and writing skills. *The Reading Teacher* 31 (1977):262–268.

Plessas, G.P., and Oakes, C.R.   Prereading experiences of selected early readers. *The Reading Teacher* 17 (1964):241–245.

Price, E.H.   How thirty-seven gifted children learned to read. *The Reading Teacher* 30 (1976):44–48.

Purves, A.C., and Beach, R.   *Literature and the reader: Research in response to literature, reading interests, and the teaching of literature.* Urbana, Ill.: National Council of Teachers of English, 1972.

Read, C.   Pre-school children's knowledge of English phonology. *Harvard Educational Review* 41 (1971):1–34.

Read, C.   Children's categorization of speech sounds in English. NCTE Research Report no. 17, 1975.

Reddy, M.J.   The conduit metaphor—a case of frame conflict in our language about language. In A. Ortony (Ed.), *Metaphor and thought.* New York: Cambridge University Press, 1979.

Reger, R.   The child who could read before he could talk. *Journal of School Psychology* 4, no. 2 (1966):50–55.

Reid, J.F.   Learning to think about reading. *Educational Research* 9, no. 1(1966):56–62.

Rhodes, L.K.   Visible language acquisition: A case study. Paper presented at the twenty-fourth annual International Reading Association convention, Atlanta, May 1979.

Roberts, J.M. Arth, M.J., and Bush, R.R.   Games in culture. *American Anthropologist* 61 (1959):597–605.

Robinson, E., Goelman, H., and Olson, D.R.   Children's understanding of the relation between expressions (what was said) and intentions (what has meant). *British Journal of Developmental Psychology*, 1983, 1, 75–86.

Rosenblatt, L.M.   *The reader, the text, the poem.* Carbondale, Ill.: Southern Illinois University Press, 1978.

Rosenblatt, L.M.   What facts does this poem teach you? *Language Arts* 57 (1980):386–394.

Saint Augustine.   *The confessions.* London: Suttaby, 1883.

Schaefer-Simmern, H.   *The unfolding of artistic activity.* Berkeley, Calif.: University of California Press, 1948.

Scheffler, I.   *The language of education.* Springfield, Ill.: Charles C. Thomas, 1960.

Schickendanz, J.A.   Hey! This book's not working right. *Young Children* 37 (1981):18–27

Schieffelin, B.B.   Getting it together: An ethnographic approach to the study of the development of communicative competence. In E. Ochs and B.B. Schieffelin (Eds.), *Developmental pragmatics.* New York: Academic Press, 1979.

Schieffelin, B.B.   Talking like birds: Sound play in a cultural perspective. In J. Loy (Ed.), *The paradoxes of play.* West Point, N.Y.: Leisure Press, 1982.

Schieffelin, B.B.   *How Kaluli children learn what to say, what to do and how to feel.* New York: Cambridge University Press. In press.

Schieffelin, E.L.   *The sorrow of the lonely and the burning of the dancers.* New York: St. Martin's Press, 1976.

Scollon, R.   Communicative style and research style: A problem in discovery, application, and reportage. Paper presented at the fortieth annual meeting of the Society for Applied Anthropology, Denver, March 1980.

Scollon, R.   Computers and linear thinking. *The Computing Teacher* 9, no. 4, (1981a): 59–60.

Scollon, R.   The organization of gates in a public institution. Paper presented at the annual meeting of the American Anthropological Association, Los Angles, December 1981b. (To appear as "Gatekeeping: Access or retention?" in *Working Papers in Sociolinguistics*, Southwest Educational Development Laboratory, Austin.)

Scollon, R.   Human knowledge and the institution's knowledge. Final report to the National Institute of Education, 1981c.

Scollon, R., and Scollon, S.B.K.   *Linguistic convergence: An ethnography of speaking at Fort Chipewyan, Alberta.* New York: Academic Press, 1979.

Scollon, R., and Scollon, S.B.K.   Literacy as focused interaction. *Quarterly Newsletter of the Laboratory of Comparative Human Cognition* 2, no. 2 (1980):26–29.

Scollon, R., and Scollon, S.B.K.   *Narrative, literacy and face in interethnic communication.* Norwood, N.J.: Ablex, 1981a.

Scollon, R., and Scollon, S.B.K.   Cooking it up and boiling it down: Abstracts in Athabaskan children's story retellings. In D. Tannen (Ed.), *Spoken and written language.* Norwood, N.J.: Ablex, 1981b.

Scollon, R., and Scollon, S.B.K.   Computer conferencing in instruction. Report to the University of Alaska Instructional Telecommunications Consortium, 1981c.

Scollon, R., and Scollon, S.B.K.   Face in interethnic communication. In J. Richards and R. Schmidt (Eds.), *Communicative competence.* London: Longman, 1982a.

Scollon, R., and Scollon, S.B.K.   Face in interethnic telecommunications at the University of Alaska: Computer conferencing as non-focused interaction. Paper presented at the Conference on Native American Interaction Patterns, University of Alberta, Edmonton, April 1982b.

Scollon, R., and Scollon, S.B.K.   The problem of language problems in Alaskan Society. Forthcoming.

Scollon, S.B.K.   Professional development seminar: A model for making higher education more culturally sensitive. Paper presented at the third annual conference of the National Association for Asian and Pacific American Education, Honolulu, April 1981.

Scollon, S.B.K.   Reality set, socialization and linguistic convergence. Ph.D., Department of Linguistics, University of Hawaii, 1982.

Scribner, S.   Modes of thinking and ways of speaking: Culture and logic reconsidered. In R.O. Freedle (Ed.), *New directions in discourse processing.* Norwood, N.J.: Ablex, 1979.

Scribner, S., and Cole, M.   Unpackaging literacy. *Social Science Information* 17, no. 1 (1978):19−40.

Scribner, S., and Cole, M.   *The psychology of literacy: A case study among the Vai.* Cambridge: Harvard University Press. 1981.

Searle, J.R.   Intentionality and the use of language. In A. Margalit (Ed.), *Meaning and use.* Jerusalem, Israel: The Magnes Press, The Hebrew University, 1979.

Sheldon, W., and Carrillo, L.   Relation of parents, home, and certain developmental characteristics to children's reading ability. *Elementary School Journal* 52 (1952):262−270.

Silverstein, M.   Language as a tool of culture. In J. Wertsch (Ed.), *Culture, communication, and cognition.* New York: Academic Press, 1983.

Simons, H.D.   Black dialect and reading interference: A review and analysis of the research evidence. 1974.

Slobin, D.   Language change in childhood and in history. In J. Macnamara (Ed.), *Language, learning and thought.* New York: Academic Press, 1977.

Smethurst, W.   *Teaching young children to read at home.* New York: McGraw-Hill, 1975.

Smith, F.   *Understanding reading.* New York: Holt, Rinehart and Winston, 1971; 2nd ed. 1978.

Smith, F.   *Writing and the writer.* New York: Holt, Rinehart and Winston, 1981a.

Smith, F.   Demonstrations, engagement and sensitivity: A revised approach to language learning. *Language Arts* 58, no. 1 (1981b):103−112.

Smith, F.   Demonstrations, engagement and sensitivity: The choice between people and programs, *Language Arts* 58, no. 6 (1981c):634−642.

Smith: F.   A metaphor for literacy: Creating words or shunting information? In F. Smith, *Essays into Literacy.* Exeter, N.H.: Heinemann Educational Books, 1983.

Snow, C.   Conversations with children. In P. Fletcher and M. Garman (Eds.), *Language acquisition: Studies in first language development.* Cambridge: Cambridge University Press, 1979.

Snow, C., and Ferguson, C. (Eds.). *Talking to children.* Cambridge: Cambridge University Press, 1977.

Snow, C., and Goldfield, B.   Building stories: The emergence of information structures from conversation. In D. Tannen (Ed.), *Analyzing discourse: Text and talk.* Washington, D.C.: Georgetown University Press, 1982.

Söderbergh, R.   *Reading in early childhood.* Stockholm: Almqvist and Wiksell, 1971.

Söderbergh, R.   *Reading in early childhood: A linguistic study of a preschool child's gradual acquisition of reading ability.* Washington, D.C.: Georgetown University Press, 1977.

Spencer, M.   Stories are for telling. *English in Education* 10 (1976):15−23.

Staton, J., Shuy, R., and Krefft, J.   Analysis of dialogue journal writing as a communicative event, vol. 2. Final report to the National Institute of Education (NIE-G-80-0122), 1982.

Steinberg, D.D., and Steinberg, M.T.   Reading before speaking. *Visible Language* 9 (1975):197–224.

Steiner, George.   George Steiner on literature, language, and culture. Interview with Bill Moyers, Public Broadcasting System, May 22, 1981.

Stern, D. Hofer, L., Haft, W., and Dore, J.   Interpersonal communication: The attunement of affect states by means of intermodial fluency. Paper presented at the international conference on infancy studies, Austin, Texas, March 1982.

Stevenson, R.L.   *Essays of travel.* London: Chatto and Windus, 1920. First published 1879.

Sulzby, E.   A scale for judging emergent reading of favorite storybooks. Paper presented at the thirty-second annual meeting of the National Reading Conference, Clearwater Beach, Fla., December 1982.

Sulzby, E., and Otto, B.   "Text" as an object of metalinguistic knowledge: A study in literacy development. *First Language* 3 (1982):181–199.

Sutton, M.H.   Readiness for reading at the kindergarten level. *The Reading Teacher* 17 (1964):234–240.

Sutton-Smith, B.   *Play and learning.* New York: Gardner Press, 1979.

Swartzmann, H.B.   The anthropological study of children's play. *Annual Review of Anthropology* 5 (1976):189–328.

Sylva, K., Bruner, J., and Genova, P.   The role of play in the problem-solving of children 3–5 years old. In J. Bruner, A. Jolly, and K. Sylva (Eds.), *Play—its role in development and evolution.* New York: Basic Books, 1976.

Taylor, D.   *Family literacy: Young children learning to read and write.* Exeter, N.H.: Heinemann Educational Books, 1983.

Taylor, D.   Learning to "read" stories. Kean College of New Jersey, n.d.

Teale, W.H.   Toward a theory of how children learn to read and write naturally. *Language Arts* 59 (1982):555–570.

Teale, W.H., and Anderson, A.B.   La lecto escritura como practica cultural. Paper presented at Simposio international: Nuevas perspectivas sobre los procesos de lectura y escritura, July 1981.

Teale, W.H., Anderson, A.B., Cole, M., and Stokes, S.   Literacy activities in the homes of low-income preschool children. Paper presented at the conference on the influence of home background on school achievement, Madison, Wisc., October 1981.

Teale, W.H., and Lewis, R.   The nature and measurement of secondary school students' attitudes toward reading. *Reading Horizons* 21 (1981):94–102.

Terman, L.M.   *Genetic studies of genius,* Stanford: Stanford University Press, 1918.

Tobin, A.W.   Social and psychological correlates of precocious reading achievement. Paper presented at the annual meeting of the American Educational Research Association, New York, March 1982.

Tolman, E.C.   *Purposive behavior in animals and men.* New York: Appleton-Century, 1932.

Torrance, N., and Olson, D.   Oral language competence and the acquisition of literacy. In D. Olson, N. Torrance, and A. Hildyard (Eds.), *The nature and consequences of literacy.* In press.

Torrey, J.W.   Learning to read without a teacher: A case study. *Elementary English* 46 (1969):550–556, 658.

Torrey, J.W.   Learning to read without a teacher: A case study. In F. Smith (Ed.), *Psycholinguistics and reading.* New York: Holt, Rinehart & Winston, 1973.

Tough, J.   *Report of a longitudinal study.* Leeds, England: University of Leeds Institute of Education, Language, and Environment, 1970.

232 Awakening to Literacy

Trevarthen, C. Interpersonal abilities of infants as generators for transmission of language and culture. In A. Oliverio and M. Zappella (Eds.), *The behaviour of human infants*. London and New York: Plenum Press. In press.

U.S. Bureau of the Census. *Census of the population: 1970. General social and economic characteristics, Puerto Rico.* Washington, D.C.: Government Printing Office, 1972.

Varenne, H. *Americans together.* New York: Teachers College Press, 1977.

Varenne, H., Hamid-Buglione, V., McDermott, R.P., and Morison, A. The acquisition of literacy for learning in working class families. Final report to the National Institute of Education (NIE no. 400-79-0046), Teachers College, Columbia University, New York, 1981.

Vendler, Z. Say what you think. In J.L. Cowan, (Ed.), *Studies in thought and language.* Tucson: University of Arizona Press, 1970.

Vukelich, C. The development of writing in young children. *Childhood Education* 57 (1981):167–170.

Vygotsky, L.S. *Thought and language.* Cambridge: MIT Press, 1962.

Vygotsky, L.S. *Mind in society.* Cambridge: Harvard University Press, 1978.

Vygotsky, L.S. The genesis of higher mental functions. In J.V. Wertsch (Ed.), *The concept of activity in Soviet psychology.* White Plains, N.Y.: Sharpe, 1981.

Walker, G.H., and Keurbitz, I.E. Reading to preschoolers as an aid to successful beginning reading. *Reading Improvement* 16 (1979):149–154.

Watson, R.S. Smiling, cooing and the game. *Merrill-Palmer Quarterly* 18 (1972):323–329.

Weir, R. *Language in the crib.* The Hague: Mouton, 1962.

Wells, G. *Learning through language: The study of language development,* vol. 1. Cambridge: Cambridge University Press, 1981.

Wells, G. Story reading and the development of symbolic skills. *Australian Journal of Reading* 5 (1982):142–152.

Wells, G. Preschool literacy-related activities and success in school. In D. Olson, N. Torrance, and A. Hildyard (Eds.), *The nature and consequences of literacy.* In press.

Wells, C.G., and Raban, B. Children learning to read. Final report to the Social Science Research Council, University of Bristol, March 1978.

White, D.N. *Books before five.* Wellington, New Zealand: New Zealand Council for Educational Research, 1956.

Yinger, R.J., and Hill, J. Learning by doing: Locating learning in student teachers' practicum experiences. Paper presented at the meeting of the American Anthropological Association, Washington, D.C., December, 1982.

Ylisto, Ingrid. Early reading responses of young Finnish children. *The Reading Teacher* 31 (1977):167–172.

NAME INDEX

SUBJECT INDEX

Active learning, 213, 217–218
Adult-child interaction, culture and, 203; importance of, 51–71; literacy development and, 117–118, 122–125, 127–129; literacy events in, 209; story-reading and, 51–52, 59–67, 111–114, 210
Adult mind, child mind and, 100
Aesthetic reading, 119
Anthropology, approach to literary development of, 215, 217, 221–222
Art, self-taught, 96, 101; writing and, 108, 155–158, 181–184; See also Drawing
Attitude, literacy development and, 115–116

Bedtime reading, 6; See also Storybook time, Story-reading
Black families, initiation of literacy events in, 33–34; preschool literacy in, 51–71
Bolt, Beranek, and Newman, 199–200
Book-reading, changes due to, 70; effects of, 52–71; in low-income families, 52–53; in middle-class families, 51–52; parent-child interaction during, 51–52, 58–71
Books, children's knowledge of, 102–103; cultural value of, 6; equation of literacy with, 24–25; lower-class children's experiences with, 25; in nonliterate cultures, 13
Brain, creativity and, 131, 206
Bulletin board, as literacy event, 44–45
Bush consciousness, 132

Capitalization, children's use of, 127
Child mind, vs. adult mind, 99–101
Children, artistic development in, 96; benefits of reading to, 110–120; book-reading in, 24–25; evaluation of literacy skills of, 45–46; family environments of, 38–48; language development in, 57–71; learning in, 73–83, 149–152; nonbook literacy experiences of, 27–36; in nonliterate cultures, 11–15; preschool reading in, 51–71, 102; reading fluency in, 122–130; searching for order by, 100–101; as teacher, 15–20, 87–101; See also Preschool literacy
Children Learning to Read Project, 120
Chinese families, literacy in, 15–20
Cognitive conflicts, in literacy development, 172
Communication, bush vs. modern, 132–133; community-wide, 132–133; computers and, 134–140; literacy events associated with, 30; as motivation for literacy, 176, 184n; parent and child, 8, 57–71; See also Adult-child interaction
Computer games, interaction and, 136–138, 139–140
Computer-mediated conferencing, 134

Computers, communication and, 134–140; educational use of, 135–136; linear logic of, 138; literacy development and, 210–211; preschool literacy and, 107; reading and, 139–140
Conduit metaphor, 134
Confessions (St. Augustine), 177
Consonants, learning of, 100
Contextualization, 146–148, 194–195
Conventionalization, 146, 148–149, 194
Counting, defined, 75; in play, 77–79, 82
Coupons, as literacy event, 44–45
Creativity, in learning, 151–152; literacy and, 143–152; as motivation for reading, 196; written language and, 206–207
Culture, adult-child interaction and, 203; learned in play, 73; literacy and, 3–22, 34–36, 100–101, 131–133, 140, 152, 201–203, 204–205, 208–209; middle-class transmission of, 52; reading strategies and, 117

Daily living, literacy events in, 28–29, 31–33, 36
Demonstrations, in learning, 149–151
Dialect, literacy patterns and, 35
Dialogue, role in learning, 90–91
Drawing, learning and, 91–96; as representative, 106; story-telling and, 91–96; writing and, 108, 155–158, 181–184; See also Art

Education, computer and, 135–136; within families, 38–48; informal, 38–48; See also Learning, School, Teaching
Elbenwood Center for the Study of Family as Educator (Teachers College, Columbia University), 39
Engagement, 151
Emic observations, defined, 37n; in ethnography, 26
Emotional climate, within families, 45–46
Emotional relationships, effect on preschool literacy, 40
Entertainment, literacy events associated with, 29–33, 35, 36
Ethnic minorities, literacy in, 24–36
Ethnographic observations, issues involved in, 39; value of, 26–27
Ethnographic research, 16, 39
Ethnography, defined, 4; literacy and, 3–22
Evaluation, role of literacy skills in, 45–46
Extensive research, vs. intensive research, 47

Family, emotional climate in, 45–46; as environment for literacy, 38–48, 107; informal instruction in, 38–48; literacy development and, 103, 207–208, 220; motivational climate